CHRISTIAN
HERITAGE
COLLEGE
LIBRARY

PRESENTED BY

The Crowell Foundation

English Romantic Irony

821.709
M527e

English Romantic Irony

Anne K. Mellor

HARVARD UNIVERSITY PRESS

CAMBRIDGE, MASSACHUSETTS

AND LONDON, ENGLAND

1980

51989

Copyright © 1980 by the President and Fellows of Harvard College
All rights reserved
Printed in the United States of America

Publication of this book has been aided by a grant from the
Andrew W. Mellon Foundation

Library of Congress Cataloging in Publication Data

Mellor, Anne Kostelanetz.
English romantic irony.

Includes bibliographical references and index.
1.   English literature—19th century—History and
criticism.   2.   Romanticism.   3.   Irony in literature.
I.   Title.
PR468.R65.M44   821'.7'091   80-10687
ISBN 0-674-25690-5

For Carl Woodring

Preface

The theory of romantic irony, which was most clearly formulated by Friedrich Schlegel between 1799 and 1801, provides a conceptual framework within which we can better understand both the content and the structure of several major English romantic works. Romantic irony is a way of looking at the universe and the artistic process that is very different from the perspective embedded in the secularized Judaeo-Christian traditions whose impact on English romanticism Meyer Abrams has masterfully summarized in *Natural Supernaturalism*. Romantic irony grows out of philosophical skepticism and the social turbulence of the French Revolution and the American War of Independence; it posits a universe founded in chaos and incomprehensibility rather than in a divinely ordained teleology.

The English literary works I have chosen to discuss are intended to be exemplary, not exhaustive. The writings of Byron, Keats, and Carlyle illustrate the range of literary structures, styles, and tonalities of romantic irony, as do other poems by Shelley and Blake which I have not analyzed. I have taken certain works by Coleridge and Lewis Carroll as representative of the point where, both psychologically and historically, romantic irony becomes something else. Psychologically, the romantic ironist's enthusiastic response to process and change terminates where the perception of a chaotic universe arouses either guilt or fear, the guilt so intensely experienced by Coleridge or the fear felt by Carroll and later existentialist writers. The writings of Coleridge and Carroll do not constitute fixed historical termini for romantic irony; one can easily read works by Sterne, Yeats, Woolf, and Joyce, among others, as romantic irony. But the bulk of authentically romantic-ironic writing in England occurred in the early nineteenth century, during a cultural period of profound political and economic change.

In this book I do not attempt a complete account of the development of the concept of romantic irony among German theorists and artists; that account has already been written by Ingrid Strohschneider-Kohrs in *Romantische Ironie in Theorie und Gestaltung*. Nor do I try to show that the writings of these German theorists and authors had a direct influence upon the English writers I discuss. In some instances, Schlegel's notion of *romantische Ironie* was familiar to these Englishmen (Carlyle knew Schlegel's work, as did Coleridge); in other instances, it was not. By far the most direct and pervasive source of romantic irony as a mode of consciousness in England was the native eighteenth-century Deist "higher criticism" of the Bible, as Elinor Shaffer has shown in *"Kubla Khan" and The Fall of Jerusalem: The Mythological School in Biblical Criticism and Secular Literature, 1770-1880*. Romantic irony was a significant part of the nineteenth-century English "spirit of the age," a recurrent skeptical reaction to the egotistical sublime of Christian fundamentalism, apocalyptic poetry, and Victorian myths of progress and imperialism.

I am grateful to Macmillan & Co. Ltd. for permission to quote from Yeats's "What Then?" and to John Murray and Harvard University Press for permission to quote from Byron's *Letters and Journals*.

This book would not have been written without the constant encouragement and affectionate support of my husband, Ronald, the cheerful acquiescence of my son, Blake, the assistance of the John Simon Guggenheim Foundation and the National Endowment for the Humanities, the stimulation of the students in my graduate seminars on romantic irony, and the generous help of my colleagues and friends. I particularly thank those whose suggestions and criticisms substantially improved this book: Patricia Alden, George Dekker, Stuart Ende, Albert Guerard, Janice Haney, George Levine, Peter Manning, Stephen Parrish, David Perkins, Robert Polhemus, Lucio Ruotolo, Craig Seligman, David Wellbery, and above all, Herbert Lindenberger. To the man who taught me both the shapings of romanticism and the meaning of the word *humane* I gratefully dedicate this book.

Note on the Title Page Vignette

The vignette on the title page, which appears in Thomas Bewick's *British Birds* (London, 1797), is an excellent visual example of romantic irony. Here we see an idyllic pastoral landscape with thatched cottage and rider on horseback, about an inch and a half wide, that is almost obliterated by a thumbprint. This vignette can be read in several ways. The thumbprint is Bewick's own (he engraved it again, with the words "Thomas Bewick his mark," on the bottom of a receipt for his illustrated *Fables of Aesop*, dated January 1, 1824). Hence it could be seen as a gigantic signature over the landscape. But this thumbprint, which is roughly actual size, draws attention to the smallness and fragility of a pastoral idyll that can be blotted out by a fingertip. Thus the thumbprint also functions as a parabasis, a disruption of the artistic illusion, forcing us to acknowledge the engraver's control over his fictional image (the Lord giveth and the Lord taketh away). Alternatively, we might see the thumbprint as a smudge upon a windowpane through which we perceive the landscape at a distance, thus setting the scene into pictorial perspective and insisting upon its realism. However, since the picture field is not outlined, it is impossible for the viewer to assess either his exact distance from the image or the intended dimensions of the pictured image. And finally, the canceling thumbprint may only indicate that the artist made a mistake. In this way, Bewick subtly creates and de-creates his idyllic English landscape. (I am indebted to Henri Zerner's review of Bewick's *Memoir* in *The New York Review of Books*, September 30, 1976, for drawing my attention to this remarkable vignette.)

Contents

PART ONE

Romantic Irony

1

The Paradigm of Romantic Irony

The publication in 1748 of David Hume's *An Enquiry Concerning Human Understanding* heralded a cultural and historical era of profound and sweeping change. As is well known, in England and Europe the late eighteenth century was a time of revolutions: the American Revolution, the French Revolution, the beginning of the Industrial Revolution. By the end of the eighteenth century, belief in the Elizabethan world picture of a Great Chain of Being had waned among the educated. Several factors contributed to this loss of faith in a God-ordained, hierarchical universe. The rise of the middle classes during the seventeenth and eighteenth centuries challenged the traditional class system, as well as the prerogatives of the Crown. Peasant food riots throughout England and Europe in the eighteenth century, brought on by the Enclosure Acts and by the start of the Industrial Revolution—with its influx of workers into the cities and factory towns, mechanization of labor, rising prices, high unemployment, and subsequent starvation—further attacked the rectitude of a class system. The increasing popularity, especially among the middle and lower classes, of a new "heart religion" (Methodist, Quaker, Baptist, and other Dissenting Protestant sects), which preferred private emotions and the "inner light" of conscience over reason as the guide to spiritual truth and consequently denied the necessity for outward religious ceremonies, rituals, or priesthood, undermined the power and privileges of the established churches.[1] Moreover, Hume powerfully denied that human reason could discover any universal natural laws or absolute truths. Instead, he argued, men could have knowledge only of their immediate, subjective sensations. The intellectual confusion caused by Hume's radical skepticism was compounded by John Locke's earlier conclusion, in *An Essay Concerning Human Understanding* (1690), that there is no *necessary* connection between objects, the ideas that the primary and secondary quali-

3

ties of objects produce in the human consciousness, and the words people use to express those ideas. This widespread confusion was brilliantly recorded in Lawrence Sterne's *Tristram Shandy* (1759-67). This is a novel about a world that has no necessary form or causal connections. Hence it is a novel that barely gets written; a novel in which every character rides his own hobby-horse, obsessed with ideas he cannot verbally communicate; a novel that finally suggests that the only way people can reach each other, if at all, is through emotions and sexuality and not through rational discourse. Finally, the great political events of the late eighteenth century—the American Revolution, the French Revolution, and the English publication of Thomas Paine's *Rights of Man* in 1791-92—undermined the authority and viability of traditional governing institutions and thus opened the way to new and changing concepts of man, of the structure of society, and of the nature of the universe.

It is from this background of political revolution and post-Enlightenment distrust of the capacity of human reason to ascertain the laws of nature, or, indeed, any absolute truths concerning the ways of the world, that romantic irony emerges. Romantic irony is a way of thinking about the world that embraces change and process for their own sake. As the finest literary exponent of romantic irony wrote, "The great object of life is Sensation—to feel that we exist—even though in pain—it is this 'craving void' which drives us to Gaming—to Battle—to Travel—to intemperate but keenly felt pursuits of every description whose principal attraction is the agitation inseparable from their accomplishment." And so, Byron continued, "*I* can't *stagnate*."[2]

Romantic irony is both a philosophical conception of the universe and an artistic program. Ontologically, it sees the world as fundamentally chaotic. No order, no far goal of time, ordained by God or right reason, determines the progression of human or natural events. This chaos is abundantly fertile, always throwing up new forms, new creations. But insofar as these forms are static and finite, they are inevitably overwhelmed by and reabsorbed into the process of life. To borrow the terms used by modern physics, we might think of this chaos as pure energy. This energy flows in "force-fields" that to our crude vision appear as material objects but that are more precisely understood as only momentary conjunctions of differently charged forces. And the motion of these forces is ultimately unpredictable: universal chaos has no specifiable direction, no telos, no comprehensible pattern or purpose.

The artist who shares this conception of the universe as chaos must find an aesthetic mode that sustains this ontological reality, this never-ending becoming. Clearly, he cannot merely impose a man-made form or system upon this chaos: that would distort motion into stasis. Instead, the romantic ironist must begin skeptically. He must acknowledge the inevitable limitations of his own finite consciousness and of all man-made structures or myths. But even as he denies the absolute validity of his own perceptions and structuring conceptions of the universe, even as he consciously deconstructs his mystifications of the self and the world, he must affirm and celebrate the process of life by creating new images and ideas. Thus the romantic ironist sustains his participation in a creative process that extends beyond the limits of his own mind. He deconstructs his own texts in the expectation that such deconstruction is a way of keeping in contact with a greater creative power.

In this sense, the romantic ironist must be sharply distinguished from modern deconstructors. A radical demystifier like Paul de Man subjects all linguistic discourse to skeptical analysis and rejects poetic symbolism as "ontological bad faith."[3] In so doing, de Man arbitrarily privileges one form of literary discourse, the allegorical, over another, the symbolic. In other words, modern deconstructionists choose to perform only one half of the romantic-ironic operation, that of skeptical analysis and determination of the limits of human language and consciousness. But the authentic romantic ironist is as filled with enthusiasm as with skepticism. He is as much a romantic as an ironist. Having ironically acknowledged the fictiveness of his own patternings of human experience, he romantically engages in the creative process of life by eagerly constructing new forms, new myths. And these new fictions and self-concepts bear with them the seeds of their own destruction. They too die to give way to new patterns, in a never-ending process that becomes an analogue for life itself. The resultant artistic mode that alone can properly be called romantic irony must therefore be a form or structure that simultaneously creates and de-creates itself.

Romantic irony was as significant and important a way of thinking about the nature of the universe and the artistic process for nineteenth-century English writers as was that other great intellectual tendency of the age, natural supernaturalism. Meyer Abrams has cogently and persuasively argued that English and German romantic works frequently present a secularized Judaeo-Christian conception of an ordered, teleological universe in which mankind progresses toward an apocalyptic marriage with the divine and a return to paradise.[4] He is correct, but his failure to discuss either Friedrich Schlegel's concept of romantic irony or its greatest exemplar, Byron's *Don Juan*, should alert us to what Abrams left out of his description of "the spirit of the age." Not all romantic works present a confident movement from innocence to experience to a higher innocence, that circuitous journey which leads the protagonist spiraling upward to a more self-aware and therefore more meaningful communion with the divine. To the contrary, many central romantic works exhibit a structure that is deliberately open-ended and inconclusive. Byron's improvised *Don Juan*; Keats's unresolved Odes, love poems, and *The Fall of Hyperion*; Carlyle's self-consuming *Sartor Resartus*; and, at the outward limits of romantic irony, Coleridge's guilt-ridden "The Rime of the Ancient Mariner" and Lewis Carroll's defensive *Alice* books—all present a simultaneously creative and de-creative form. In these works, symbols are generated only to be qualified and rejected; mythic patterns, including the Christian one of fall-penance-redemption, are tested and found wanting. And yet they affirm the creative process. Giving up their ladders, these romantic ironists begin again and again, "in the foul rag-and-bone shop of the heart."

The failure to recognize the openness of romantic-ironic structures has led to radically divergent readings of specific texts. The critical disagreements that have circled round such oft-studied poems as "The Eve of St. Agnes," "The Rime of the Ancient Mariner," and *Don Juan*, to name only a few famous examples, have been engendered by the critics' eagerness to impose systematic interpretations upon these intrinsically antisystematic works. Rather than trying to fit these open-ended poems into an inherently inadequate logical or emotional structure, we must see them as liminal rites of passage (to borrow terms from Victor Turner and Arnold van Gennep),[5] as movements *between* one structure and another. At the center of these works lies an all-important liminal experience of unstructured openness (what Turner calls *communitas*), a sacred participation in the process of life.

Before I discuss these poems, however, the concept of romantic irony itself needs more attention and elucidation. And here I turn for guidance to the writings of its first and most profound theorist, Friedrich Schlegel. In the chapters that follow, I shall be using Schlegel's conceptualization of romantic irony as a paradigmatic model, in terms of which I shall discuss various English works. Many of these English writers did not know Schlegel's work but were responding similarly to the same intellectual, sociological, economic, and political milieu. Others, like Coleridge and Carlyle, may have been directly influenced by Schlegel, and I shall note their debts in the appropriate places. It will clarify the discussion of romantic irony, I think, to distinguish the philosophical or ontological dimension of Schlegel's concept from its artistic or literary application.

PHILOSOPHICAL IRONY

Philosophical irony is grounded on the denial of any absolute order in natural or human events. Schlegel frequently insists that the universe is essentially chaotic; in his essay "On Incomprehensibility," he asks rhetorically, "isn't this entire, unending world constructed by the understanding out of incomprehensibility or chaos?"[6] And in the *Dialogue on Poetry* he confirms, "the highest beauty, indeed the highest order, is yet only that of chaos."[7] Schlegel regards this ontological chaos positively, as a fertile abundance or *Fülle*. In an early essay, "On the Limits of the Beautiful" (1794), he glosses *Fülle* thus: "By Abundance (*Fülle*) I must here be understood to mean, the exhaustless fund of life which is constantly developing itself in nature, in matchless but evergrowing beauty." He then locates it at the heart of reality: "The most prominent characteristic of nature is an everflowing and exhaustless vital energy."[8] This creative chaos becomes, in Schlegel's *Dialogue on Poetry*, identical with poetry itself:

> The world of poetry is as infinite and inexhaustible as the riches of animating nature with her plants, animals, and formations of every type, shape, and color. Nor are the artificial or natural products which bear the form and name of poems easily included under the most inclusive term. And what are they, compared with the unformed and unconscious poetry which stirs in the plant and shines in the light, smiles in a child, gleams in the flower of youth, and glows in the loving bosom of women? This, however, is the primeval poetry without which there would be no poetry of words. Indeed, there is not and never has been for us humans any other object or source of activity and joy but that one poem of the godhead the earth, of which we, too, are part and flower. (DP, 53-54)

This "infinite and inexhaustible" world of poetry is life itself, a neverending life of joy and rich potentiality, for "the poetry of earth is never dead." Schlegel here defines the essence of reality, not as matter or *being* (a thing or substance in itself), but as *becoming*. Moreover, he argues that a "spiritual intuition" or direct perception of this chaotic becoming is possible, through the smile of a child or the loving bosom of a woman. Ultimately, as we shall see, Schlegel identifies this intellectual or spiritual perception of infinite becoming with artistic irony and the only genuine freedom.

But, Schlegel insists, finite human perceptions can never completely capture an infinite chaos. For if they did so, becoming or change would no longer be possible and life would cease. This is true on both the ontological and the epistemological levels. Schlegel equates the ontological process of universal change with the epistemological movement from unconsciousness to increasing consciousness. This cognitive process is stimulated, he says, by an emotional longing for an ever-greater participation in the *Fülle*, a longing that ends only with death. "Never will the mind that knows the orgies of the true Muse journey on this road to the very end, nor will he presume to have reached it; for never will he be able to quench a longing which is eternally regenerated out of the abundance of gratifications" (DP, 53). And just as the individual consciousness can never be fully satisfied (for it can never attain an infinite self, even theoretically, without ending its own becoming), so any theoretical formulation of reality can never be infinite or complete, but only "an approximation" that must ultimately be transcended by being negated and rejected. Therefore, Schlegel concludes, "Scepticism is as eternal as philosophy [the creation of a specific system] . . . The idea of philosophy is to be attained through an infinite progression of systems."[9] As he says elsewhere, "When the goal is reached, metaphysics should *begin again and again from the beginning*—alternating between chaos and system, chaos preparing for a system and then new chaos."[10] Emphatically, Schlegel insists, "One can only become a philosopher, but not be one. As soon as one believes he is a philosopher, he stops being one."[11] Or as Byron would later put it, "So little do we know what we're about in / This world, I doubt if doubt itself be doubting" (*Don Juan*, 9.17).

Schlegel then translates this conception of the universe as an abundant chaos into psychological terms. He argues that the conception of reality as becoming entails a psychological conflict or tension in the individual. Every person is dominated by two opposing psychic drives: one seeks order and coherence (to become being), while the other seeks chaos and freedom (to be becoming or to become nonbeing). Emotionally, the drive toward order, system, or being is experienced as love. In his novel *Lucinde* (1799), Schlegel enthusiastically celebrates the experience of becoming a unity with the beloved object through the attracting, harmonizing, and fusing power of romantic love. In content, Schlegel's novel is a paean to a new and holy kind of love, a fusion of sexuality and spirituality that achieves an ideal marriage of the self with the other. Lucinde is the priestess, Julius the priest of this new religion of love, which purifies, anoints, and even (in a vision) beatifies them.

Intellectually, the drive toward order is experienced as imagination or what Schlegel called wit. Schlegel's concept of wit (*Witz*) is central to his aesthetic theory. He defines it thus: "If wit in all its manifestations is the principle and the program of universal philosophy, and if all philosophy is nothing but the spirit of universality, the science of the eternally uniting and dividing sciences, a logical chemistry: then the value and importance of that absolute, enthusiastic, thoroughly material wit is infinite" (A, 220). By "material wit" and "logical chemistry," Schlegel means that wit is an activity that fuses the physical and mental realms: it is a catalyzing and synthesizing faculty that can suddenly unite two opposed ideas or phenomena in new and strikingly fertile relationships. Wit thus has a dual function. First, it destroys old ideas and relationships: "A witty idea is a disintegration of spiritual substances which, before being suddenly separated, must have been thoroughly mixed."[12] Secondly, wit unites hitherto dissociated concepts; it becomes the matchmaker of ideas and the founder of new societies or moral orders. "Many witty ideas are like the sudden meeting of two friendly ideas after a long separation" (A, 37). By thus actively engaging in the creative process of always-becoming life, the faculty of wit (which Antonio's "Letter about the Novel" in Schlegel's *Dialogue on Poetry* explicitly identifies with the imagination; DP, 100) can lead one to a perception of "the infinite . . . the one eternal love and the sacred fullness of creative nature" (DP, 100).

Schlegel's concept of wit or imagination thus closely approximates the eighteenth-century English notion of poetic wit as the perception of a striking relationship between two seemingly incongruous thoughts, or as a mental alertness to resemblances in general.[13] Moreover, it anticipates Coleridge's famous definition of the secondary imagination as a conscious and willed act of perception that "dissolves, diffuses, dissipates, in order to recreate."[14] The capacity of wit to unite friendly but hitherto separated ideas leads Schlegel further to characterize wit as "geniality,"[15] "logical sociability" (L, 56), and an "absolute social feeling" (L, 9). By wedding dissociated ideas, the wit or imagination lays the foundations for new psychological structures and social institutions and thus has the capacity to create the "new mythology" that Ludovico calls for (DP, 81).

Remembering that wit begins by destroying old orders and received truths, we can see that wit satisfies one's desire for freedom. This association of wit with freedom had been anticipated in Schlegel's early essay on Aristophanic comedy, *On the Aesthetic Value of Greek Comedy* (1795?), where he linked the comic wit to the joyful, Dionysian assertion of freedom:

A person . . . who is governed only by his own will and makes it evident that he is subject to neither inward nor outward barriers, exemplifies complete inward and outward personal freedom. His inward freedom is made evident by his acting in happy enjoyment of him-

self, from pure caprice and whim alone, deliberately without reason
or contrary to reasons; his outward freedom by the mischievous
spirit in which he violates outward barriers, while the law magnanimously forgoes its rights.[16]

According to Schlegel, our psychic desire for freedom, chaos, or becoming is energized by our consciousness of that law which "magnanimously forgoes its rights." Inherent in every individual's self-consciousness is the knowledge of one's own limitations: human beings must die.
Being mortal, we are finite. Our perceptions of the infinite must therefore
be but partial and in that sense false. "One's poetry is limited, just because it is one's own," insists Schlegel (DP, 54). Insofar as we attempt to
structure the chaos of becoming into comprehensible systems, we are
confined within the Kantian categories or deep structures of the phenomenal world. This awareness of the limitations of the self is what Schlegel
meant by philosophical "irony" or the "critical faculty" (a term he derived from Kant's *Critiques*). A skeptical awareness of the limitations of
one's knowledge is necessary, Schlegel felt, to detach imagination from
an excessive commitment to its own finite creations. Irony must "toll" the
"forlorn" poet back from illusions of perfection to his "sole self."

By doing so, irony can free the imagination to discover or create ever-
new relationships, to participate once again in the fertile chaos of life. For
if a person were ever to believe that his reason had fully comprehended
this chaos, that conviction would in itself destroy his capacity to participate in the mystery and primeval power of life. As Schlegel explains,
"Yes, even man's most precious possession, his own inner happiness, depends in the last analysis, as anybody can easily verify, on some such
point of strength that must be left in the dark, but that nonetheless shores
up and supports the whole burden and would crumble the moment one
subjected it to rational analysis."[17]

Not only can finite human beings never fully comprehend the chaotic
abundance of becoming; they can never adequately express the limited
perceptions they do have. Language itself, says Schlegel, is a structured,
rational system that by its very nature cannot capture or articulate the
unstructured and chaotic. Schlegel insists upon both "the impossibility
and the necessity of complete communication" (L, 108). He explicates this
paradox further in *Lyceum* fragment 37: "As long as the artist is in the
process of discovery and inspiration, he is in a state which, as far as communication is concerned, is at the very least intolerant. He wants to blurt
out everything, which is a fault of young geniuses or a legitimate prejudice of old bunglers." The mystery of becoming can be linguistically ex-

pressed only as hints, cyphers, and hieroglyphs, and never as lucid, logical discourse. "For in what words, known to these profane times," Carlyle's Teufelsdröckh would later ask, can one "speak even afar off of the unspeakable?" Through symbolism, one enthusiastically attempts to contain the whole within a part, only to be forced to acknowledge one's failure to do so; through allegory, one can continue to hint *at* this infinite and reflect upon one's failed attempts to encompass it. Thus a powerful symbolism generates a powerful allegory; the capacities of figural discourse are celebrated even as they are finally found inadequate.[18]

Philosophical irony, this inevitable and all-important consciousness of the limitations of human knowledge and of human language, is thus the necessary prerequisite and counterforce to love and creative imagination. It criticizes and thus negates one's excessive commitment to the fictions of one's own mind, thereby enabling one to sustain contact with reality. It insists that "The fancy cannot cheat so well / As she is fam'd to do." And thus it renews one's direct participation in an always-becoming life. In denying the validity of *all* orders, philosophical irony grants us the freedom to become whatever we desire; for this reason, "Irony is necessary" (LN, 481). For Schlegel, nature's movement from chaos to order and back to chaos, from life to death and new life, is psychologically paralleled by a movement back and forth between a desire for change and a desire for order. And it is intellectually paralleled by an unceasing debate between the infinite and the finite, the free and the conditioned. This philosophical dialectic, unlike the artistic process, begins with a skeptical negation, with a "critical examination" and rejection of existing beliefs and errors. It thus frees the imagination to create a new conception of the self, of society, of nature. But this new conception must, in turn, be subjected to the same ironic, critical analysis, an analysis that recognizes its limitations and failings. It is in this sense that Schlegel insists that "Irony is analysis of thesis and antithesis" (LN, 802).

We must be careful here to distinguish Schlegel's concept from Hegel's later formulation of the dialectic in his *Phaenomenologie des Geistes* (1807) and *Encyklopaedie der philosophischen Wissenschaften im Grundrisse* (1817). Hegel's dialectic is progressive and transcendental. The thesis generates its antithesis, which is then reconciled with the thesis in a higher synthesis. This new perspective or synthesis then generates its antithesis, which again leads to a broader synthesis in an upward and outward spiraling growth of human consciousness. In contrast, Schlegel's dialectic allows for no genuine resolution or synthesis. The thesis and antithesis remain always in contradiction: being or system can never be united with becoming or chaos. These two opposed principles stay in constant conflict; and the function of philosophical irony is to examine their intrinsic and insuperable contradiction.

Philosophical irony can thus be summed up, in Schlegel's words, as "an absolute synthesis of absolute antitheses, the continual self-creating interchange of two conflicting thoughts" (A, 121). By "synthesis" here, as we have seen, Schlegel means not reconciliation or harmonization but rather conjunction: being and becoming stand side by side, in unresolved and unresolvable conflict. Borrowing a phrase from F. Scott Fitzgerald's *The Crack-Up*, we might say more simply that philosophical irony is the ability to hold two opposed ideas in the mind at the same time, while still retaining the ability to function.

In his *Lyceum* fragment 108, Schlegel celebrates this capacity (which he here calls "Socratic irony"):

> Socratic irony is the only involuntary and yet completely deliberate dissimulation. It is equally impossible to feign it or divulge it. To a person who hasn't got it, it will remain a riddle even after it is openly confessed. It is meant to deceive no one except those who consider it a deception and who either take pleasure in the delightful roguery of making fools of the whole world or else become angry when they get an inkling they themselves might be included. In this sort of irony, everything should be playful and serious, guilelessly open and deeply hidden. It originates in the union of savoir vivre and scientific spirit, in the conjunction of a perfectly instinctive and a perfectly conscious philosophy. It contains and arouses a feeling of indissoluble antagonism between the absolute and the relative, between the impossibility and the necessity of complete communication. It is the freest of all licenses, for by its means one transcends oneself; and yet it is also the most lawful, for it is absolutely necessary. It is a very good sign when the harmonious bores are at a loss about how they should react to this continuous self-parody, when they fluctuate endlessly between belief and disbelief until they get dizzy and take what is meant as a joke seriously and what is meant seriously as a joke.

Socratic irony was encapsulated in Socrates' famous defense in the *Apology*: "I know nothing." Socrates knew the limitations of his own knowledge; thus from the viewpoint of the absolute, he knew nothing. But he also knew that his accusers and questioners knew less than he. Hence he knew that they, in their ignorance of their own limitations, were not lovers of wisdom but rather fools. From the viewpoint of mortal men, he lied to his questioners; but from the viewpoint of eternity, he told the necessary, "involuntary" truth. Socrates saw reality as a series of opposi-

tions or contradictions between the given, the absolute, the instinctive—
and the created, the relative, the conscious. These contradictions simultaneously forced him to recognize the limitations of his own mind and
freed him from the illegitimate limitations of other minds. Like Byron's
narrator, Socrates felt that "There's no such thing as certainty, that's
plain / As any of mortality's conditions" (*Don Juan*, 9.17). Socrates'
constant self-parody, his perennial awareness of his own weaknesses and
failures as well as his strengths, thus enabled him to be simultaneously
playful and serious, exultant and anxious, free and yet bound to what is
necessary. Only such self-parody can enable one to transcend all unnecessary human limitations and to approach as near as human beings can
to a valid perception of the infinite chaos that is reality.

To be an ironist, then, one must constantly engage in such Socratic
self-parody. One must be always aware of both the value and the falsity
of one's perceptions and ideas. If one fails to do this, one falls into what
Schlegel called the irony of irony, which happens if

> one speaks of irony without using it . . . ; if one speaks of irony iron-
> ically without in the process being aware of having fallen into a far
> more noticeable irony; if one can't disentangle oneself from irony
> anymore . . . ; if irony turns into a mannerism and becomes, as it
> were, ironical about the author; if one has promised to be ironical
> for some useless book without first having checked one's supply and
> then has to produce it against one's will, like an actor full of aches
> and pains; and if irony runs wild and can't be controlled any longer.[19]

Instead, one must always sustain the incredibly difficult but not impossible dual awareness that everything one believes is both true and false;
that what one is both exists and is constantly changing; that nature and
society are as stable as they appear and yet are built on the quicksand of
chaos.

Whenever one does this, one becomes Schlegel's hero: the person of
"urbane" or "liberal" imagination,[20] the Byronic ideal, the philosophical
ironist. In doing so, one also approaches divinity: "Every good human
being is always progressively becoming God. To become God, to be human, to cultivate oneself are all expressions that mean the same thing"
(A, 262). Schlegel thus redefines divinity as the human consciousness of
becoming. The only true goal of spiritual longing is activity, the never-
ending activity of self-becoming. For Schlegel, this self-becoming is a
process of enlargement: one develops from conceptions of the self as a
unity to ever-clearer conceptions of the self as flowing into a rich and
manifold chaos. Schlegel thus defines the moral life as a dynamic activ-

ity, a dialectical movement between destruction and creation, creation and destruction, that produces an ever-expanding consciousness of life as becoming.

ARTISTIC IRONY

Schlegel's conception of philosophical irony has fascinating implications for the artistic process and product. The artist who is a philosophical ironist must always play a dual role. He must create, or represent, like God, a finite, ordered world to which he can enthusiastically commit himself; and *at the same time* he must acknowledge his own limitations as a finite human being and the inevitable resultant limitations of his merely fictional creations. The artistic process, then, must be one of simultaneous creation and de-creation: a fictional world must be both sincerely presented and sincerely undermined, either by showing its falsities or limitations or, at the very least, by suggesting ways of responding to it other than whole-hearted assent. The artist must achieve the distance of Yeats's authorial voice in "The Circus Animals' Desertion": "Winter and summer till old age began / My circus animals were all on show."

In Schlegel's terms, the ironic artist must constantly balance or "hover" between self-creation (*Selbstschöpfung*) and self-destruction (*Selbstvernichtung*) in a mental state that he calls *Selbstbeschränkung*, a rich term variously translated as self-determination, self-restraint, or self-restriction. Self-determination thus involves the artist in a process in which he simultaneously projects his ego or selfhood as a divine creator and also mocks, criticizes, or rejects his created fictions as limited and false. He must show that "the poet is a god, or, the young poet is a god. The old poet is a tramp." Such self-restraint is for Schlegel "the first and the last, the most necessary and the highest duty" (L, 37) for the artist as well as for the individual. He develops this idea at length in *Lyceum* fragment 37:

> Most necessary because wherever one does not restrict oneself, one is restricted by the world; and that makes one a slave. The highest because one can only restrict oneself at those points and places where one possesses infinite power, self-creation, and self-destruction. Even a friendly conversation which cannot be broken off at any moment, completely arbitrarily, has something intolerant about it. But a writer who can and does talk himself out, who keeps nothing back for himself, and likes to tell everything he knows, is to be pitied. There are only three mistakes to guard against. First: What

appears to be unlimited free will, and consequently seems and should seem to be irrational and supra-rational, nonetheless must still at bottom be simply necessary and rational; otherwise the whim becomes willful, becomes intolerant, and self-restriction [*Selbstbeschränkung*] turns into self-destruction. Second: Don't be in too much of a hurry for self-restriction, but first give rein to self-creation, invention, and inspiration, until you're ready. Third: Don't exaggerate self-restriction. (L, 37)

Or, as Schlegel puts it more cryptically in his notebooks, "Irony is self-polemic overcome [*überwundene Selbstpolemik*]" (LN, 506).

Schlegel means that the philosophically aware artist must engage in the chaotic creativity of life; in so doing, he will appear arbitrarily willful to the philosophically ignorant, but will in fact be doing what is not necessary and rational. But he must remain true to the actual contradictions of life, lest he become purely willful and thus lose contact with reality and destroy his authentic self. In creating his own chaotically ordered worlds, the artist must beware not to restrain himself too much: the de-creative process must make way for a new creation; enthusiasm and inspiration must, at least for a moment, overwhelm irony, for "nothing is duller than the empty form of irony without enthusiasm" (LN, 1047). Nonetheless, detachment from one's enthusiastic assertions is necessary. For only when detached can one create that ultimate poetry, that "transcendental poetry" which is the authentic manifestation of Schlegel's transcendental philosophy or critical idealism, and which Keats portrays as a never-ending process of "soul-making" in *The Fall of Hyperion*. For, Schlegel argues,

> just as we wouldn't think much of an uncritical transcendental philosophy that doesn't represent the producer along with the product and contain at the same time within the system of transcendental thoughts a description of transcendental thinking: so too this sort of poetry should unite the transcendental raw materials and preliminaries of a theory of poetic creativity—often met with in modern poets—with the artistic reflection and beautiful self-mirroring that is present in Pindar, in the lyric fragments of the Greeks, in the classical elegy, and, among the moderns, in Goethe. In all its descriptions, this poetry should describe itself, and always be simultaneously poetry and the poetry of poetry. (A, 238)

The ironic artist should constantly mirror himself, his desires and beliefs, and even as he mirrors them, reflect critically upon them. He must write what Wallace Stevens later called "The poem of the mind in the act of finding / What will suffice." Or as Schlegel said in his laudatory review of Goethe's *Wilhelm Meister*, "We must raise ourselves above our own love and be able to annihilate in thought what we worship: otherwise we lack, whatever other capabilities we might have, the faculty [sense] for the infinite and with it the sense for the world."[21] The philosophical ironist who successfully performs this difficult maneuvering between enthusiastic self-creation and skeptical self-destruction produces that self-expanding, "progressive, universal poetry" which Schlegel hailed as the only genuinely "romantic poetry" in his *Athenaeum* fragment 116:

> It alone can become, like the epic, a mirror of the whole circumambient world, an image of the age. And it can also—more than any other form—hover at the midpoint between the portrayed and the portrayer, free of all real and ideal self-interest, on the wings of poetic reflection, and can raise that reflection again and again to a higher power, can multiply it in an endless succession of mirrors . . . Romantic poetry is in the arts what wit is in philosophy, and what society and sociability, friendship and love are in life. Other kinds of poetry are finished and are now capable of being fully analyzed. The romantic kind of poetry is still in the state of becoming; that, in fact, is its real essence: that it should forever be becoming and never be perfected. It can be exhausted by no theory and only a divinatory criticism would dare try to characterize its ideal. It alone is infinite, just as it alone is free; and it recognizes as its first commandment that the will of the poet can tolerate no law above itself. The romantic kind of poetry is the only one that is more than a kind, that is, as it were, poetry itself: for in a certain sense all poetry is or should be romantic. (A, 116)

To produce such romantic poetry, to sustain the incredibly difficult hovering or balancing between self-assertion and self-reflection, requires, as Schlegel freely acknowledged, both enormous energy and great mental agility. "The energetic man always makes use of only the moment, and is always ready and infinitely flexible. He has an infinite number of projects or none at all; for energy is really more than mere agility: it is effective, certainly externally effective, but it is also universal power, through which the whole man shapes himself and acts" (A, 375). Moreover, as Schlegel later insisted in the *Ideas*, "Irony is the clear consciousness of eternal agility, of an infinitely teeming chaos."[22] With energy and agility, then, the ironic artist constantly views and projects himself as simultaneously free and governed by instinct, as sentimental and naive, as committed to no system and yet deeply involved in a system, for as Schlegel said, "It's equally fatal for the mind to have a system and to have none. It will simply have to decide to combine the two" (A, 53).

This ironic hovering of the artist, this self-restraint, manifests itself in the work of art as what Schlegel called "transcendental buffoonery" (L, 42). This phrase has been mocked and dismissed,[23] but it deserves to be taken seriously. Schlegel meant that the work of art must reveal the presence of an authorial consciousness that is simultaneously affirming and mocking its own creation: "There are ancient and modern poems that are pervaded by the divine breath of irony throughout and informed by a truly transcendental buffoonery. Internally: the mood that surveys everything and rises infinitely above all limitations, even above its own art, virtue, or genius; externally, in its execution: the mimic style of an averagely gifted Italian *buffo*" (L, 42). We have already seen that by "transcendental" Schlegel refers to a poetry that hovers between the real and the ideal, between the chaos of becoming and the order of being (A, 238). But outwardly, the work of art should create the same impression as that created by the *buffo* or harlequin figure in commedia dell'arte plays, a dramatic character who both controls the plot and mocks the play. For instance, in Carlo Gozzi's *The Love of Three Oranges*, Arlecchino is an intriguer who manipulates the action, even interrupting it to speak directly to the audience and to comment wittily upon the plot and the other actors. He frequently mimics the gestures and parodies the language of the other characters. But even as he undermines the credibility of the play as a dramatic illusion, he enables the plot to go forward and engineers the play's denouement. He thus simultaneously creates and de-creates the play and does so with zest and wit.[24] That this is what Schlegel had in mind by "transcendental buffoonery" is confirmed by his description of irony as a permanent parabasis.[25] The parabasis in Greek Old Comedy was an interruption of the action, usually in the middle of the play, in which the author's spokesman addressed the audience directly, often either speaking of the author's personal circumstances or attacking the faults of various contemporary personages. One good modern example of parabasis is *Blazing Saddles*, a comic film directed by Mel Brooks, in which the dramatic frame is constantly broken, every convention of the film western is mocked, and every stereotype is parodied, and yet the story gets told and Cleavon Little, the black, Gucci-bag-toting sheriff sent to save the town, becomes a hero. In these examples, the ironic author (or director) always makes his audience aware of his presence behind and in the work of art, a presence that simultaneously creates and wittily mocks the work before them.

This authorial presence may, but *need not*, take the form of a deliberate destruction of the dramatic illusion. The traditional, and overly restrictive, interpretation of romantic irony as an artistic device in which the author appears as a figure in his own play or novel, disrupting or commenting upon the action, has been persuasively refuted by Ingrid Strohschneider-Kohrs, Raymond Immerwahr, and others.[26] Schlegel himself considered such a destruction of the artistic illusion primarily as a means of achieving a powerful comic effect, as his comments on Ludwig Tieck's deft use of this device make clear.[27] More generally, artistic irony can manifest itself in the work of art as a process of simultaneous creation and de-creation: as two opposed voices or personae, or two contradictory ideas or themes, which the author carefully balances and refuses to synthesize or harmonize—as in the opposition of Juan and the narrator in Byron's *Don Juan* or in the conflicting ontological systems presented by the text and the gloss of Coleridge's "The Rime of the Ancient Mariner." And in his own essay "On Incomprehensibility," Schlegel asserts simultaneously that the essential nature of reality is incomprehensible and that he will write comprehensibly about this very incomprehensibility.[28] The use of opposing voices, ideas, and even artistic structures operates both to affirm and to undermine the artist and his vision. The effect achieved by the genuinely ironic work is like that of a circus clown on a trapeze who almost falls off. The clown is a master of the art of trapeze-swinging who mocks that very mastery by pretending to be clumsy and to lose his balance—only to go too far and nearly fall off.[29]

In form as well as content, then, the ironic work of art must join together chaos and order. As Schlegel said, it should be an "artfully ordered confusion, [a] charming symmetry of contradictions, [a] wonderfully perennial alternation of enthusiasm and irony which lives even in the smallest parts of the whole" (DP, 86). It necessarily rejects the use of classical genres as too limited: one must not try "to produce [poetry], invent it, establish it, and impose upon it restrictive laws as the theory of poetics would like to" (DP, 54). Instead, the ironic work must be an "arabesque," a term Schlegel borrowed from art history and more directly from Goethe's essay *Die Arabesken*.[30] As Karl Polheim has shown, "arabesque" came to connote for Schlegel the creative, enthusiastic, and transcendental (as opposed to the skeptical) activity of romantic irony, the positive participation in an infinite abundance (*unendliche Fülle*).[31] More precisely, Schlegel denoted by the arabesque the decorative, linear, capricious designs of Pompeian Third Style wall-painting, the kind of designs rediscovered in the Golden House of Nero by Italian Renaissance painters and frequently utilized by Raphael and Giovanni da Udine in the Vatican Logge, the Loggetta del Cardinal Bibbiena, and the Villa Farnesina. Known as *grottesche*, these delicately drawn, brightly painted, cur-vilinear designs arbitrarily blend architectural, vegetal, animal, and human motifs in irrational but balanced patterns.[32] Goethe saw Raphael's *grottesche* as contributing to a monument of abundance and opulence (*ein Denkmal der Fülle und des Reichtums*) and described the blossoming human forms and gaily fluttering genii as balancing between a striving toward a defined goal and a pure delighting in the love of energetic mo-tion.[33] Schlegel too saw the arabesque as a form that released the creative excess of the imagination. Its profusion of motifs and irrational but bal-anced linear patterns became for Schlegel a visual analogue for the bal-ancing of caprice with purposefulness, of abundant chaos with psycho-logically necessary orders, that is transcendental buffoonery or artistic irony.

For Schlegel, the most appropriate art form for the philosophical iron-ist to use was the novel. As Hans Eichner has argued, Schlegel's concep-tion of the *Roman* and the *romantisch* ("Ein Roman ist ein romantisches Buch," he proclaimed in a statement that is and is not tautological; DP, 101) depended on traditional notions of the novel or *Roman*. As the novel developed in German and other literatures, it was a prose work written in the vernacular (the secular or romance languages as opposed to Latin), utilizing nonclassical forms. In content, it drew on the legends, fairy tales, and supernatural or fantastic materials of popular folklore ballads and plays; increasingly, the *Roman* was associated specifically with love stories.[34] By the late eighteenth century, the terms *Roman* and *romantisch* had acquired a further derogatory connotation. People who allowed their view of life and their conduct to be unduly influenced by the extravagantly imaginative popular novel or *Roman* were called *ro-mantisch*. But as this literature became more influential, the term roman-tic was further identified with the "ineffable" quality that such people insisted they experienced in their relationships with their beloved or with nature. Thus, "romantic" came to connote an "inexpressible yet spiritual" experience.[35] As Schlegel proclaimed, "that is romantic which presents a sentimental theme in a fantastic form" (DP, 98).

The truly romantic book is thus an arbitrary mixture (a *Mischgedicht*) of all known literary genres: poetry, song, prose, dramatic exchanges, epic, pastoral, satire, mock-heroic, and so on. As such, Schlegel's con-ception of the novel is fundamentally opposed to the "great tradition" of the English novel propounded by F. R. Leavis: a tradition that demands a unified and logical structure, an overt yet subtle moral stance, and a con-cern with the realizable possibilities of life; a tradition that dismisses the novels of Sterne as "irresponsible (and nasty) trifling."[36] Instead, the genre of romantic irony is much closer to what Northrop Frye has called Menippean satire or the "anatomy": a form that combines prose, dialogue, and verse in an elaborate dissection and playing off, one against another, of varying mental attitudes, as in the examples cited by Frye— *Tristram Shandy, Gulliver's Travels, Don Quixote,* Burton's *Anatomy of Melancholy,* and Boethius's *Consolation of Philosophy.*[37] But these diverse styles, genres, characters, and points of view must all join together, says Schlegel, in an activity, in the chaotic becoming of life. Thinking specifically of *Tristram Shandy, Don Quixote, Wilhelm Meister,* and Diderot's *Jacques le Fataliste,* Schlegel concluded, "Novels are the Socratic dialogues of our time" (L, 26).

The form of Schlegel's own novel *Lucinde* is deliberately chaotic and thus mirrors the chaotic abundance of life. The novel begins with a letter that is interrupted by an "unkind chance" that kindly enables Schlegel to show his reader how chance or chaos controls both life and this work of art. This interruption also provides Schlegel's protagonist, Julius, with an opportunity to develop and deepen his thoughts about love before writing the autobiography that occurs at the center of the book. Next come a fantasy, a character sketch, an allegory, a conversation, and, finally, the promised autobiography—all these genres appear in fragments, which nonetheless organically cohere around the sentimental theme of Julius's physical and psychological development as man, lover, father, friend, and self-conscious prophet of love. This development, born out of conflict and frustration (one of his early mistresses committed suicide), hope and agony (at one point he is convinced that Lucinde is dying of a fatal disease), despair and fulfillment, is never completed. Just as the novel is unfinished and can therefore "never *be* a novel, but must forever be attempting to *become* one,"[38] so the love of Julius and Lucinde and their individual yet closely entwined psychological and physical growth are never ending, always in process.

Irony enters this novel not only as this formal chaos but also as the "self-restraint" or self-awareness of the narrator. Julius entitles his writings "Confessions of a Blunderer": he is an unreliable narrator or, at least, a person whose perceptions are limited by his subjectivity. Perhaps he is too enthusiastic? or mad? or immature? As readers, we must beware of taking him completely seriously. Irony must guide our responses to Julius as it guides Julius's responses to life. In an unpublished fragment for the novel, Julius tells Lorenzo it was irony that helped him to reject his own limitations, to seek an ever more expansive and fulfilling love and life. Irony, says Julius, "attached itself profoundly only to what was just and, after a brief experiment, despised all that was unjust; it affirmed itself, expanded, became clear and conscious of its power, became wise, just as everything that is human becomes wise, through action."[39]

In addition to the novel, Schlegel cited other examples of "fantastic forms" appropriate to the expression of philosophical irony. The form he preferred and used most often was of course the fragment or aphorism. As he announced, "Wit is absolutely sociable spirit or aphoristic genius" (L, 9). The aphorism enabled him to express a particular *aperçu* or idea without being forced to relate it to other thoughts or to a complete system. It allowed him, as it later allowed Nietzsche and Wallace Stevens, to include in the same literary work extremely contradictory ideas, or to approach the same idea from widely divergent points of view. In both cases, he was able to avoid imposing a false system or an unjustified rational order upon his ideas. "A fragment, like a miniature work of art, has to be entirely isolated from the surrounding world and be complete in itself like a porcupine" (A, 206). Each fragment contains a single complete idea, yet carries with it sharp and immediate relevance to all other thoughts on the subject. In this sense, Schlegel argued, "fragments are the real form of universal philosophy" (A, 259). In addition to avoiding systematization, the fragment permitted Schlegel to develop his ideas dialectically, putting forth both an assertion and its antithesis in the same work without being forced toward a falsifying synthesis; Schlegel's *Lyceum* and *Athenaeum* fragments thus present the mind in the very *act* of thinking.

The paradox is another "fantastic" form that permits the expression of two contradictory ideas as equally valid. As in Shakespeare's famous example, "Caesar never did wrong but with just cause," evil and good are equally weighted since the wrong, however "justified," remains a wrong. As Schlegel said, "Irony is the form of paradox. Paradox is everything simultaneously good and great " (L, 48)—by which he means, I think, that the genuinely ironic paradox simultaneously reveals both the absolute chaos of nature (the "great") and the limited, but nonetheless valuable ("good") attempts of men to comprehend and express this. Essentially, paradox is the literary manifestation of one's ability to hold two opposed ideas in the mind at the same time; it is thus "for irony the *sine qua non*, the soul, source and principle; what liberality is for the urbane imagination" (LN, 1068).

Both these forms, the fragment and the paradox, were included in the broader form that Schlegel developed to present the full complexity of his ideas: the dialogue. By introducing different characters (all of whom are nonetheless clearly elements of Schlegel's own personality and mental life, albeit filled out with allusions to members of his Jena circle), he could present his views from very different assumptions and contexts: philosophical, literary-critical, literary-historical, even religious. In addition, the dialogue form could contain diverse genres: essay, eulogy, letter, public speech, academic lecture, casual conversation and repartee, dramatic interlude, even song and verse. Such flexibility of form and speaker allowed Schlegel to include earlier drafts and stages of his intellectual development. As Ernst Behler has noted, "By including such contradictory stages, the work mirrors thinking-in-process."[40] Or as Schlegel himself said, "the present dialogue . . . is intended to set against one another quite divergent opinions, each of them capable of shedding new light upon the infinite spirit of poetry from an individual standpoint, each of them striving to penetrate from a different angle into the real heart of the matter" (DP, 55).

Other artistic manifestations of philosophical irony besides those used or enumerated by Schlegel are possible and were employed by the writers I shall discuss in the following chapters. The poem as an unresolved debate (Keats's Odes), the poem as a never-ending improvisation (Byron's *Don Juan*), and the poem that de-creates the poet's favorite symbols (Yeats's "Sweet Dancer" and "A Crazed Girl") are only a few of the ways other artists have found to embody in literature the basic perceptions of romantic irony.

Fundamental to such ironic literary discourse, as Paul de Man and Cyrus Hamlin have argued, is the distinction between allegory or metaphor and symbol. Allegory or metaphor acknowledges and preserves the difference between the way the world is in reality and the way it appears in language, between the object and the subject, between eternity and temporality, between the infinite and the finite. Symbolism, on the other hand, asserts a fundamental unity of the object with the subject, of the signifier with its semantic significance. Both de Man and Hamlin one-sidedly argue that only metaphor and allegoric irony accurately reflect the human condition. Despite the symbolist's attempt to make the temporal structure of the poem mimetically reveal the infinite, asserts Hamlin, "the language of the poem, the situation it represents, and the voice of the self which speaks through it, are all necessarily finite and limited, subject to the processes of time, human experience, and human history." Therefore, he insists, "some degree of tension or discontinuity always remains between the finite means and the infinite end, the temporal structure and the transcendent goal, which poetic language and poetic experience cannot overcome."[41] This tension or discontinuity is the basis of the metaphoric or allegoric—as distinct from the symbolic—mode of poetry. De Man and Hamlin correctly analyse the nature of ironic discourse. But they fail to see that both modes of discourse, allegory and symbolism, are appropriate to romantic irony.[42] Just as the romantic-ironic work sustains two opposed ideas without reconciling them, so it sustains two modes of figural discourse without privileging one over the other.

The romantic-ironic artist must both affirm and question the claims of the symbol to have accurately achieved "a translucence of the special in the individual, or of the general in the special, or of the universal in the general, above all . . . the translucence of the eternal through and in the temporal."[43] Even as he enthusiastically generates a symbol in a mimetic representation of life-creating chaos, the "sentimental" or self-conscious ironist must acknowledge the gap between that infinite chaos and his symbol which, being man-made, can only partially render that reality intelligible. Despite the unalterable opposition of symbol and metaphor, romantic-ironic discourse must allow room for both linguistic modes to operate with equal validity.

Because for Schlegel both symbolism and allegory, both enthusiasm and irony, are equally valid, the constant consciousness of the limits of human comprehension is not accompanied by despair, frustration, or existential *angst*. Most modern commentators on irony have ignored the enthusiastic creativity inherent in Schlegel's concept of romantic irony. Perhaps they have been overly influenced by Hegel's description of irony as "infinite absolute negativity," which Kierkegaard endorsed in *The Concept of Irony* (1841). In any case, they have assumed that romantic irony, or what Wayne Booth calls "Unstable-Overt-Infinite Irony," leads only to an absurdist vision of a world where, as in the works of Samuel Beckett, "all is chaos, when there is no point in living, when there is, in fact, no point in writing either."[44] Even D. C. Muecke's excellent analysis of romantic irony in *The Compass of Irony* subtly shifts the emotional emphasis of Schlegel's concept from celebration to desperation. Muecke selects Thomas Mann's *Dr. Faustus* as the best literary example of romantic irony, even though he recognizes that it is a more "modern" and hence "less optimistic" work. In Mann's novel, the romantic-ironic vision becomes frightening and the chaos of the universe is purely destructive. Overly influenced by Mann's pessimism, Muecke one-sidedly concludes,

> What the theory of Romantic Irony achieved . . . was a (highly generalized) programme for modern literature . . . It recognized, to begin with, man's ironic predicament as a finite being, terrifyingly alone in an infinite and infinitely complex and contradictory world

of which he could achieve only a finite understanding, and in his art only a finite presentation, but a world for which he, and particularly the artist, the artist as God since there was no other, had nevertheless to accept responsibility and give it meaning and value. It went on to recognize that implicit even in the artist's awareness and acceptance of his limitations there lay the possibility, through the self-irony of art, of transcending his predicament, not actually yet intellectually and imaginatively . . . Wishing to keep open the place of art in an open world, the theorists of Romantic Irony prescribed a "dynamic" literature which would ironically accept and ironically express within itself the general ironies of art and of the human predicament at large and so preserve itself against "the destructive power of the whole."[45]

But for Schlegel, as for Byron, Keats, and Carlyle, the chaos of the universe was fertile rather than destructive, and an ironic awareness of the limits of human understanding only posed a more exciting challenge to the alert and enthusiastically creative mind: to participate ever more expansively in the abundance of creative becoming. Life, and the ironic artistic process that actively participates in life, is play, insists Schlegel. "We demand that events, men, in short the play of life, be taken as play and be represented as such" (DP, 89). In seeing this active embracing of chaos as an enjoyable game, as *Spiel*, Schlegel is echoing Schiller's affirmation in his letters on aesthetic education that man "is only wholly man when he is playing."[46] But for Schlegel, play involves a balancing between the naive and the sentimental, between an apprehension of the beauty and truth of the natural world and a recognition of the incomprehensibility of infinite becoming. It is just this playful balancing that Schiller rejected in *Naive and Sentimental Poetry* as the unacceptable equivocation of the sentimental poet's bucolic idyll.

Romantic irony, then, is a mode of consciousness or a way of thinking about the world that finds a corresponding literary mode. The artist who perceives the universe as an infinitely abundant chaos; who sees his own consciousness as simultaneously limited and involved in a process of growth or becoming; who therefore enthusiastically engages in the difficult but exhilarating balancing between self-creation and self-destruction; and who then articulates this experience in a form that simultaneously creates and de-creates itself is producing the literary mode that Schlegel called romantic irony. As a literary mode,[47] romantic irony characteristically includes certain elements: a philosophical conception of the universe as becoming, as an infinitely abundant chaos; a literary structure that reflects both this chaos or process of becoming and the systems that men impose upon it; and a language that draws attention to its own limitations.

THE ORIGINS OF PHILOSOPHICAL IRONY

What led Schlegel to deny so emphatically the existence of an underlying order in nature? Both the philosophical challenges posed by Kant and Fichte and specific political, cultural and literary events in Europe in the late eighteenth century influenced Schlegel's thinking. On the epistemological level, philosophical irony is Schlegel's answer to Kant's frustrating insistence upon the limits of human knowledge. Kant had theoretically divided the universe into two realms, the *noumenon* (the *Ding-an-sich* or the world as it actually is) and the *phenomenon* (the world as it is perceived by the human mind); he had further insisted that these two realms are not, and can never be, the same. The very act of perception is a process of structuring or organizing sensory data; the mind thus responds not to raw sense-data but to already categorized experience. As the Kantian Gestalt psychologists have argued, "Experience as such exhibits an order *which is itself experienced*"; therefore, "the right psychological formula" for human perception is *"pattern of stimulation—organization—response to the products of organization."*[48] The determinate objects of experience are thus the products of a synthesis of raw data with the mental categories of unity, causality, space, time, and so forth, a process that takes place before cognition occurs. Human cognition is thus limited to categorized experience; Kant called this realm of human understanding or knowledge *Verstand*. This realm is necessarily finite, because it is limited materially to specific concrete experiences and formally to a knowledge of the mental structures or categories of all possible experiences.

Biologically the human mind is so designed that it can receive sensory information only through the categories or structures that it itself imposes upon experience; from this it followed for Kant that the subject can only truly know what it itself makes, structures, or forms. In the case of man, all such knowledge must be finite. And because human knowledge is not infinite and therefore is not self-caused, Kant held that man's "sensible intuitions" must be caused by an external being, the noumenal world. Insofar as the human mind attempts to transcend the realm of phenomenal, structured experience and to discover the noumenon directly, to come into contact with the unconditioned basis for the conditional, it engages in acts of what Kant called "pure reason" or *Vernunft*.

Pure reason has developed such unexperienceable ideas as totality and infinity.

The dual functioning of *Verstand* and *Vernunft* leads to a contradiction, the famous Kantian antinomy. The human mind must simultaneously affirm both the existence of an unconditioned, free first cause and the fact that there is no completed causal series in nature and hence no freedom. For Kant, this contradiction demonstrated the invalidity of pure reason's attempt to ascertain any truth about the noumenon. It is crucial to see here that Kant has accepted the Aristotelian principle of identity and contradiction ($p = p$; $p \neq$ not-p) as not only a principle of thought or structural category determining the way the human mind functions but also a constitutive principle of reality or the noumenon itself. He has further assumed that the category of causality applies not only to the unending causal series of the phenomenal world but to the constitutive relationship between the noumenal and the phenomenal world (that is, the noumenal world, the thing in itself, causes our perceptions of it). Since Kant firmly believed that the world could not be both free and not free, and that freedom could not cause nonfreedom, he resolved these contradictions by denying the validity of any human or finite understanding of the world as it actually is, even though he acknowledged the moral necessity for postulating the existence of a noumenal realm in which God functions as first cause and as ultimate authority for the categorical imperative.[49]

Kant thus left his followers with a human desire to know the absolute, the *Ding-an-sich*, that can never be satisfied. This can easily lead to despair, as it did in the dramas and fiction of Heinrich von Kleist, in which humanity is imprisoned in its own finitude and feels always incomplete, frustrated, inadequate; in which one finally ends in psychic atrophy. In an attempt to save humanity from such despair, Fichte criticized Kant's limitation of human knowledge to what can be known from sensible intuitions. He argued that the mind is capable of an "intellectual intuition" in which it has a direct experience of the infinite. In his *Theory of Knowledge* (1794), Fichte asserted that Kant's noumenal world does not exist, that human consciousness creates its own universe (the Ego posits itself). Further, the Ego itself creates its antithesis, the Non-Ego (what I am not) or finite world, in order to stimulate the Ego to greater creativity and an expanding consciousness that alone constitutes the experience of freedom. But Fichte thereby denied the reality of an external, non-self-created, objective world. The burning question for Schlegel and his contemporaries, who were all convinced by Spinozistic pantheism (as advocated by Lessing, Jacobi, Mendelsohn, Goethe, and others) that an objective, external reality exists, was "How can the finite world of sensible knowledge (the phenomenal realm) and the infinite world of pure being (the noumenal realm) be brought together?"

Philosophical irony, or the conception of the noumenon as an abundant chaos, is Schlegel's answer to this question. By defining essential reality or the noumenal realm as becoming, Schlegel relegates the principles of identity and contradiction to the phenomenal realm. Identity and contradiction are useful categories for dealing with the exigencies of daily life, and especially in matters relating to the corporeal world, but they have no *absolute* validity. Instead, Schlegel asserts that reality *is* contradiction or, more precisely, becoming. For becoming is a type of contradiction. In the process whereby p becomes not-p, there must be a period when it must be considered to be both p and not-p. Hence, p = not-p in-the-act-of-becoming. In the process of becoming, then, every thing is simultaneously itself and something other; the all is simultaneously one and diverse. Schlegel thus rejects the Aristotelian thesis that substance (being) underlies all change (becoming) for the Heraclitian thesis that becoming underlies all substance. Schlegel can therefore unite the infinite and the finite "as a living becoming activity at the most only differentiated by degree; and the contradiction [between the infinite and the finite that Kant found unacceptable] is only an appearance that arises when one fixes and kills life by making it into a thing (substance)."[50] The finite-in-change is thus an analogue for, and a way into, infinity, which the human mind can apprehend as an unceasing activity, as pure energy or a process of becoming underlying all being.

Political, religious, and literary events also influenced Schlegel's conception of the universe as becoming. The political situation in late eighteenth-century Germany (the existence of many small but well-defended states) made a revolution similar to that taking place in France impossible. Perhaps this is why the German intellectuals, inspired by the ideals of the French Revolution, gave birth to an intellectual revolution instead.[51] As Schlegel insisted in the controversial *Athenaeum* fragment 216, which he defended at length in the essay "On Incomprehensibility," "The French Revolution, Fichte's philosophy, and Goethe's *Meister* are the greatest tendencies of the age . . . Even in our shabby histories of civilization, which usually resemble a collection of variants accompanied by a running commentary for which the original classical text has been lost; even there many a little book, almost unnoticed by the noisy rabble at the time, plays a greater role than anything they did" (A, 216). This sympathy for revolution, both political and intellectual, led to an affirmation of change as such and thus to an acceptance of paradox and contradiction as normal.

In addition, the philosophical revolution effected by Kant, whom Schlegel hailed as "the Copernicus of philosophy" (A, 220), led to an emphasis upon the phenomenal over the noumenal world, upon the ways in which the human mind shaped (rather than passively received) sense-data. Simplifying drastically, we might say that Fichte extended Kant's Idealist philosophy by insisting that the Ego alone created the knowable universe. Schelling, in opposition to Fichte, laid more emphasis upon the independence of a dynamic nature. Hegel then combined these two opposing views in his dialectic of an evolving consciousness. The tradition of German Idealism as it developed through all these thinkers was anti-materialistic and dynamic: it stressed the mind's power to create its own universe of consciousness, freed from any absolute natural law. This affirmation of the freedom of the individual mind to determine its own identity and moral being, according to the categorical imperative defined by Kant, garnered further support from the prevailing Protestant "inner light" theology in Germany at this time. In addition, the Neoplatonic concept of a world created from the radiation of a divine light or energy, a world in which matter was merely the absence of light or spirit, lent further credibility to this Idealist tradition.

Finally, Schlegel was directly and powerfully influenced by Schiller's application of Kant's epistemology to the realm of aesthetics in *Naive and Sentimental Poetry* (1795-96).[52] In this essay, Schiller characterized the naive poet as one who existed wholly within, and who was completely satisfied by, the finite phenomenal realm. Being integrated himself, the naive poet shaped the world into a corresponding harmony. Nature or the object "possesses him entirely";[53] "he feels all the powers of his humanity active in such a moment, he stands in need of nothing, he is a whole in himself; without distinguishing anything in his feeling, he is at once pleased with his spiritual activity and his sensuous life" (NSP, 155). While the naive poet is at home in the world perceived by the understanding (*Verstand*), the sentimental or modern poet feels a constant disjunction between the actual and the ideal. He self-consciously uses his pure reason (*Vernunft*) in an attempt to apprehend the spiritual or noumenal world. This attempt fills him with longing for a perfect knowledge of reality and a direct experience of the infinite. But this longing must remain forever frustrated, since Schiller followed Kant in denying to the human mind an accurate apprehension of the noumenal world. But even though the sentimental poet does not achieve his goal, just because "his task is an infinite one" (NSP, 156), he is perhaps superior to the naive poet. He at least extends our minds "beyond their natural circumscription" (NSP, 156) and thus encourages our moral striving to transcend the merely phenomenal and become pure spirit.

Nevertheless, for Schiller as for Kant, any rational attempt to unite the phenomenal and noumenal worlds was contradictory and therefore intellectually deceptive or an equivocation. Earlier, in the 1793 series of letters *On the Aesthetic Education of Man*, Schiller had tried to resolve the Kantian antinomies by limiting them to a psychological context. Schiller there defined the human condition as dualistic. As a natural animal, man desires abundant and varied sensuous gratification (what Schiller called the *Stofftrieb*, which corresponds to Kant's *Sinnlichkeit*); as a thinking animal, man desires a permanent identity and an enduring rational and moral order (what Schiller called the *Formtrieb*, which includes Kant's *Verstand* and *Vernunft*). Schiller argued that these opposing psychic drives could be reconciled in the experience of play, where rules are freely chosen and dynamic motion creates an enduring pattern. Schiller had further argued that only the aesthetic experience of freedom, of the union of desire and law (Kant's "purposiveness without purpose" or *Zweckmässigkeit ohne Zweck*), produced by a beautiful object could fully satisfy the psychological desire for the condition of play (*Spieltrieb*). "With beauty man shall *only play*, and it is with *beauty only* that he shall play. For, to declare it once and for all, Man only plays when he is in the fullest sense of the word a human being, and *he is only fully a human being when he plays*" (AE, 107).[54]

But Schiller's subsequent study of the sublime persuaded him that such a gratifying psychological reconciliation of the compulsions of duty (of reason and morality) and the compulsions of nature (of bodily needs and desires) through play occurs at the expense of rational truth. As Schiller acknowledged in *On the Sublime* (c. 1795), since man cannot escape death, he is *not free*.[55] The experience of freedom aroused by the aesthetic contemplation of beauty is therefore limited or naive and must historically give way to man's conscious and *willed* struggle to transcend his sensuous nature and physical limitations by becoming pure spirit or form. This effort is aided, not by beauty, but by the sublime, an aesthetic experience that simultaneously arouses our consciousness of the infinite and our painful recognition of human finitude. Therefore, in *Naive and*

Sentimental Poetry, Schiller criticized the bucolic idyll of the sentimental poet who attempted to realize the ideal (the noumenal) within the natural or phenomenal world:

> He will, indeed, satisfy all classes of readers without exception up to a certain point because he strives to unite the naive with the sentimental, and consequently discharges to a certain degree the two opposed demands that can be made on a poem; but because the poet, in the effort to unify both, fails to do justice to either one, and is neither wholly nature nor wholly ideal, he cannot for that very reason be quite acceptable to a rigorous taste that cannot forgive half-measures in aesthetic matters. (NSP, 151)

Schiller's own attempt to define a new kind of idyll that would completely reconcile *"all opposition between actuality and the ideal"* and lead those "who cannot now go back to Arcady forward to Elysium" (NSP, 153) stumbles on the contradictory insistence that this new "higher harmony" must be both static ("calm") and in constant, dynamic motion. "The highest unity must prevail," demands Schiller; "but not at the expense of variety; the mind must be satisfied, but not so that aspiration ceases on that account" (NSP, 154). Schiller's "rigorous" classical taste found it theoretically difficult to reconcile such logical oppositions (although one could read his *Wilhelm Tell* as their successful *poetic* reconciliation). But Friedrich Schlegel could and did embrace such contradictions easily in his ontology of chaotic becoming and his aesthetic of "hovering" self-restraint.

By 1800, then, the Kantian tradition of German Idealism and the English Deist "higher criticism of the Bible"[56] had given birth to romantic irony, a radically new way of thinking about the nature of the universe and the role of the artist. This conceptualization of the world and the creative process is artistically manifested in the writings of Byron, Keats, and Carlyle. Committed to an enthusiastic affirmation of change at all levels of psychological and social experience, they tested a variety of formal structures in their effort to include such change in their written works. In doing so, they deliberately rejected the structural plot and the symbolic imagery of the "circuitous journey" back to paradise—the controlling design of a secularized Judaeo-Christian literary tradition.

2

Byron:
"Half Dust, Half Deity"

Byron's mature works are probably the most masterful artistic examples of romantic irony in English. From the time of the fourth canto of *Childe Harold's Pilgrimage* to his death, Byron artistically presented his "self" as that mode of consciousness I have been defining as romantic irony. "Byron" is Schlegel's hero, the urbane man of liberal imagination and tolerance. Engaging in continuous self-creation, Byron deliberately blurred the lines between his "real" self and his "artistic" self. More and more, he lived the role he imagined for himself, a heroic balancing between enthusiastic commitment and sophisticated skepticism. In this process of self-fictionalization, this deliberate incarnation of philosophical irony and "self-restraint," Byron paralleled the achievement of *The Prelude*, the transformation of autobiography into myth. But where Wordsworth's egotistical sublimity enabled him to present the details of his own life as heroic exempla, a paradigm for salvation, Byron more modestly chose to embody a mode of consciousness in a fictive "self" rendered in sufficient detail to be credible as an actual person.[1] The name of that fictive person is never in doubt—he is called "Byron." The fictive Byron and the empirical Byron are and are not the same; this is but one of many examples of what Byron confessed was his "natural love of contradiction and paradox."[2]

Even before *Don Juan*, that *locus classicus* of English romantic irony, Byron had philosophically envisioned the universe as a dynamic chaos. His perception of life as vital motion animates *Childe Harold's Pilgrimage* where "pilgrimage" is finally celebrated as a process of becoming, not "the Truth but the way to Truth," as Jerome McGann puts it.[3] And as such, Byron's concept of pilgrimage closely parallels Victor Turner's: the pilgrimage is a protracted liminal experience in which the participant leaves a highly structured society or world-view and enters for a time an unstructured *communitas*.[4] The poet-narrator of *Childe Harold* moves away from a rigid, narrow definition of the self and the universe into a more open-ended, self-expanding awareness of the possibilities of life. But Childe Harold himself, rather than proceeding to a postliminal reintegration with natural and social processes, turns back to a preliminal, constrictive, and separated selfhood. In *Childe Harold's Pilgrimage* Byron's philosophical irony had not yet found an adequate artistic form.

Validating Byron's intuition that all men should travel, because "it is from *experience* not *Books*, we ought to judge of mankind,"[5] the poet-narrator of *Childe Harold* psychologically moves from a conventional, youthful impressionability through an alienated and bitter world-weariness to a romantic-ironic apprehension of the never fully knowable glory of human life. His mental and physical movements embody Byron's emphatic assertions to Annabella Milbanke: "The great object of life is Sensation—to feel that we exist—even though in pain—it is this 'craving void' which drives us to Gaming—to Battle—to Travel—to intemperate but keenly felt pursuits of every description whose principal attraction is the agitation inseparable from their accomplishment." Therefore, he continues, "*I* can't *stagnate* . . . if I must sail let it be on the ocean no matter how stormy—anything but a dull cruise on a level lake without ever losing sight of the same insipid shores by which it is surrounded."[6] The stormy, often painful mental passages of the poet-narrator finally lead him to a growing consciousness of the possibilities of life.

By the time he reaches St. Peter's in Rome, the poet-narrator has experienced the sense of momentary freedom from human limitations that love and imagination can bring to mortal man. Inspired by the Venus de Medici, that artistic embodiment of the ideal in the real,[7] he intuitively apprehends that love can make man feel divine and thus transcend for a moment the ironic consciousness of boundaries dividing heaven from earth:

> Glowing and circumfused in speechless love,
> Their full divinity inadequate
> That feeling to express or to improve,
> The gods become as mortals, and man's fate
> Has moments like their brightest; but the weight
> Of earth recoils upon us;—let it go!
> We can recall such visions, and create,
> From what has been or might be, things which grow
> Into thy statue's form and look like gods below.   (CHP, 4. 52)

And the imaginative powers of the human mind, as manifested by Michaelangelo, Alfieri, Galileo, Machiavelli, and Canova, are themselves "sublimities" that "might furnish forth creation" (CHP, 4.54-55). Convinced now that man is born with a "faculty divine," consciousness itself, the poet-narrator pronounces his curse of forgiveness. Having become a romantic ironist, he magnanimously accepts the limitations as well as the open possibilities of the human condition. Like the daughter who breast-fed her imprisoned, starving father, he gives back love rather than hatred and thus breaks the closed and vicious circle of vengeance that has reduced the history of human civilization to a succession of tyrannies.[8]

Entering St. Peter's, he participates in the sublime process of mental and emotional growth that is Byron's paradigm for the abundant chaos of life. Feeling his mind expand, he realizes that all human knowledge is but "piecemeal": what we are capable of understanding now is far less than what we shall come to know as we continually participate in the process of life and self-transcendence. Yet Byron shows us too how this traditional experience of the sublime can lead directly to philosophical irony: paradoxically, the recognition of the potential infinity of the human mind entails an intensified awareness of its present limitations.

> Enter: its grandeur overwhelms thee not;
> And why? it is not lessen'd; but thy mind,
> Expanded by the genius of the spot,
> Has grown colossal, and can only find
> A fit abode wherein appear enshrined
> The hope of immortality; and thou
> Shalt one day, if found worthy, so defined,
> See thy God face to face as thou dost now
> His Holy of Holies, nor be blasted by his brow.
>
> Thou movest—but increasing with the advance,
> Like climbing some great Alp, which still doth rise,
> Deceived by its gigantic elegance;
> Vastness which grows, but grows to harmonise—
> All musical in its immensities;
> Rich marbles, richer painting, shrines where flame
> The lamps of gold, and haughty dome which vies
> In air with Earth's chief structures, though their frame
> Sits on the firm-set ground—and this the clouds must claim.
>
> Thou seest not all; but piecemeal thou must break
> To separate contemplation the great whole;
> And as the ocean many bays will make,
> That ask the eye—so here condense thy soul
> To more immediate objects, and control
> Thy thoughts until thy mind hath got by heart
> Its eloquent proportions, and unroll
> In mighty graduations, part by part,
> The glory which at once upon thee did not dart,

> Not by its fault—but thine. Our outward sense
> Is but of gradual grasp: and as it is
> That what we have of feeling most intense
> Outstrips our faint expression; even so this
> Outshining and o'erwhelming edifice
> Fools our fond gaze, and greatest of the great
> Defies at first our Nature's littleness,
> Till, growing with its growth, we thus dilate
> Our spirits to the size of that they contemplate.   (CHP, 4.155-158)

Here the poet-narrator simultaneously acknowledges his own mortal limitations ("our Nature's littleness") and his capacity to move beyond his initial, overly narrow perceptions (the "immediate objects" of his condensed soul). As his gaze rolls in "mighty graduations" over the increasing beauty and grandeur of the bays and domes of St. Peter's, his mind dilates to encompass the "outshining and o'erwhelming edifice" that rises above the highest Alpine mountain into the realm of the clouds. And even though a finite human language can never hope to capture the immensities of this "gigantic elegance"—"as it is / That what we have of feeling most intense / Outstrips our faint expression"—the poet-narrator's consciousness nonetheless transcends the limits of language and mortality to experience momentarily a power and harmony beyond its grasp: "we thus dilate / Our spirits to the size of that they contemplate." This is the experience of philosophical irony embodied in the processual ritual of pilgrimage: the awareness of the capacities of the human mind to leap beyond the givens of its former experience, to participate in a never-ending process of growth, self-destruction, and self-creation.

The poet-narrator can now definitively reject his lesser selves, of whom Childe Harold himself was one. That spiritually inert, self-indulgent, melancholic alter-ego is now given over to the past.[9] He consumes his time nostalgically trying to recapture a forever-lost innocence in an isolated paradise near the castled crags of Drachenfels. His proud alienation, which once so tempted the narrator ("I have not loved the world, nor the world me") has been rendered slightly grotesque ("his sandal-shoon and scallop-shell") by the magnanimous spirit of generosity and commitment to all the contradictions, sufferings, limitations, and glories of the human condition voiced by the poet. The eye of the poet now widens even beyond the bays and dome of St. Peter's, and opens upon the broad and turbulent expanse of the ocean itself, Byron's concluding image for the chaotic abundance of life.

> . . . boundless, endless, and sublime—
> The image of Eternity—the throne

Of the Invisible; even from out thy slime
The monsters of the deep are made; each zone
Obeys thee; thou goest forth, dread, fathomless, alone.
And I have loved thee, Ocean!   (CHP, 4.183.5-184.1)

The poet-narrator "Byron" can now celebrate both the monsters of the deep, the destructive forces which prepare the way for new creations, and the invisible, fathomless principle of boundless life. Within the zone of that life, his own self must be continually made and remade—"I am not now / That which I have been."

Although the poet-narrator of *Childe Harold's Pilgrimage* becomes a philosophical ironist committed to continuous self-definition and self-transcendence, he does not become an artistic ironist. The projection of the Childe as an alter-ego does allow Byron to explore two closely related but finally antithetical modes of being, but the structure of the poem—a series of vignettes loosely cohering around a voyage and meditations upon those scenes—does not provide for a complex interplay of antithetical modes of vision or paradoxical situations. The few instances of gentle mockery that the narrator permits himself—the deliberately affected diction with which he introduces the Childe ("in sooth he was a shameless wight, / Sore given to revel and ungodly glee; / Few earthly things found favour in his sight / Save concubines and carnal companie / And flaunting wassailers of high and low degree.") and his dismissal of the Childe's "sandal-shoon and scallop-shell"—hardly challenge the pervasively serious, even on occasion lugubrious, tone with which the poet recounts his experiences. That Byron had not yet fully embraced philosophical irony as a mode of openness and comic freedom is clear when we look at *Manfred*, that "dramatic poem" or "mental theatre"[10] written between the third and fourth cantos of *Childe Harold* in 1816-17.

Manfred is obsessed with the pessimistic elements of philosophical irony, the skeptic's insistence upon the limits of human consciousness and power. He is the Faustian soul who seeks infinite knowledge and total control over the universe but who is repeatedly forced to recognize the ironic disjunction between finite man and infinite chaos. "The Tree of Knowledge is not that of Life," he learns. Man's mental systems, no matter how complex and sophisticated (and Manfred's are more extensive than most), still can never encompass the infinity of life. But rather than accepting this ironic awareness of human finitude as a mode of possibility and part of the process of self-transcendence—as does the poet-narrator of *Childe Harold*—Manfred bitterly rebels against the limitations of his own humanity. He thus locks himself into a tragic view of life. For him, the knowledge that man is half dust as well as half deity is a "fatal truth," full of sorrow. This is because Manfred is obsessed with the past, with the mistakes made by his earlier, smaller self. Rejecting out of hand the possibility that the future may bring experiences of human love and glory as great as his lost relationship with Astarte, Manfred can experience his present life only as a cruel curse.

Yet Manfred heroically defies any attempt to ease his guilt-ridden suffering. He rejects the temptations of the Witch of the Alps to deny the value of the merely human Astarte and to forget his love for her. He turns away from the overly naive pastoral life of the shepherd and the chamois hunter. He emphatically refuses the services of the kindly Abbot and the self-mystifying Christian theology he would insert between Manfred and "the overruling infinite" (2.4.416). Instead, Manfred maintains his superabundance of consciousness and his equality with the "destinies" or powers that be. As Manfred tells the Spirit who, like the Devil in Goethe's *Faust*, unsuccessfully tries to claim his soul, his mind has achieved knowledge and control over the elements by

> . . . superior science, penance, daring,
> And length of watching, strength of mind, and skill
> In knowledge of our fathers when the earth
> Saw men and spirits walking side by side
> And gave ye no supremacy.   (3.4.375-379)

The mind, Manfred triumphantly asserts, is its own creator and destroyer:

> The mind which is immortal makes itself
> Requital for its good or evil thoughts,
> Is its own origin of ill and end,
> And its own place and time; its innate sense,
> When stripp'd of this mortality, derives
> No colour from the fleeting things without,
> But is absorbed in sufferance or in joy,
> Born from the knowledge of its own desert.   (3.4.389-396)

Because Manfred's mind has chosen a "wretched identity"[11] that cannot change, Manfred is inevitably swallowed up by the chaos from which he came. His life, like the "pathless comet" under which he was born, "still rolling on with innate force, / Without a sphere, without a course" (I,1:120-121), has shaped its own finite form. Aspiring as high as the Alps he deftly climbs, hoping to make his own "the mind of other men, / The enlightener of nations" (3.1.107-108), then falling "even as the mountain-cataract" (3.1.110) into the depths of inadvertent cruelty and guilty self-recrimination, Manfred has embodied the ironist's consciousness of human finitude. And he has borne that painful consciousness with courage and dignity. He has remained what the Abbot perceptively describes—a noble creature with enormous energy fully absorbed in "chaos—light and darkness, / And mind and dust, and passions and pure thoughts, / Mix'd and contending without end or order" (3.1.164-166).

But in his obsession with his agonizing loss of Astarte, his inability to look to the future for a new and expanded consciousness that would re-shape and reinterpret the past, Manfred has allowed his critical, skeptical intelligence to overwhelm his creative enthusiasm. He has failed to see that the hope aroused by the apparition of Astarte in the first Act—"O God! if it be thus, and *thou* / Art not a madness and a mockery, / I yet might be most happy" (I,1:188-190)—is not only the illusion he perceives but also a possibility for his future growing self. Manfred, by insisting on the irreplaceability of the past and the absolute value of a particular relationship, has closed himself inside a tragic view of the human condition. And in doing so, Manfred has embodied the "Byronic hero," the Calvinistically guilt-obsessed, self-recriminatory protagonist of the *Turkish Tales* who has threatened to absorb Byron's personal identity and creative life.[12] Only in the culminating scenes of *Manfred*, when the Demons finally disappear and Manfred dies, does Byron move toward an exorcism of this life-negating alter-ego, and begin to free himself from a total immersion in his own neurotic guilt and self-destructive melancholy.

That Byron came to see Manfred's fixation on an irretrievable past as willfully self-destructive is suggested not only by the play's final scenes, which establish a dramatic distance from Manfred's obsessive sense of sin and ethos of retaliatory justice, but also by the hesitation with which Byron sent the manuscript of *Manfred* to Murray and by the dismissive terms in which he described it:

> I forgot to mention to you—that a kind of poem in dialogue (in blank verse) or drama—from which "the Incantation" is an extract —begun last summer in Switzerland is finished—it is in three acts— but of a very wild—metaphysical—and inexplicable kind.—Almost all the persons—but two or three—are Spirits of the earth & air—or the waters—the scene is in the Alps—the hero a kind of magician who is tormented by a species of remorse—the cause of which is left half unexplained—he wanders about invoking these spirits—which appear to him—& are of no use—he at last goes to the very abode of the Evil principle in propria persona—to evocate a ghost—which appears—& gives him an ambiguous & disagreeable answer—& in the 3d. act he is found by his attendants dying in a tower—where he

studied his art.—You may perceive by this outline that I have no
great opinion of this piece of phantasy—but I have at least rendered
it *quite impossible* for the stage.[13]

Byron the poet, of course, took his play very seriously (it was, at a profound psychological level, a cathartic release from his personal obsession
with incest and Augusta Leigh), but Byron the letter-writer and man of
the world recognized its fantastic and overly self-indulgent aspects. As
Leslie Marchand comments, Byron's writings present a "divided self"; he
is "a romantic with a balance of commonsense which always brings him
back to earth and to an honest recognition of his own frailties and limitations."[14] To put the case in the terms I have been using, the poetry of
Manfred, the *Turkish Tales*, and the first two cantos of *Childe Harold*
presents a naive enthusiasm or mystifying "self-creation" without a de-
creative skepticism, while Byron's letters of the same period reflect his
critical wit and ironic "self-destruction" without a passionate commitment to his own fictions. Not until *Don Juan*, his never-ended masterpiece, did Byron manage to combine the antithetical impulses of his being
in a work of artistic irony.

To reach *Don Juan*, however, he had to make the transition from the
rejected tragic view of *Manfred* to a comic and potentially ironic view.
The agent of that transition was human love. Byron's affair with Marianna Segati, his Venetian antelope, persuaded him that, despite the agonizing losses of Augusta Leigh and Lady Byron, he could still love and be
loved. Thereby released to a saving degree from his own obsession with
the past, Byron could once again participate vigorously in the life of the
present, as his list of lovers between 1817 and 1819 (a list that would do
credit to the mythical Don Juan himself) convinces us:

> since last year I have run the Gauntlet; . . . the Tarruscelli—the Da
> Mosti—the Spineda—the Lotti—the Rizzato—the Eleanora—the
> Carlotta—the Giuletta—the Alvisi—the Zambieri—The Eleanora da
> Bezzi—(who was the King of Naples' Gioaschino's mistress—at least
> one of them) the Theresina of Mazzurati—the Glettenheimer—& her
> Sister—the Luigia & her mother—the Fornaretta—the Santa—the
> Caligari—the Portiera [Vedova?]—the Bolognese figurante—the
> Tentora and her sister—cum multis aliis[.]—some of them are
> Countesses—& some of them Cobblers' wives—some noble—some
> middling—some low—& all whores . . . I have had them all & thrice
> as many to boot since 1817.[15]

To these we must of course add Teresa Guiccioli, the captivating count-
ess who was, if not his first, certainly his last passionate love. And from
his own accounts, it was a love as absorbing and satisfying as his earlier

grand passions for Mary Chaworth, John Edleston, Caroline Lamb, Ladies Jersey, Holland, and Webster, Augusta Leigh, and Marianna Segati. What is important to see in these lists is not the Don Juanesque promiscuity so often emphasized but rather Byron's remarkable capacity to repeat, with intriguing variations, the experiences that brought him the greatest personal pleasure.

The glories of human love that Byron learned upon his pulses are celebrated in *Heaven and Earth* and *The Island*. Here, the romantic vision that generates half of *Don Juan* is presented without irony. To appreciate the affirmations of *Heaven and Earth*, however, we must look first to *Cain*, which is in effect its ironic antithesis. Cain, like Manfred, is a tragic figure. He is obsessed with the consciousness of death, with man's finitude and mortality. Despite his passionate love for Adah, he cannot accept the limitations of the human condition. Led by Lucifer, the incarnation of unfeeling thought, Cain seeks to defy the limits of his being and know the infinite. Having traversed immense spaces and times, Cain proudly refuses to submit to a Jehovah who ordains that man must die. In his anger both at Abel's cruel sacrifice of a living lamb and at Abel's blind conviction that Jehovah is "sole Lord . . . of good, and glory, and eternity" (3.1.231-232), Cain destroys both Abel's altar and his brother's life. In so doing, he has acted without love; he has tried like Lucifer to impose his own metaphysical system on another human being. Paradoxically, in trying to preserve Abel's flock from future slaughter (and Abel himself from the mind-forged manacles of a belief in a cruel, oppressive, and life-denying Jehovah—"I love God more than life," says Abel), Cain has created the very death he sought to prevent. Cain thereby experiences to the full the contradictions of the human condition. Again like Manfred, Cain can understand those contradictions, the inevitable limitations of the human body and mind, only as a curse. Not even the companionship of his innocent child Enoch or the beauty of his beloved Adah can reconcile him to his existence. Fixated upon the limits of the self, Cain remains the archetypal murderer, the man who denies future possibilities and thus kills life.[16] Cain, then, is the pure ironist, for whom self-consciousness is only a melancholy conviction of loss and death.

But the renewal of life through love proffered to Cain by Adah and Enoch, a renewal Cain can see only as a movement toward death, provides an alternative mode of human consciousness. In *Heaven and Earth* and *The Island*, Byron fully develops a romantic humanism that is the antithesis to Cain's ironic pessimism. These poems enthusiastically celebrate the power of human love to fuse the mortal with the divine and to

restore paradise to earth. Passionate love, and the acts of sexual reproduction that naturally grow from that emotion—together with the awareness that this altogether human activity is a paradigm for the abundant
life-force and hence an act of death-transcending glory—are here presented as the ultimate human consciousness. Aholibamah and Anah, the
descendents of Cain, are women so beautiful in their humanity that the
Seraphim Samiasa and Azaziel have fallen in love with them. And their
love has implicitly broken the barrier that Noah tries to maintain between heaven and earth ("Has not God made a barrier between earth /
And heaven, and limited each, kind to kind?" l. 740). When the flood
waters descend, blurring the boundaries of land, sea, and sky, when "the
heavens and the earth are mingling" (l. 1060), we see the paradox and the
dual possibilities inherent in Byron's romantic humanism. Either one can
follow Noah and the reluctant Japhet onto the ark and assume that God
has indeed ordained a human world forever separated from him and at
his mercy, or one can, like Anah, Aholibamah, and the Seraphim,
proudly assert that love unifies the divine and the mortal and thereby
attempt to transcend the human condition as Noah conceives it. As the
floodwaters cover the earth with a crushing weight of death and destruction, the Seraphim fly off with their beloved women—not to the heaven
of Jehovah, from which that authoritarian and intolerant god has forever
barred them, but to an alternative world of divine human experience.[17]

Some of the qualities of that experience are portrayed in *The Island*.
Torquil, a child of the ocean and a worshipper of freedom, follows the
mutinous Christian back to Otaheite, the land of plenty. In this "general
garden" where freedom and love flourish abundantly, Torquil finds
again his bride Neuha. She too is a child of nature, highborn, beautiful,
sensual, innocent, and fearless. Together, these two lovers recreate the
experience of paradise. Rapt in the infinite variety of their mutual passion, they live entirely in the present, oblivious to the burdens of the past
(the weight of vengeance and remorse born by Christian) and confident
that the future holds but finer tones of pleasure.

The corruptions of civilization pursue these lovers, however, in the
form of the navy sent to capture or kill the mutineers of the *Bounty*.
Loyal to his leader, Torquil leaves Neuha to fight by his comrades' side.
But at the moment of their defeat, Neuha appears, offering once again
that love which can transform earth to heaven. As she embraces the
wounded but living Torquil, "paradise was breathing in the sigh / Of
nature's child in nature's ecstasy" (3. 199-200). Sending Christian and his
two men in the larger canoe, Neuha steers Torquil alone across the sea to

what seems a totally barren, death-reeking rock. "Has Neuha brought me
here to die?" asks Torquil's half-upbraiding eye, when suddenly Neuha
leaps into the sea, calling to Torquil to follow fearlessly. Immediately
diving behind her, Torquil dies into life. Like the sun of the South Sea,
that "plunged with red forehead down along the wave, / As dives a hero
headlong to his grave" (1.364-365), Torquil sinks deep into the water,
only to rise again into vital life. His willingness to follow his love even
into apparent death has restored him to paradise; the pursuing crew correctly if ignorantly invoke images of Christ's transfiguration and resur-
rection to describe what they have and have not seen:

> Some said he had not plunged into the wave,
> But vanish'd like a corpse-light from a grave;
> Others, that something supernatural
> Glared in his figure, more than mortal tall;
> While all agreed that in his cheek and eye
> There was a dead hue of eternity.   (4.85-90)

Here Torquil, like the poet-narrator of *Childe Harold's Pilgrimage*, becomes a "pilgrim of the deep" (4.95), committing himself to self-renewal
and self-expansion. For the barren rock conceals a life-sustaining cave,
structured like "a self-born Gothic canopy" and as dimly lit as an "old
cathedral." In this sacred spot of nature, the lovers gain "a central realm
of earth" again, a place where the "olden tale of Love" can be retold forever. "For love is old, / Old as eternity, but not outworn, / With each
new being born or to be born" (4.192-194). In this paradise regained,
Neuha and Torquil manifest their enduring innocence in their capacity to
repeat that olden tale of love and to make every sacrifice necessary (even
the apparent one of death) to sustain it. They show us Byron's mature
conviction that human love, which is as renewable as the daily rising
sun, brings man ultimate experiences of glory and an innocence that
transcends civilization's closed cycles of destruction and revenge. Christian, a tragic figure who like Cain and Manfred is cursed with a past that
cannot be escaped, hurls himself to his self-chosen and violent death.
And Ben Bunting, the brave (but motley) ironist who mockingly comments that Neuha's and Torquil's passionate farewell embraces "will do
for the marines" (2. 531), is killed off by the king's navy. But Torquil and
Neuha proffer an alternative vision. As Jerome McGann enthusiastically
concludes,

> As an allegory, then, *The Island* should probably be regarded as
> normative rather than definitive. It describes the term of man's fur-
> thest hopes but does not offer—any more than *Prometheus Un-*

bound does—the picture of a necessary personal or political future. Both poems are prophecies in the basic sense: they delineate a form of human possibility which yet requires the choice that determines accomplishment, a choice, moreover, that must be reaffirmed constantly. The vision of *The Island* is true because it may be true, always.[18]

But this romantic humanism, this natural supernaturalism, is only half the story Byron has to tell. Ben Bunting's ironic skepticism, and the heroic death he suffered, could not be forgotten or ignored. Nor could Byron repress his "temporary melancholy."[19] Finally, in *Don Juan*, Byron found a vehicle for his divided, romantic-ironic consciousness. In this poem, Byron carefully balances a romantic enthusiasm against a skeptical conviction of human finitude.

Don Juan

The world of *Don Juan* is founded on abundant chaos; everything moves, changes its shape, becomes something different. Time never stands still, but arbitrarily shifts about. Beginning in the present tense with Southey's fall and the narrator's pressing need of a hero, the poem then leaps into the past tense to create its fictive plot, the life and loves of Don Juan. Repeatedly passing from fictive past to authorial present and back again, the poem further extends its time-scape to encompass Cuvier's pre-Adamite ages and that far goal of future time, an unreachable eternity. Byron's never-spoken "lost advice," for instance,

> will one day be found
> With other relics of 'a former world,'
> When this world shall be *former*, underground,
>   Thrown topsy-turvy, twisted, crisped and curled,
> Baked, fried, or burnt, turned inside-out, or drowned,
>   Like all the worlds before, which have been hurled
> First out of and then back again to Chaos,
> The Superstratum which will overlay us.   (9. 37)

And yet "an age may come, Font of Eternity, / When nothing shall be either old or new" (14. 3.5-6). In the chaotic time of this poem, past, present, and future intersect, bringing both the destruction of sometime worlds and the creation of possible ages.

Nor does space stay put in this ironic universe. Starting in England and/or Spain, the poem moves abruptly to Greece, then crosses to Turkey, Ismail, and Russia and races back across the Continent to England

—the place so often revisited by the narrator during Don Juan's travels. The poem refuses to confine itself to that territory already explored by man: "full soon / Steam-engines will conduct him to the Moon" (10.2.8). While expanding to encompass the galaxies, the poem also describes the smallest, most concentrated spaces. Seeking an adequate comparison for Lady Adeline, Byron fastens on a bottle of champagne,

> Frozen into a very vinous ice,
>   Which leaves few drops of that immortal rain,
> Yet in the very centre, past all price,
>   About a liquid glassful will remain;
> And this is stronger than the strongest grape
> Could e'er express in its expanded shape:
> 'Tis the whole spirit brought to a quintessence. (13.37.3-38.1)

Voyaging hither and thither, both Don Juan and the narrator traverse psychological as well as physical space, exploring the boundaries of the possible. "The new world would be nothing to the old, / If some Columbus of the moral sea / Would show mankind their soul's Antipodes" (14.101.6-8). The distances traveled by this poem are wide, various, and haphazardly covered. Sent to France and Italy, Don Juan is thrown naked upon a Greek island. Sold into slavery and condemned to death by the jealous Gulbeyaz, Don Juan disappears while we readers suddenly find ourselves at the siege of Ismail. Fifty-six stanzas later, Don Juan and Johnson suddenly join us there. Such abrupt spatial transitions contribute to the poem's pervasive restlessness.

In a poetic universe where space and time behave so capriciously, it would be difficult for things to sustain lasting identity or unity. In *Don Juan*, things fall apart, often rather violently. Julia's bedroom is reduced to a shambles by her irate husband. Her last love letter is torn up to make lots for the starving, shipwrecked crew, while both Juan's dog and his tutor are carved up for breakfast. Haidée's heart is broken. And the entire city of Ismail is savagely beaten down into rubble. In a world that so clearly moves in and out of chaos, human relationships are no more stable than physical objects. Juan's love-affairs with Julia, Haidée, Dudu, Gulbeyaz, and Catherine all end. Yet every lost relationship is followed by a new one. In this poem, acts of destruction make way for new births, and Haidée, the child of nature, is abundantly recompensed by Aurora Raby, the child of nurture. Even Don Juan is replaceable; Donna Inez "informed him that he had a little brother / Born in a second wedlock" (10.32.6-7).

Yet while individual relationships perish and are created anew, the human community endures. The court of Catherine, always producing new lovers for its queen, and the high society of England, making and unmaking matches and heirs, are paradigms for the human condition. The community makes it possible for its members to engage in a never-ending process of self-creation, self-destruction, and self-transcendence. Thus the universe of *Don Juan* images the chaotic abundance of life itself: constantly changing, infinitely various, merrily multiplying. "Love, war, travel, tempest" are but a few of Byron's topics; and his ranging eye encompasses not only the navigable globe and the heavens above, but every class and condition of men, from sultans and lords through lawyers, soldiers, clergymen, and artists to whores and highwaymen.

A world of such infinite variety and incessant change defies reduction to a rational, comprehensible system or explanation.[20] The narrator of *Don Juan*, attacking Bishop Berkeley's egotistical attempt to reduce the world to pure spirit, insists that however hard he tries to discover the metaphysical order of the universe, he yet can "find no spot where man can rest eye on, / Without confusion of the sorts and sexes, / Of being, stars, and this unriddled wonder, / The World, which at the worst's a glorious blunder—" (11. 3.4-8). Man must therefore acknowledge his inability ever to know this infinite, hence incomprehensible, universe. Turning appropriately to Socrates, like Schlegel before him, the narrator asserts:

> Socrates said, our only knowledge was
>   "To know that nothing could be known"; a pleasant
> Science enough, which levels to an ass
>   Each man of wisdom, future, past or present.
> Newton (that proverb of the mind), alas!
>   Declared, with all his grand discoveries recent,
> That he himself felt only "like a youth
> Picking up shells by the great ocean—Truth."   (7.5)

Hence, the narrator concludes, he must hold up "the Nothingness" (that is, the mystery or unknowability) of life.[21]

Since finite man can never unriddle the incomprehensible wonder of the world, he can never be certain of his beliefs or attain any absolute truth.

> "Que sçais-je?" was the motto of Montaigne,
>   As also of the first academicians:
> That all is dubious which man may attain,
>   Was one of their most favourite positions.

> There's no such thing as certainty, that's plain
>   As any of Mortality's conditions:
> So little do we know what we're about in
> This world, I doubt if doubt itself be doubting.   (9.17)

Here Byron strikingly anticipates Ludwig Wittgenstein's assertion in *On Certainty* (1949-51) that no verbal proposition can claim a certainty that gives it an absolute validity, a validity beyond its meaning or function in the language-game in which it is used. Since Wittgenstein implicitly accepted the Kantian antinomy between the phenomenal and the noumenal worlds, he was finally unwilling to accept the absolute truth of any proposition of the type "I know *x*" unless its contradiction is inconceivable. Wittgenstein's language-games operate solely in the phenomenological realm; hence, every statement's claim to certainty is false insofar as it implies valid knowledge of the noumenal world. Nonetheless, like Byron's narrator, Wittgenstein could not dismiss the possibility that a reality exists beyond man's capacity to know or linguistically apprehend it.[22] For Byron's narrator, this commitment to ironic doubt, that "sole prism / Of the Truth's rays" (11.2.6-7), is liberating rather than debilitating. In a masterful piece of rhetorical irony, he affirms those voyages beyond Newton's sea-shores onto the great ocean of truth itself:[23]

> It is a pleasant voyage perhaps to float,
>   Like Pyrrho, on a sea of speculation;
> But what if carrying sail capsize the boat?
>   Your wise men don't know much of navigation;
> And swimming long in the abyss of thought
>   Is apt to tire: a calm and shallow station
> Well nigh the shore, where one stoops down and gathers
> Some pretty shell, is best for moderate bathers.   (9.18)

This narrator, who like Byron has swum the Hellespont (2.106), has never been a moderate bather,[24] never been content with merely picking up pretty seashells when an exciting sea-voyage beckoned, never been willing to settle for a calm and shallow station or a comfortable and conventional "truth" (falsehood) when he might explore the dangerous regions of the unknown. He courageously rejects the illusory security of philosophical systems, for he has seen that "One system eats another up" (14.1.5)—and too often destroys its faithful followers in the process. He commits himself instead to sustaining romantic irony's difficult balancing between a passionate desire for knowledge and a recognition that all human knowledge is inadequate and hence uncertain.

> For me, I know naught; nothing I deny,
>   Admit, reject, contemn; and what know *you*,

> Except perhaps that you were born to die?
>   And both may after all turn out untrue.   (14.3.1-4)

Such an ironic hovering between belief and doubt is, as Schlegel knew, an act of self-liberation and human freedom. The narrator is well aware of the political implications of his ironic stance.

> And I will war, at least in words (and—should
>   My chance so happen—deeds) with all who war
> With Thought;—and of Thought's foes by far most rude,
>   Tyrants and sycophants have been and are.   (9.24.1-4)
>   —I wish men to be free
> As much from mobs as kings—from you as me.
> The consequence is, being of no party,
>   I shall offend all parties:—never mind!   (9.25.7-26.2)

The narrator's skeptical self-extrication from all warring systems, parties, and partial truths alternates with his romantic commitment to the creative process, both in life and in art. Man must fall in love, get drunk, experience ecstasy, multiply, die (in both the Elizabethan and the modern sense)—if he is to participate fully in the abundance of life.

> The best of life is but intoxication:
> Glory, the grape, love, gold, in these are sunk
>   The hopes of all men, and of every nation;
> Without their sap, how branchless were the trunk
>   Of life's strange tree, so fruitful on occasion.   (2.179.2-6)

The passionate, romantic love of Juan and Haidée can bring a perfect happiness ("for to their young eyes / Each was an angel, and earth paradise"; 2.210.7-8), which narrator sympathetically celebrates:

> Oh beautiful! and rare as beautiful!
>   But theirs was love in which the mind delights
> To lose itself when the old world grows dull,
>   And we are sick of its hack sounds and sights . . .   (4.17.1-4)

Such rare and enthusiastic responses to the beautiful creatures of the living world provide bored men and women with pleasurable, satisfying, meaningful experiences. In such moments of intoxication, they experience a kind of self-transcendence—an expansion of human possibility, a widening of the senses and the spirit that is the closest they can come to divinity. One should therefore seek such encounters and, to rephrase Byron slightly, make love, inconstant love, one's constant guest. For

> that which
> Men call inconstancy is nothing more

Than admiration due where nature's rich
 Profusion with young beauty covers o'er
Some favour'd object; and as in the niche
 A lovely statue we almost adore,
This sort of adoration of the real
Is but a heightening of the "beau ideal."

'Tis the perception of the beautiful,
 A fine extension of the faculties,
Platonic, universal, wonderful,
 Drawn from the stars, and filter'd through the skies,
Without which life would be extremely dull;
 In short, it is the use of our own eyes,
With one or two small senses added, just
To hint that flesh is form'd of fiery dust.   (2.211-212)

The agents of such fleshly transfigurations and supreme fictions, as Schlegel knew, are love and wit, or women and art. Byron never underestimated the power of a woman to make and unmake a world. His narrator hails her creative and destructive capacities:

Some call thee "the worst Cause of war," but I
 Maintain thou art the *best:* for after all
From thee we come, to thee we go, and why
 To get at thee not batter down a wall,
Or waste a world? Since no one can deny
 Thou dost replenish worlds both great and small:
With, or without thee, all things at a stand
Are, or would be, thou sea of life's dry land!   (9.56)

The sea of women, like Newton's great ocean of truth, is an incomprehensible abundance of destroying and satisfying fertility.

The human imagination, too, has the power to "replenish worlds both great and small," to create from mortal clay a figure of glory that momentarily redeems the human enterprise. Since we live in a phenomenological realm, confined to what our minds can comprehend of the incomprehensible, we must look to the imagination for all prefigurations of what man and his world may come to be. Together with love, that human pathway to the sublime, art transfigures the human into the divine:

Oh Love! O Glory! what are ye who fly
 Around us ever, rarely to alight?
There's not a meteor in the Polar sky
 Of such transcendent and more fleeting flight.
Chill, and chain'd to cold earth, we lift on high
 Our eyes in search of either lovely light;
A thousand and a thousand colours they
Assume, then leave us on our freezing way.

And such as they are, such my present tale is,
    A non-descript and ever-varying rhyme,
A versified Aurora Borealis,
    Which flashes o'er a waste and icy clime.
When we know what all are, we must bewail us,
    But, ne'ertheless, I hope it is no crime
To laugh at *all* things—for I wish to know
What after *all*, are *all* things—but a *show*?   (7.1-2)

Since the perceivable world is but a partial vision of the unknowable, an illusory show, the images of art are as valid as those of the senses. One can therefore embrace their "entusimusy" with laughter, rather than despair. For insofar as artistic fictions often endure as a lasting recognition of a human possibility not realized in the present world, their bonds with the abundant chaos of noumenal reality may be the stronger. As the poet-narrator asserts of his creation,

Don Juan, who was real, or ideal,—
    For both are much the same, since what men think
Exists when the once thinkers are less real
    Than what they thought, for mind can never sink,
And 'gainst the body makes a strong appeal;
    And yet 'tis very puzzling on the brink
Of what is call'd Eternity, to stare,
And know no more of what is here than there.   (10.20)

Always ironically aware of his human limitations, the poet has nonetheless never avoided the challenge or dangers of exploring the unknown. Sailing his "slight, trim, / But *still* sea-worthy skiff" of Poesy always against the wind, he has "shunn'd the common shore, / And leaving land far out of sight, would skim / The ocean of eternity," undaunted by "the roar of breakers" (10.4.3-6), just as the poet-narrator at the end of *Childe Harold* "wantoned" with the ocean's breakers in "pleasing fear" (CHP, 4.184).

But just as every intense passion ends, so every artistic creation finally proves inadequate to the ever-growing, ever-changing human condition it would image and glorify. The poet is keenly aware that his caper-cutting muse but throws a straw in the wind of a more vigorous, chaotic reality:

. . . such a straw, borne on by human breath,
    Is poesy, according as the mind glows;
A paper kite which flies 'twixt life and death,
    A shadow which the onward Soul behind throws:
And mine's a bubble, not blown up for praise,
But just to play with, as an infant plays.   (14.8.3-8)

Byron's play, however, is as serious as Schiller's, for whom the relaxing function of art constituted a mode of liberation, an access to freedom.[25] We should think too of Wordsworth's apotheosized child in "Ode: Intimations of Immortality," for whom play is still a mode of abundant creation:

> See, at his feet, some little plan or chart,
> Some fragment from his dream of human life,
> Shaped by himself with newly-learned art. (7.90-92)

And in Coleridge's "Frost at Midnight," thought itself becomes a toy in the playful hands of the exuberant imagination, which everywhere seeks and finds a harmonizing echo or mirror of itself.

Through love and the imagination, man engages in romantic irony's constant process of creation and de-creation, of commitment and detachment, of self-projection and self-criticism. For the growing self, that "onward Soul" that yearns for the greater glory, always passes beyond the necessarily finite boundaries of every man-made artifact. The poetic fiction then is both a mode of liberation, imaging a possibility not yet realized by some, and also a rejected prison, the shadow cast behind by those whose expanding consciousness has burst into a wider space. This "paper kite," then, which "flies 'twixt life and death," is in itself a metaphor for the Schlegelian act of hovering (*schweben*), that balancing between self-creation and self-destruction, between commitment and detachment, which Byron perceives as human growth and the process of life itself.

> Between two worlds life hovers like a star,
>   'Twixt night and morn, upon the horizon's verge.
> How little do we know that which we are!
>   How less what we may be! The eternal surge
> Of time and tide rolls on, and bears afar
>   Our bubbles; as the old burst, new emerge,
> Lash'd from the foam of ages; while the graves
> Of empires heave but like some passing waves. (15.99)

Don Juan, that best-balanced and most flexible of paper kites, hovers accordingly between two worlds, two modes of consciousness: between dawning, loving self-creation and darkling, skeptical self-destruction. In the felt disjunction between the naive, romantic, experiencing character (Don Juan) and the reflective, ironic, experienced narrator occurs the vital play and "eternal surge" of life itself. The poem's constant alternation between these widely divergent characters or modes of consciousness is itself an analogue for the process of human growth, of self-crea-

tion and self-transcendence. For as we learn in reading the poem, Don
Juan's experiences lead him ever closer to the narrator and the heroic
vision of romantic irony, while the ironic narrator becomes increasingly
aware of his potential sterility and need for romantic commitment.

Don Juan, handsome, well-born, healthy, courageous, begins life as
the Schillerian realist or naive man.[26] He is innocent, receptive, unself-
conscious, full of energy. When we first encounter him, he seems almost
without identity or personality; he is rather a potentiality, a seed not yet
sprouted into a self. Thus, he seems passive, the instrument of others' desires and will. Yet he is notable for one capacity that he has in superabundance, the capacity to love. His passionate attachments to Julia and especially to Haidée develop his consciousness of a transcendent state. The
long, heart-quaking kiss Juan tastes with Haidée persuades them both, in
the glory of this first total love, that there is "no life beneath the sky /
Save theirs, and that their life could never die" (2.188.7-8). Being so
caught up in the sensations and language only lovers know, they become
in their perfect innocence a renewal of "our first parents," so loving and
so lovely that to them all earth is "another Eden" (4.10). Juan's ability to
commit himself completely to this first love, to feel as passionately and
purely as man can, merits him the title ironically bestowed by the narrator: "what we mortals call romantic, / And always envy, though we
deem it frantic" (4.18.7-8). Juan qualifies for the romantic half of the hero
of romantic irony: the man of passion and enthusiastic commitment who
can give himself wholly to a love that enlarges his self by fusing his being
with another person.

Juan, then, is the romantic lover. But his love-affairs do not last. In
this regard, Juan's career parallels that of his literary namesake, the Don
Juan of dramatic, operatic, and pantomime fame whom Byron had recently seen "sent to the devil, somewhat ere his time" (1.1.8).[27] Before the
nineteenth century, Don Juan had been artistically presented, most notably by Tirso de Molina, Molière, and Mozart, as a callous, clever de-
ceiver who intentionally seduces and abandons women, ever on the look
for new sensual pleasures. In 1812, unknown to Byron, E. T. A. Hoff-
mann profoundly reinterpreted Don Juan as the embodiment of that
erotic desire which perpetually seeks a complete fusion with the ideal
woman or perfect love-object and is constantly frustrated by the limitations of the mortal body.[28] Like Tristan and Isolde, this romanticized
Don Juan can experience the consummation or cessation of his desire
only in death.[29]

While Byron's Don Juan is neither the heartless seducer nor the *Lie-*

bestod lover of literary and operatic tradition, he does embody Byron's conception of the nature of erotic desire. He is capable not only of intense passion but also of loyalty and great kindness. He gallantly saves Leila from the slaughter of Ismail; and every one of his love-affairs is ended, not by his own personal dissatisfaction or cruelty, but by circumstances beyond his control. Julia's husband runs him out of town, Haidée's father sells him into slavery, Suwarrow separates him from Dudu, and Catherine herself sends him away to England. Nonetheless, Juan's love-affairs do end, often with great pain both to Juan and to the women involved (Julia is confined to a convent; Haidée dies of a broken heart). Moreover, erotic passion as such can be destructive, engulfing rather than expanding one's self—is not the serpent in Haidée's very eyes?[30] But while they last, these love-affairs provide delight and satisfaction, as well as anxiety and pain, for *both* partners. Juan thus manifests Byron's profound perception about the nature of eros on earth, a perception that liberates man from the total pessimism inherent in Platonism and the *Liebestod* tradition. Erotic passion, as the Don Juan myth affirms, does not last, but it does return again and again, each time bringing both pain and ecstasy, both the danger of self-annihilation and the exhilarating sensation of powerful union. And for Byron, the pleasures of such self-expanding love delicately balance the frightening violence of its stimulation and the anguish of its ending.

Byron frequently insists upon Juan's identification with eros. At the court of Catherine, the mythical Cupid comically declines into the all-too-human Juan:[31]

> His bandage slipp'd down into a cravat;
>   His wings subdued to epaulettes; his quiver
> Shrunk to a scabbard, with his arrows at
>   His side as a small sword, but sharp as ever;
> His bow converted into a cock'd hat;
>   But still so like, that Psyche were more clever
> Than some wives (who make blunders no less stupid),
> If she had not mistaken him for Cupid.   (9.45)

As the lover who, forced by circumstances, leaves behind his beloved women, as the lover who, however unwittingly, finds himself again and again involved with new women, Juan incarnates erotic desire. As such, he becomes a comic image of Schiller's sentimental idealist or Schlegel's romantic spirit, always striving to transcend his single self, to experience the infinite. Moreover, Juan's capacity to grow through his love-experiences, to develop an ever more perceptive consciousness of his own capacities and values, also defines him—like the poet-narrator of the fourth canto of *Childe Harold*—as a pilgrim of eternity.

Juan's personal growth is clear. Confined by Donna Inez's overly theoretical education, he progresses from innocence and abstraction toward reality. He learns the sensations of love and the physical capacities of his own body, both in bed and on the battlefield; he learns the limitations of mortal man in the face of nature (the tempest and shipwreck) and of society (Lambro's hostile forces). By the time Juan reaches Catherine's court, his naive innocence and open, simple responses have given way to a more effective sophistication. Juan is, from one point of view, now a little spoilt, responding to Catherine's desire with self-love rather than affection. From another point of view, he is becoming more the master of his circumstances, now "able / For love, war or ambition" (10.22.5-6) and thus capable of seizing what opportunities offer. No longer so passive, Juan is becoming more assertive, self-confident, perhaps selfish. But this self-awareness, this concern with gaining his own pleasures (rather than being the tool of circumstances), does enable Juan to make choices. When he reaches England and encounters the matchmaking Lady Adeline, he can reject her selfish suggestions and propose instead the radiant Aurora Raby. Juan's experiences, if they have taught him to hide his honest feelings and to calculate his responses to gain what he wishes, have also taught him to see beneath the surfaces of social glitter and to appreciate what is truly fine in human civilization. He can now interact with women he doesn't desire without being overwhelmed by their advances and seek out the subtler perfections of an Aurora Raby. In this sense, Juan's experiences have led him toward self-definition, toward a conscious self-creation. The personality Juan has developed by the English cantos is of course limited, and would certainly have been subjected to further change had the poem continued (he has a way to go before he could be compared to the revolutionary Anacharsis Clootz), but it is a character that enables Juan to achieve a greater personal freedom and control than he has hitherto known.

> Serene, accomplish'd, cheerful but not loud;
> Insinuating without insinuation;
> Observant of the foibles of the crowd,
> Yet ne'er betraying this in conversation;
> Proud with the proud, yet courteously proud,
> So as to make them feel he knew his station
> And theirs:—without a struggle for priority,
> He neither brook'd nor claim'd superiority.   (15.15)

With this sophistication and self-confidence, we suspect, Juan will be able to escape the nets of the Ladies Fitz-Fulke and Amundeville when he wishes to, however "wan and worn" (17.14) he may become in the process—something he could not have done earlier in Spain, Turkey, or Russia.

As Juan becomes more worldly-wise, the antithetical voice of the narrator begins to acknowledge the limitations of the sophistication *he* has achieved. The narrator is identified by Byron in his rejected preface as "either an Englishman settled in Spain—or a Spaniard who had travelled in England"; as the narrator later claims England as his place of birth (10.66), we can suppose him the former. He is a well-born gentleman, educated at the university (1.52), unmarried, with a keen interest in the ways of the world. He is, above all, the urbane man of liberal imagination so much admired by Schlegel. At thirty, he has grown beyond the passions of his youth, that time when he gave away his heart and lost forever the pure feelings of innocence (6.5). Nonetheless, he is still attracted by beautiful women (1.61), even though he claims that his "days of love are over" (1.216.1). He has replaced the passionate indiscretions of his hot youth with "a deal of judgment" (1.215.7) and that "good old-gentlemanly vice," avarice (1.216.8). More important, in his maturity the narrator has acquired much of that mode of consciousness I have been calling romantic irony—the simultaneous recognition of the blessing and curse of passionate love, the ability to balance an enthusiastic commitment to the values of love and freedom against a skeptical awareness of man's inability ever to comprehend the universe or to act in a way capable of realizing his goals.

> Ambition was my idol, which was broken
>   Before the shrines of Sorrow, and of Pleasure;
> And the two last have left me many a token
>   O'er which reflection may be made at leisure:
> Now, like Friar Bacon's brazen head, I've spoken,
>   "Time is, Time was, Time's past:"—a chymic treasure
> Is glittering youth, which I have spent betimes—
> My heart in passion, and my head on rhymes.   (1.217)

As the poem grows and the narrator's digressions increase, the narrator's consciousness often dominates the poem. As this happens, readers have been tempted to identify the narrator with the historical Byron, seduced by such autobiographical details as the narrator's claim to have swum the Hellespont (2.106) or to have taken the details of Juan's shipwreck and survival in part from "my grand-dad's Narrative" (2.137).[32]

But it would be a mistake, I think, to say simplistically that Byron himself is the narrator or even the elusive "English editor" of *Don Juan*. Rather, the author Byron is creating in the narrator an alter-ego or mode of consciousness that includes some of his own experiences, excludes others (such as incest), and involves some further experiences not directly known by him (such as a visit to a harem).[33] Although the rhetorical mode of the digressions is definably confessional (the diction of the plain, blunt speaker; the plethora of personal references; the tone of sincerity or self-criticism; the structure of self-examination—albeit without guilt or penance), this is confession objectified—perhaps even an "objective correlative" for the confessional process.

The distance between the narrator and the author is subtly defined. Insofar as the passionate love of Juan and Haidée or Juan and Aurora is presented sympathetically, it involves feelings that are no longer experienced by the narrator, whose days of love are over, but that are still part of the author's ongoing affair with Teresa Guiccioli. In contrast to Juan's capacity for emotional passion, the narrator increasingly seems overly blasé. Moreover, the narrator's growing avarice, which culminates in a thirteen-stanza-long eulogy of gold, comes to seem excessive. While we might agree that at thirty-five one has lost the illusions of one's first loves and it may be late to marry, yet as the narrator himself acknowledges, "love lingers still" (12.2.5) and is not so easily replaced by gold as he suggests:

> Love or lust makes man sick, and wine much sicker;
>   Ambition rends, and gaming gains a loss;
> But making money, slowly first, then quicker,
>   And adding still a little through each cross
> (Which *will* come over things), beats love or liquor,
>   The gamester's counter, or the statesman's *dross.* (12.4.1-6)

The narrator's assertion that the miser's obsession with each cheese-paring is a valid substitution for the fool's manias—"Wars, revels, loves" (12.11.5)—would persuade us, perhaps, if he assured us that he too has "great projects in his mind, / To build a college, or to found a race, / A hospital, a church" or to "liberate mankind / Even with the very ore that makes them base" (12.10.1-3, 5-6). But these are ambitions to which the narrator does not lay claim—and his failure to do so helps to chart the space between his values and the author's. The narrator is selfishly materialistic; Byron is not. Perhaps most telling is the narrator's exclusion from the life of action. A detached observer, he reflects upon Juan's escapades and his own responses to the infinite variety of life, but he does not engage in that life—he currently carries on no love-affairs, no family relationships, no social battles. He observes, comments, criticizes, condemns—but does not reform or revolutionize. His own uneasiness with such passivity, which reflects his growing sense of the limitations and sterility of his wholly ironic character, is sharply revealed on one occasion. Asserting his hatred of Catherine's autocracy, he comments:

> And I will war, at least in words (*and—should*
> *My chance so happen—deeds*), with all who war
> With Thought;—and of Thought's foes by far most rude,
>   Tyrants and Sycophants have been and are.
>
> (9.24.1-4; italics added)

By the time the poem breaks off, then, the reader is aware of the limitations as well as the admirable urbanity of the narrator's mode of consciousness. The skeptical narrator who has been structurally opposed to the romantic Juan is thus also engaged in a process of self-analysis and self-criticism. Erring on the side of critical detachment and emotional impotence, he is now beginning to perceive—as we have already perceived —his error in overvaluing intellectual skepticism at the expense of emotional commitment and noble action.

It seems thematically appropriate that at this point in the poem the narrator and Juan encounter each other again. Juan is becoming more sophisticated and self-aware; the narrator is becoming more aware of the emotional paralysis involved in his cynical detachment. As these two figures psychologically move closer together, they physically meet—at Lord Henry Amundeville's electioneering banquet where, penned among the Boring and the Bored, the narrator is deafened by the loud wit of Parson Pith (16.81) and Juan, still distracted by his unnerving encounter with the ghostly Black Friar, is unusually gauche. Does this geographical contiguity imply a closer biographical contiguity than we had suspected? Would the narrator finally have come to confess that he and Don Juan are the same person? The questions are unanswerable, of course, but they point toward a tantalizing possibility: a nearly perfect literary manifestation of that "absolute synthesis of absolute antitheses, the continual self-creating interchange of two conflicting thoughts" that Schlegel defines as romantic irony.

Don Juan's celebration of life as process, change, growth, openness, tolerance, expansion and abundance necessarily entails an attack on death, stasis, repetition, retrogradation, closed minds and systems, bigotry, and sterility. The poem is therefore dedicated to (an attack on) Robert Southey, the antithesis of all Byron most values. Southey, the "representative of all the race," embodies a closed, retrogressive mind and ideology. A political turncoat, he is both poetically and sexually impotent (in Regency slang, "a dry bob" is sexual intercourse without ejaculation):

> . . . you overstrain yourself, or so,
> And tumble downward like the flying fish
> Gasping on deck, because you soar too high, Bob,
> And fall, for lack of moisture, quite a-dry, Bob!   (Ded 3.5-8)

Having sold his soul into slavery for a tyrant-king, Southey has lost all capacity to create, tolerate, or forgive; instead, he rages self-righteously and viciously against Byron's "Satanic School of Poetry." Southey is the real devil in Byron's universe, the incarnation of intolerance, and is appropriately in league with the "other Bob," the anti-Christ himself— Robert Stewart, Viscount Castlereagh. Even more than Southey and his shore-bound, King-bought Lakers, the "intellectual eunuch Castlereagh" embodies all the evils Byron opposes. As the leading Tory minister from 1812 to 1822, Castlereagh rigidly opposed all political reform. He further encouraged the suppression of movements of national independence abroad, in Ireland, Italy, and France. A cold-blooded slave-maker, Castlereagh was "blind / To worth as freedom, wisdom as to wit." Emasculated in mind and body, he was without feeling, sterile and stagnant, a tool of tyranny "with just enough of talent, and no more, / To lengthen fetters by another fix'd, / And offer poison long already mix'd" (Ded 12.6-8). His barren mind could produce only deformities; he was an "orator of such set trash of phrase / Ineffably—legitimately vile, / That even its grossest flatterers dare not praise" (Ded 13.1-3). Castlereagh's mixed metaphors, maladroit phrases, and long, tedious, and confused speeches were notorious. In contrast to the romantic ironist who soars, balances, hovers, and soars again, Castlereagh's impotent body and imagination go round and round in the same rut, an Ixion grindstone that "turns and turns to give the world a notion / Of endless torments and perpetual motion" (Ded 13.7-8).

But even as Byron levels his guns against all mind-forged barricades, he is usually careful to target the ideology rather than the person. Distinguishing what Blake called the "state" from the individual, Byron attacks the system while acknowledging the personal virtues of its proponents. Despite their arrogance, Southey and the Lake poets are "poets still, / And duly seated on the immortal hill" (Ded 6.7-8), while "carotid-artery-cutting Castlereagh" is credited with at least the wisdom of committing suicide. Even that mad tyrant, George III, is finally allowed to slip into paradise in *The Vision of Judgment;* Byron's tolerance can embrace individuals even while it excludes their hated ideas or principles.[34] As he wrote to John Murray, "Opinions are made to be changed—or how is truth to be got at? we don't arrive at it by standing on one leg? or on the first day of our setting out—but though we may jostle one another on the way that is no reason why we should strike or trample—*elbowing's* enough."[35]

Don Juan, then, presents Byron's romantic-ironic vision of the universe as an abundant chaos, as becoming, change, and growth, in which the most appropriate human activities are creativity, love, mental flexibility or *mobilité*,[36] and tolerance both for alternative opinions and for the thousand natural shocks that flesh is heir to. Most important, Byron's philosophical irony here finds its appropriate artistic manifestation. The form of *Don Juan* is what Schlegel would call an arabesque—it unites order and chaos in an "artfully ordered confusion," in a "charming symmetry of contradictions." Above all, *Don Juan* is a work of transcendental buffoonery.

> There are ancient and modern poems that are pervaded by the divine breath of irony throughout and informed by a truly transcendental buffoonery. Internally: the mood that surveys everything and rises infinitely above all limitations, even above its own art, virtue, or genius; externally, in its execution: the mimic style of a good Italian buffo (L, 42).

The opening lines of the poem introduce its buffoonery, its artfully ordered confusion of genres.[37]

> I want a hero: an uncommon want,
>> When every year and month sends forth a new one,
> Till, after cloying the gazettes with cant,
>> The age discovers he is not the true one.   (1.1.1-4)

An impulse toward epic ("I want a hero"—"Arma virumque cano") here opposes an impulse toward satire ("The age discovers he is not the true one"). These antithetical impulses are sustained throughout the poem. The narrator frequently insists that his poem is an epic. He invokes his Muse ("Hail, Muse! *et cetera*"; 3.1.1); treats an enormous range of subjects ("love, tempest, travel, war"; 8.138.3), indeed, "treats all things, and ne'er retreats / From any thing" (16.3.1-2); would have begun *in medias res* save that the satiric impulse to be a plain, blunt speaker demanded that he begin at the beginning (1.6-7); and writes in twelve—or twenty-four—books. As he insists,

> My poem's epic, and is meant to be
>> Divided in twelve books; each book containing,
> With love, and war, a heavy gale at sea,

> A list of ships, and captains, and kings reigning,
> New characters; the episodes are three:
> A panoramic view of hell's in training,
> After the style of Virgil and of Homer,
> So that my name of Epic's no misnomer.   (1.200)

The narrator's epic impulse to depict an entire civilization and to embody its values in the figure of the hero directly conflicts with his satiric impulse to tell the truth, to correct the faults of men and hence to deny the heroism of any given individual.

> There's only one slight difference between
> Me and my epic brethren gone before,
> And here the advantage is my own, I ween; . . .
> They so embellish, that 'tis quite a bore
> Their labyrinth of fables to thread through,
> Whereas this story's actually true.   (1.202.1-3, 6-8)

This contradiction of genres involves the poem in a constant alternation between romance and realism, between the potentially tragic and the comic. Every celebration of human glory—romantic love, military courage and honor, poetic achievement, social reform—is satirically posed against the facts—that love ends, often cruelly; that the soldier is a murderer; that the poet is a liar; that the social reformer is an egotist. The tragic vision of the heroic or beautiful person wastefully sacrificed (Haidée) is here balanced against the comic vision that every individual is replaceable, every experience repeatable, perhaps in a finer tone (Aurora Raby). The achievement of *Don Juan* is to balance these antithetical impulses without reconciling or synthesizing them. The death of Haidée *is* a sad and tragic reminder of the frailty of man; and the feelings her death arouses are not denied by the dawning promise of a new world of love heralded by Aurora Raby. Since the human condition is half dust, half deity, this altogether human poem reflects the checkered human lot with "melancholy merriment" (8.89.3, 5).

Byron's model for this confusion of genres, this "Epic Satire" (14.99.6), is that "real epic," Cervantes's *Don Quixote*. But Cervantes went too far in the direction of satire—he "smiled Spain's Chivalry away; / A single laugh demolished the right arm / Of his own country; seldom since that day / Has Spain had heroes" (13.11.1-4). Byron's poem, while acknowledging the justice of Cervantes's vision—that all efforts to "redress men's wrongs and rather check than punish crimes" must fail and that virtue appears like madness in the present world (13.8-9)—still affirms the power of romance to charm and make the world give ground before her bright array (13.11.4-5).

The structural device employed by Byron to sustain the contradictory impulses of epic and satire is the alternation of plot and digression. The plot, the epic romance of Don Juan's adventures, is constantly interrupted by the satiric asides, worldly comments, or philosophical disquisitions of the narrator. In giving as much weight to the digressions as to the plot, Byron has created a poem in which two competing ontological systems stand tensely side by side. The romantic imagination enthusiastically constructs the fictive but emotionally compelling tale of Don Juan and his loves—a heroic vision of the capacity of human love to transform a barren earth into paradise. Meanwhile, the ironic critical wit of the digressions skeptically insists that all love ends, that man is mortal and can know nothing, that all fictive illusions are only an ignis fatuus or aurora borealis over a waste and icy clime. When the poem breaks off, we are equally involved in the fate of Don Juan and Aurora Raby and in the growing disenchantments of the narrator.

In creating a poem in which digressions bear as much structural importance and thematic significance as the plot, Byron has of course deliberately broken the rules of classical poetic form. In classical rhetorical theory, *digressio* and *descriptio* are considered a part of *inventio*, subsets of a larger speech and not independent forms. In medieval literature, the extension of a digression into a self-sustaining work is not only formally incorrect but ethically wrong. To stray from the straight path to God is, for the devout pilgrim, a sin—that very sin of pride which led the first criminal, Satan, to fall. Satan's fall away from truth and obedience—and the comic, anarchic impulse that fall releases (in, say, *Tristram Shandy*) —thus become the mythic equivalent to the formal device of the digression in the literary tradition inherited by Byron.[38] The narrator, assuming the voice of the neoclassical satirist and plain, blunt speaker, asserts that the "regularity" of his design "forbids all wandering as the worst of sinning" (1.7.3-4). He then proceeds in short order to grant his "chaste Muse" just such a "liberty":

> This liberty is a poetic license
> Which some irregularity may make
>   In the design, and as I have a high sense
> Or Aristotle and the Rules, 'tis fit
> To beg his pardon when I err a bit.   (1.120.4-8)

The narrator's digressions thus become a calculated sin (a transgression) which is also a "liberty," a mode of poetic (and sexual, as the reference to his "chaste" muse implies) freedom. Byron here suggests that the digressive mode is not only a defiance of the limits of a formal fictional

plot but also a mode of liberation and a vehicle of vision. While man
needs the psychological security of a system, a supreme fiction, he also
needs to diverge from that structured world to realize his full potentiality
and to discover greater truths and other pleasures. To experience the full
perplexity and abundance of a chaotic universe, one must digress:

> Man's a phenomenon, one knows not what,
>   And wonderful beyond all wondrous measure;
> 'Tis pity though, in this sublime world, that
>   Pleasure's a sin, and sometimes sin's a pleasure;
> Few mortals know what end they would be at,
>   But whether glory, power, or love, or treasure,
> The path is through perplexing ways, and when
> The goal is gain'd, we die, you know—and then—
> What then?—I do not know, no more do you—
>   And so good night.   (1.133.1-134.2)[39]

Sinning or digressing becomes, in the romantic ironic world of *Don Juan*,
a mode of learning—the necessary detour to heaven on earth.

> But sweeter still than this, than these, than all,
>   Is first and passionate love—it stands alone,
> Like Adam's recollection of his fall;
>   The tree of knowledge has been pluck'd—all's known—
> And life yields nothing further to recall
>   Worthy of this ambrosial sin, so shown,
> No doubt in fable, as the unforgiven
> Fire which Prometheus filch'd for us from heaven.   (1.127)

This brilliant stanza assures us that sinning is ambrosial, falling is knowing, fable is truth, and human fire or love is both cursed with pain and
guilt and radiant with heavenly glory. Poetic license, promiscuous sexual
procreation, political rebellion—all are transgressing modes of knowledge "unforgiven" by classical decorum, but necessary to a fuller comprehension of the human condition and its unrealized possibilities.

The structural device of the extended digression also enables Byron to
present the process of a mind constantly engaged in the act of self-reflection. The exigencies of plot confine the passive Don Juan to a life of
action and reaction; the openness of the undirected digression provides
the narrator the phenomenological space and time in which to meditate,
self-examine, analyze, reconsider, to create and de-create himself. The
Byronic digression, then, is in itself a mode of "self-restraint." Moreover,
the narrator, who hovers above yet within the poem, simultaneously
creates and de-creates its fictional plot. He creates the tale of Don Juan by
telling it; he de-creates it by digressing so far from it that for moments at

a time we forget that it exists. He creates the traditional image of Don Juan as a mythical lover and de-creates it by first turning Juan into an innocent little boy seduced by an older woman. He creates himself by projecting his authorial self, through the digressions, into a prominence as great as or greater than that of Don Juan; he undermines himself by denying himself the passionate love or political action he values most. Above, all, he engages in the activity of self-exploration, self-definition, and self-transcendence.

Byron's prosody, like his structure, is a masterful union of form and vision. The ottava rima stanza, borrowed from Pulci's *Morgante Maggiore* and Frere's *Whistlecraft* and earlier employed in Byron's *Epistle to Augusta*, suits his purposes exactly. Readers have often commented on the force of the concluding couplet. The first six lines enable the poet to set up his hypothesis—his epic vision of love or glory; the final couplet satirically undercuts such romantic visions with a harsh dose of reality. Remember, for example, Don Juan's glowing eulogy of England, "Freedom's chosen station":

> "Here are chaste wives, pure lives; here people pay
>   But what they please; and if that things be dear,
> 'Tis only that they love to throw away
>   Their cash, to show how much they have a year.
> Here laws are all inviolate; none lay
>   Traps for the traveller; every highway's clear:
> Here"—he was interrupted by a knife,
> With "Damn your eyes! your money or your life!"   (11.10)

Occasionally, the rhyme-scheme of the couplet itself provides the ironic contrast, as in the thematically functional pairing of

> . . . what we mortals call romantic,
> And always envy, though we deem it frantic.   (4.18.7-8)

In a few instances, Byron reverses this pattern and uses the ottava rima sestet comically and the concluding couplet seriously, undermining a satiric hypothesis with a profound speculation, as in the following example:

> Ecclesiastes said, 'that all is vanity'—
>   Most modern preachers say the same, or show it
> By their examples of true Christianity:
>   In short, all know, or very soon may know it:
> And in this scene of all confess'd inanity,
>   By saint, by sage, by preacher, and by poet,
> Must I restrain me, through the fear of strife,
> From holding up the nothingness of life?   (7.6)

Too many critics, however, have treated Byron's ottava rima stanza as a closed unity and have seen the usually satiric couplet as an ironic undermining of the entire epic enterprise. They forget that Byron's vision and stanzas are never end-stopped. Each stanza raises its subject, undercuts its excessively romantic or ironic pretensions, then goes on to the next stanza, the next creation, the next vision. Byron's *Don Juan* has no ending; it stops, because Byron died, but it does not end in the sense of completing a pattern or finishing a tale. Indeed, it could have no "sense of an ending," in Frank Kermode's pithy phrase. Its romantic-ironic vision defies all completed structures, all finite enclosures. As Byron wrote to John Murray, "I *have* no plan [for Donny Johnny]—I *had* no plan; but I had or have materials."[40] And the narrator more than once articulates his sense of the poem as growing beyond any literary conventions or design originally intended for it. Having begun an epic in twelve books, he soon extends it to twenty-four and then, "at Apollo's pleading," to a hundred (12.55.6-8).

The antithetical impulses to epic and satire also result in stylistic oppositions. Byron's satiric devices have been noted often: his use of the diminishing figure, of the mock-heroic, of the Horatian plain style, of the feminine rhyme ("Oh! ye lords of ladies intellectual, / Inform us truly, have they not hen-peck'd you all?"), of internal rhyme, alliteration, and assonance to link words comically.[41] But his epic or high Juvenalian style has only recently been accorded the significance it deserves in a fine discussion by Jerome McGann.[42] This poem contains not only urbane raillery but also sublime diction. Byron frequently alludes to or quotes the Bible, Shakespeare, or Milton, and not always for comic effect. In the Dedication, for instance, he invokes Milton against Southey:

> If, fallen in evil days on evil tongues,
>   Milton appeal'd to the Avenger, Time,
> If Time, the Avenger, execrates his wrongs,
>   And makes the word 'Miltonic' mean '*sublime*,'
> *He* deign'd not to belie his soul in songs,
>   Nor turn his very talent to a crime;
> *He* did not loathe the Sire to laud the Son,
>   But closed the tyrant-hater he begun.
>
> Thinkst thou, could he—the blind Old Man—arise
>   Like Samuel from the grave, to freeze once more
> The blood of monarchs with his prophecies,
>   Or be alive again—again all hoar
> With time and trials, and those helpless eyes,
>   And heartless daughters—worn—and pale—and poor;

> Would *he* adore a sultan? *he* obey
> The intellectual eunuch Castlereagh?   (Ded 10-11)

And Byron presses Shakespeare into service to strengthen his attack on Wellington:

> You are 'the best of cut-throats:'—do not start;
>   The phrase is Shakespeare's, and not misapplied;
> War's a brain-spattering, windpipe-slitting art,
>   Unless her cause by right be sanctified.   (9.4.1-4)

Even a seemingly mock-heroic use of sublime diction can cut both ways in Byron's poem. The elevated introduction of the narrator to Sir Henry's dinner-party serves both to undercut the pompous Peter Pith and to draw our attention to the heroic capacities of the narrator, a man capable of self-knowledge and self-transcendence:

> And lo! upon that day it came to pass,
>   I sate next that o'erwhelming son of heaven,
> The very powerful Parson, Peter Pith,
>   The loudest wit I e'er was deafened with.   (16.81)

Byron's use of the elegiac sublime is most apparent in his descriptions of Juan's most glorious loves, Haidée and Aurora Raby. Think of the latter:

> Early in years, and yet more infantine
>   In figure, she had something of sublime
> In eyes which sadly shone, as seraphs' shine.
>   All youth—but with an aspect beyond time;
> Radiant and grave—as pitying man's decline;
>   Mournful—but mournful of another's crime,
> She look'd as if she sat by Eden's door,
> And grieved for those who could return no more.   (15.45)

Byron's transcendental buffoonery is perhaps most apparent in his imagery. Things go forward, get pushed back, then rush forward again. More often, they leap into the air, tumble awkwardly or deftly back onto the ground, then energetically rise again. The poem behaves like an acrobatic clown, rushing in where angels might fear to tread, being unceremoniously hurled back, then rushing in again, this time with more energy, dexterity—and success. Or like a clown jumping on a trampoline, arms and legs hysterically flailing, but each leap higher than before until he somersaults several times in the air and lands deftly on his feet.

Since life goes forward, creating, multiplying, only the dead or impotent go backward. Bob Southey, finding no fame in the present, "reserves his laurels for posterity," only to discover that life goes forward

and, unlike stagnant legal systems, "does not often claim the bright re-
version" (Ded 9.1-2). Southey, like Castlereagh, is doomed to be forever
on the wrong track, going in the wrong direction. Castlereagh's grindstone simply turns round and round in the same rut of oppressive cruelty,
like Ixion's, "to give the world a notion / Of endless torments and perpetual motion" (Ded 13.7-8). To avoid such backtracking and circularity
is the reason the narrator forswears the usual epic opening *in medias res*
and begins, like life itself, with the beginning.

Rising and falling are what *Don Juan* is all about, as George Ridenour
and many others have said. But they have said too that this poem ends
with a fall, that it is a "despairing" poem, "a personal and cultural dead
end."[43] Such pessimistic readings of *Don Juan* seem to me to seriously
underestimate the open-endedness of Byron's imagery and vision. Things
fall, always and again, but they fall to rise again—in a never-ending
phoenix motion that is the pain and glory of the human condition. As
Byron said of his own spirit, it "always rises with the rebound."[44] True,
man is deity fallen to dust, but dust with the capacity to so inflame itself
that common cold clay is heated to "fiery dust" and "the precious porce-
lain of human clay" (4.11). Or, as the narrator puts it in three central
stanzas:

> When Newton saw an apple fall, he found
>   In that slight startle from his contemplation—
> 'Tis *said* (for I'll not answer above ground
>   For any sage's creed or calculation)—
> A mode of proving that the earth turn'd round
>   In a most natural whirl, called "gravitation";
> And this is the sole mortal who could grapple,
> Since Adam, with a fall or with an apple.
>
> Men fell with apples, and with apples rose,
>   If this be true; for we must deem the mode
> In which Sir Isaac Newton could disclose
>   Through the then unpaved stars the turnpike road,
> A thing to counterbalance human woes:
>   For ever since immortal man hath glow'd
> With all kinds of mechanics, and full soon
> Steam-engines will conduct him to the moon.
>
> And wherefore this exordium?—Why, just now,
>   In taking up this paltry sheet of paper,
> My bosom underwent a glorious glow,
>   And my internal spirit cut a caper:
> And though so much inferior, as I know,
>   To those who, by the dint of glass and vapour,
> Discover stars and sail in the wind's eye,
> I wish to do as much by poesy.   (10.1-3)

Unpacking these dense lines will take us to the center of Byron's mature vision. Adam fell from paradise because he loved and sexually desired Eve; he succumbed to the temptations of feminine beauty and companionship. His fall paved the way for further intercourse—sexual, emotional, and linguistic. Thus it is Eve and women who made it possible for Adam and men to know and explore the chaotic abundance of the human condition. As the narrator, contemplating the power of women, acknowledges:

> —how man *fell* I
> Know not, since knowledge saw her branches stript
> Of her first fruit; but how he falls and rises
> *Since, thou* has settled beyond all surmises.   (9.55:5-8)

Women arouse men, not only to sexual procreation, but also to imaginative creation, experiences of the sublime, and knowledge as it can be embodied in linguistic structures.

Inherent in each sexual and loving encounter, of course, are the seeds of its own destruction. Haidée's eyelids veil the serpent's poison.

> Her hair, I said, was auburn; but her eyes
>   Were black as death, their lashes the same hue,
> Of downcast length, in whose silk shadow lies
>   Deepest attraction; for when to the view
> Forth from its raven fringe the full glance flies,
>   Ne'er with such force the swiftest arrow flew;
> 'Tis as the snake late coil'd, who pours his length,
> And hurls at once his venom and his strength.   (2.117)

The serpent that tempted Eve and denied paradise to man lurks in Haidée's eyes and Juan's embrace; in this postlapsarian world, it is "fatal to be loved" (3.2.2) and "the frail beings we would fondly cherish / Are laid within our bosoms but to perish" (3.2.7-8). The living serpent in the paradise regained on earth by Juan's and Haidée's first love is specifically Lambro who in his serious moods, "calm, concentrated, and still, and slow, / . . . lay coiled like the boa in the wood" (3.48.3-4). Lambro, the Greek enraged by his nation's submission to the Turk, has become an anti-Christ, a cruel fisher of men, a vicious pirate. He brutally divorces Juan and Haidée—"In vain she struggled in her father's grasp— / His arms were like a serpent's coil" (4.48.4-5)—and destroys their love, killing Haidée and selling Juan into slavery. But their passion-perfect love would have ended in time, even without Lambro's intervention; the serpent was in her eyes, the engulfing maelstrom in their passion itself, the fated destruction in her prophetic dream (4.31-35), their deaths inherent in their own mortality.

But the serpent that lurks in each human passion, poisoning it to death, also sheds its skin and proffers a new, perhaps brighter, albeit equally fatal love. As John Johnson calmly tells Juan,

> . . . time strips our illusions of their hue,
> And one by one in turn, some grand mistake
> Casts off its bright skin yearly like the snake.
> 'Tis true, it gets another bright and fresh,
>   Or fresher, brighter; but the year gone through,
> This skin must go the way, too, of all flesh . . .   (5.21.6-22.3)

The fresher, brighter, poison-perfect love offered to Juan is of course the "young star," Aurora Raby. That Aurora is a substitution for the lost Haidée is confirmed by the narrator.

> Juan knew nought of such a character—
>   High, yet resembling not his lost Haidée;
> Yet each was radiant in her proper sphere:
>   The island girl, bred up by the lone sea,
> More warm, as lovely, and not less sincere,
>   Was Nature's all: Aurora could not be,
> Nor would be thus:—the difference in them
> Was such as lies between a flower and gem.   (15.58)

Aurora is the child of nurture, the highest gift of human civilization, who waits by Eden's door and holds out to Juan the love that can carry him back to paradise. Sitting by Aurora, he experiences once again

> . . . some feelings he had lately lost,
>   Or harden'd; feelings which, perhaps ideal,
> Are so divine, that I must deem them real:—
>
> The love of higher things and better days;
>   The unbounded hope, and heavenly ignorance
> Of what is call'd the world, and the world's ways;
>   The moments when we gather from a glance
> More joy than from all future pride or praise,
>   Which kindle manhood, but can ne'er entrance
> The heart in an existence of its own,
> Of which another's bosom is the zone.   (16.107.6-108.8)

The better world offered by Aurora is the replacement for the agonizing loss of Haidée and her pastoral idyll. And when Juan's love for Aurora ends, as end it will ("Alas! *her* star must wane like that of Dian; / Ray fades on ray, as years on years depart"; 16.109.3-4), another equally passionate commitment will eventually replace it. Adam's fall from paradise is thus a fortunate fall into finer tones of pleasure, increased knowledge, and an ever more complex hovering between melancholy and hope, between painful endings and ecstatic beginnings. The narrator therefore casually dismisses the abstract ideals of a Donna Inez, knowing that the falling and rising human world offers more intense joy—as well as pain—than a heaven beyond earth:

> Perfect she was, but as perfection is
>   Insipid in this naughty world of ours,
> Where our first parents never learned to kiss
>   Till they were exiled from their earlier bowers,
> Where all was peace, and innocence, and bliss
> (I wonder how they got through the twelve hours) . . .   (1.18.1-6)

As for the inevitable pain of mortality, we should remember what Byron wrote to Annabella Milbanke: "the great object of life is sensation—to feel that we exist—even though in pain."

Just as the poem erects the illusion of romantic love, reveals its limitations, and then recreates the illusion in a fresher, brighter, or at least subtler and more complicated form, so it de-creates and creates the Wordsworthian illusion of a nurturing nature. The devastating storm and shipwreck that drive Juan's few surviving shipmates to cannibalism effectively undercut the Wordsworthian vision of a benevolent nature that never did betray the heart that loved her and of the enduring nobility of the common man in times of stress. But this tempest carries Juan to the island paradise of Haidée's kingdom, where the natural world and the human form of the lovely girl are fused in an atmosphere of generous love.

> They look'd up to the sky, whose floating glow
>   Spread like a rosy ocean, vast and bright;
> They gazed upon the glittering sea below,
>   Whence the broad moon rose circling into sight;
> They heard the wave's splash, and the wind so low,
>   And saw each other's dark eyes darting light
> Into each other—and, beholding this,
> Their lips drew near, and clung into a kiss.   (2.185)

The possibility of pastoral is affirmed once again in the narrator's eulogy of the backwoodsman of Kentucky, Daniel Boone, who was "happiest amongst mortals anywhere; / For killing nothing but a bear or buck, he / Enjoyed the lonely, vigorous, harmless days / Of his old age in wilds of deepest maze" (8.61.5-8). Healthy, long-lived, kind to all he met, Boone spawned a race of noble savages—tall, strong, cheerful, serene, and free:

>   around him grew
> A sylvan tribe of children of the chace,

Whose young, unwakened world was ever new,
    Nor sword nor sorrow yet had left a trace
On her unwrinkled brow, nor could you view
    A frown on Nature's or on human face;—
The free-born forest found and kept them free,
And fresh as is a torrent or a tree.   (8.65)

In this poem, then, nature is both viciously destructive of human life and magnanimously abundant with nourishment for the free man.

Nature's most famous apple not only tempted Adam out of one paradise into another; it also inspired Newton to define the laws of gravity and mechanics. Here, as in *Cain*, the fall from perfect paradise brought man a greater knowledge, both of his finite limitations and of his potential achievements. Byron rightly speculates that Newtonian mechanics will enable man to develop a technology that will one day carry him (albeit in rocket ships rather than Byron's steam engines) to the moon. The resulting expansion of human consciousness is "a thing to counterbalance human woes" (10.2.5); the rise of scientific knowledge and the comprehension of the workings of the stars here follow and transcend the loss of an insipidly perfect innocence.

Military glory is yet another illusion that the poem destroys only to build again. The Russian siege of Ismail is mere butchery carried out by an aggressive queen and her venal general against a town "which never did them harm" (7.76.8). Suwarrow deliberately perverts the human form divine. "Hero, buffoon, half-demon and half-dirt" (7.55.5), a "harlequin in uniform," he equates glory with "cash and conquest" and calculates life as "so much dross" (7.55.8, 64.4, 77.3). To participate in the havoc and carnage wrought by this devil is to forgo all claims to nobility, honor, or courage; Juan's military exploits are redeemed only by the ignorance of his courage ("following honour and his nose / [he] Rushed where the thickest fire announced most foes"; 8.32.7-8) and by his determination to preserve the orphaned Leila. But even while the poem savagely attacks all illusions of military fame and glory that permit such unmitigated and unjustified slaughter, it insists that some wars are good. Battles fought in the proper causes—in "Defense of freedom, country or of laws" (7.40.4)—are justifiable, and the fame of such freedom-fighters as Leonidas and Washington, "Whose every battlefield is holy ground, / Which breathes of nations saved, not worlds undone" (8.5.3-4), is deserved. The narrator's summary comment on military action— "War's a brain-spattering, windpipe-slitting art, / Unless her cause by right be sanctified" (9.4.3-4)—sets up a brighter, fresher image of military action that transcends the merely brutal savagery of the siege of

Ismail. For old worlds must be militarily destroyed to make way for new. As Byron wrote in his Diary on January 9, 1821:

> *onward!*—it is now the time to act, and what signifies *self*, if a single spark of that which would be worthy of the past can be bequeathed unquenchedly to the future? It is not one man, nor a million, but the *spirit* of liberty which must be spread. The waves which dash upon the shores are, one by one, broken, but yet the *ocean* conquers, nevertheless. It overwhelms the Armada, it wears the rock, and, if the *Neptunians* are to be believed, it has not only destroyed, but made a world. In like manner, whatever the sacrifice of individuals, the great cause will gather strength, sweep down what is rugged, and fertillise (for *seaweed* is *manure*) what is cultivable.[45]

And poetry—is it pure illusion, a merely caper-cutting muse? or a turnpike road through the unpaved stars to a larger truth than man now comprehends? The narrator's enthusiasm for the imaginative process rises, falls, rises again. Compared to the lake-hugging, harnessed Pegasus of Wordsworth (3.98) or Southey, the narrator's winged steed soars. Even his "pedestrian muses" traverse greater spaces and tell more truths than the Lakers' constricted imaginations. But the narrator is equally well aware of the limitations of his own poetic inspiration and mental capacities:

> Nothing so difficult as a beginning
>   In poesy, unless perhaps the end;
> For oftentimes when Pegasus seems winning
>   The race, he sprains a wing, and down we tend,
> Like Lucifer when hurl'd from heaven for sinning;
>   Our sin the same, and hard as his to mend,
> Being pride, which leads the mind to soar too far,
> Till our own weakness shows us what we are.   (4.1)

The creative powers of men are finite. And their creations may well be nothing more than a beautiful delusion, "a versified Aurora Borealis, / Which flashes o'er a waste and icy clime" (7.2.304). And yet, as this stanza suggests, poetry like love and glory is the illusion that counts in a phenomenological world where *all* things are a "Show." Inspired by Newton's capacity to lift the fallen apple, "discover stars, and sail in the wind's eye" (10.3.7), the narrator's creative wit cuts a caper and confidently asserts:

> In the wind's eye I have sail'd, and sail; but for
>   The stars, I own my telescope is dim:
> But at least I have shunn'd the common shore,
>   And leaving land far out of sight, would skim
> The ocean of eternity: the roar

> Of breakers has not daunted my slight, trim,
> But *still* sea-worthy skiff; and she may float
> Where ships have founder'd, as doth many a boat.   (10.4)

Unlike Newton, who by his own admission has been content merely to pick up pebbles on the seashore, the narrator's imagination has ventured out onto the ocean of eternity. His creative wit has thus been able to apprehend and to communicate the ultimate incomprehensibility of the universe. In this sense, the imagination provides a surer road to truth, whatever the toll in self-deception, than Newton's more cautious mechanics. The narrator also implies that his light, comic, caper-cutting muse has carried him further and more successfully than the weightier ships of tragic, epic, or historical muses. It has at least shunned the common shore, the conventional platitude, and has discovered new modes of consciousness and expression.

Again and again, the poem's image-patterns affirm the process of rising over falling; the possibility of never-ending growth and self-transcendence; the triumph of communal life over individual death. The last episodes of this never-ended poem point in this direction. Juan, unnerved by his second encounter with the walking corpse of the Black Friar, nonetheless manages to look Death in the face and to thrust forth his arms—only to embrace the full, voluptuous, and very much alive breast of the Lady Fitz-Fulke, a nymphomaniac who kindles him, leaves him "wan and worn," yet still with a "virgin face," naively open to new adventures (17.13-14).[46] And the narrator's last meditation, on the fact that "intellectual Giants" often have to wait for posterity to give them the credit their ideas and works deserve since "The loftiest minds outrun their tardy ages" (17.9.5), also looks to the future rather than the past. Human knowledge increases; the mind expands; life merrily multiplies, not without pain and loss, but always with energy.

Don Juan, in addition to celebrating the abundant chaos of the universe in a mimic style and structure that reflects both this chaos and the finite systems that men impose upon it, is written in a language that constantly calls attention to its own powers and limitations. The narrator frequently discusses the process of poetic creation: the selecting of a subject ("I want a hero"), the choice of genre (an "Epic Satire") and stanza-form (Pulci's ottava rima), the impulse to undermine the chosen topic and structure ("such digressions are fair"; 6.120), the struggle to find an appropriate metaphor or rhyme. Instances of the latter are numerous. One remembers especially the successful quest for an image for Lady Adeline:

> But Adeline was not indifferent: for
>> (*Now* for a common-place!) beneath the snow,
> As a volcano holds the lava more
>> Within—*et caetera*. Shall I go on?—No!
> I hate to hunt down a tired metaphor,
>> So let the often-used volcano go.
> Poor thing! How frequently, by me and others,
> It hath been stirr'd up till its smoke quite smothers!
>
> I'll have another figure in a trice:—
>> What say you to a bottle of champagne?
> Frozen into a very vinous ice,
>> Which leaves few drops of that immortal rain,
> Yet in the very centre, past all price,
>> About a liquid glassful will remain;
> And this is stronger than the strongest grape
> Could e'er express in its expanded shape.   (13.36-37)

The exigencies of his rhyme-scheme, "that good old steamboat which keeps verses moving / 'Gainst Reason—Reason ne'er was hand-and-glove / With rhyme, but always leant less to improving / The sound than sense" (9.74.4-7), repeatedly torment the narrator. They drive him to rhyme "milk" with the Scotch "whilk" ("The rhyme obliges me to this; sometimes / Monarchs are less imperative than rhymes"; 5.77.7-8); "fact" with the French "tact" ("that modern phrase appears to me sad stuff, / But it will serve to keep my verse compact"; 1.178.3-4); and even to indulge in the outrageously comic rhymes of "intellectual" with "hen-peck'd you all" and of "liberal" with "gibber all" (12.5). The narrator also comments on his use of Biblical or literary allusions ("I like so much to quote; / You must excuse this extract, 'tis where she, / The Queen of Denmark, for Ophelia brought / Flowers to the grave"; 2.17.3-6); on his grammar ("Or *beaten* if *you* insist on grammar, though / I never think about it in a heat"; 7.42.5-6); and even on his spelling ("The Kozacks, or, if so you please, Cossacques / (I don't much pique myself upon orthography . . .)"; 8.74.1-2).

The effect created by these numerous references to the process of composing the poem is that of a man "feeling as he writes" and writing as he would talk. As the narrator says,

> I perch upon an humbler promontory,
>> Amidst life's infinite variety:
> With no great care for what is nicknamed glory,
>> But speculating as I cast mine eye
> On what may suit or may not suit my story,
>> And never straining hard to versify,

> I rattle on exactly as I'd talk
> With anybody in a ride or walk.   (15.19)

Above all, the narrator is insisting that this poem is a linguistic performance. It is poetic language as *action*, as *process*. That is why the poem
is never concluded, indeed hardly begun. As the narrator insists at stanza
fifty-four of the twelfth canto,

> But now I will begin my poem. 'Tis
>   Perhaps a little strange, if not quite new,
> That from the first of Cantos up to this
>   I've not begun what we have to go through.
> These first twelve books are merely flourishes,
>   Preludios, trying just a string or two
> Upon my lyre, or making the pegs sure;
> And when so, you shall have the overture.   (12.54)

And the overall design of the poem is always being simultaneously
created and changed:

> . . . When the body of the book's begun,
> You'll find it of a different construction
> From what some people say 'twill be when done:
> The plan at present's simply in concoction.   (12.87.2-5)

As the performer of this vigorous linguistic action, the narrator rightly
describes himself as an "Improvvisatore" (15.20). His movements are
both spontaneous and calculated. The poem he enacts occasionally runs
out of control, as when it encounters the overwhelmingly graceful walk
of the ladies of Cadiz:

> I can't describe it, though so much it strike,
> Nor liken it—I never saw the like:
> An Arab horse, a stately stag, a barb
>   New broke, a cameleopard, a gazelle,
> No—none of these will do;—and then their garb!
>   Their veil and petticoat—Alas! to dwell
> Upon such things would very near absorb
>   A canto—then their feet and ankles—well,
> Thank Heaven I've got no metaphor quite ready
> (And so, my sober Muse—come, let's be steady—
>
> Chaste Muse!—well, if you must, you must)—the veil
> Thrown back a moment with the glancing hand, . . . (2.5.7-7.2)

The narrator insists that he never knows what word is coming next, can
never decide what he should say (9.41). At the same time, he claims with
equal validity that his poem is an epic and has the requisite unity (11.44).

As a maker of poetry, an improviser, the narrator is constantly moving, creating and de-creating his fictive world. His mind never stagnates. Exuberantly it asserts the object of its consciousness ("The coast—I think it was the coast that I / Was just describing—Yes, it *was* the coast—"; 2.181.1-2); arbitrarily changes its intentions ("I feel this tediousness will never do— / 'Tis being *too* epic, and I must cut down / (In copying) this long canto into two"; 3.111.1-3); even forgets what it was going to do ("Oh, ye great Authors!—"Apropos des bottes"— / I have forgotten what I meant to say"; 9.36.1-2). Thus the ongoing creation of the poem reflects the narrator's ever-changing, ever-expanding consciousness. The process of the poem, an activity, a performance through time, imitates the process of life itself, making and unmaking patterns and forms. The narrator's claim to achieving neoclassical mimesis, to re-presenting the nature of life, to showing the truth, is thus far validated.

But not entirely. While the language of *Don Juan* self-consciously performs its symbolic action, it also acknowledges its own limits. In the parallel relationships between Juan and Haidée and between Juan and Aurora Raby, Byron deliberately explores the boundaries of language. Unable to speak each other's language, Haidée and Juan discover a *natural* language, a language in which the signifier is not arbitrary but rather the signified itself. As Haidée gazes on the shipwrecked Juan, her love enables her to "read . . . the lines / Of his fair face" and see in his every look "a world of words" (2.162). They have no need of actual words; they communicate in a language "like to that of birds" (4.14), a language of physical gesture and pure sound; for "though their speech / Was broken words, they *thought* a language there" (2.189). The symbiotic experience that Juan and Haidée share, which unites them not only with each other but with the landscape as well (their dark eyes dart the same light that the broad moon reflects at their nuptial hour when their lips cling into a long, long kiss, "all concentrating like rays / Into one focus, kindled from above"; 2.186.2-3), takes place *beyond* language. Or rather, it takes place in a realm where things *are* words, where eyes and faces convey their own and only meaning, where signifiers and signifieds cannot be separated. Only at the moment of parting, in Haidée's premonitory dream, does the gap between sign and meaning intrinsic to ordinary language recur. In the unwinding scroll-like shroud before her feet, Haidée pursues a meaning that she cannot read, and she wakes to find the allegorical gap confirmed: Juan's face has been replaced by Lambro's.

At the other limit of language, Juan's and Haidée's natural or naive expression is replaced, for the sophisticated Juan and Aurora Raby, by silence. Aurora Raby, that "baby" who engenders the rebirth of Juan's capacity for love, remains "silent, lone" (15.197.2), saying "nothing" to the "gay nothings" Juan speaks to her at dinner (15.78). And although she eventually responds to his tactful, deferential conversation and even asks him a few questions, she remains linguistically apart from the chattering coquettes, reserved and refined. At the breakfast-table banter concerning the Black Friar and Juan's wan appearance, she again says nothing and moreover looks "as though / She approved [Juan's] silence" (16.106). Aurora's care in choosing her words, together with her preference for silence, suggest the birth of a new form of communication between her and Juan. Perhaps it would become a refined form of that natural language he shared with Haidée, a language of look and gesture in which sign and meaning are fused. Or perhaps it would become a silence too pregnant with meaning to be contained in words.

Between these two boundaries of extralinguistic communication, the language of the poem itself continues to hover, a versified Aurora Borealis flashing over a waste and icy clime. Linguistically as well as epistemologically, the poem knowingly operates within the boundaries of a romantic-ironic consciousness, creating and de-creating itself.

> For me, I know nought; nothing I deny,
>   Admit, reject, contemn; and what know *you*,
> Except perhaps that you were born to die?
> And both may after all turn out untrue.   (14.3.1-4)

A Postscript on a Preface

Byron's rejected preface to *Don Juan* is in itself a brilliant example of his romantic irony. After an opening attack on the trivial details of Wordsworth's poetry and the self-serving conservatism of his political prose, Byron asks the reader—in a parody of "The Thorn"—to suppose that the narrator of *Don Juan* is a Spanish gentleman who is either a native Englishman or a Spaniard who has traveled in England. The narrator tells the long tale we are to hear while sitting at a table, drinking wine, smoking a cigar, as the sun sets upon a village in the Sierra Morena near Seville. His audience, significantly, is both small and "elderly." He might have attracted more listeners, but for the fact that nearby a group of peasants are dancing to the sound of a flute. The narrator is not "much moved by the musical hilarity," but many others (including one of the two foreign travelers present at the scene) are drawn to the striking spectacle presented among the peasants: "the beautiful movements of a tall peasant Girl whose whole Soul is in her eyes & her heart in the dance of which she is the Magnet to ten thousand feelings that vibrate with her Own."[47] The author's ironic attitude toward his narrator is clear. The narrator's long story is not nearly so involving, except to a few "elderly" persons, as the sight and sound of a young girl dancing enthusiastically. Implicitly, the preface acknowledges the superiority of passion, love, and abundant life over the finite and hence limiting boundaries of art. Nonetheless, the Spanish gentleman's tale is told—art has its valid function— but by whom? The author of the preface proceeds to de-create the very character he has just created: "Having supposed as much of this as the utter impossibility of such a supposition will admit . . ." Having given and taken away his narrator, Byron then creates another authorial persona: "the reader is requested to extend his supposed power of supposing so far as to conceive that the dedication to Mr Southey—& several stanzas of the poem itself are interpolated by the English editor." This "English editor" who may be supposed to be the author of the Dedication but who does not otherwise identify himself as the author of "several stanzas" in the poem that follows (where the teller of Don Juan's adventures and the speaker of the digressions are presented as the same persona) can further be supposed to hate Mr. Southey for any of several supposed reasons: the editor is a turncoat who gained less by the exchange than Southey and is therefore jealous; the editor is a rival poet denied his just present and future fame by Southey's self-granted success; the editor has been libelously insulted by Southey. The piling up of suppositions simultaneously substantiates the very shadowy figure of the editor and undermines it by calling repeated attention to its fictional or suppositional character. The preface ends abruptly, in a half-sentence which Byron later canceled, as the author's hostility to Southey mounts: "this Pantisocratic apostle of Apostacy—who . . . feeds the cravings of his wretched Vanity disappointed in its nobler hopes . . . by the abuse of whosoever may be more consistent—or more successful than himself;— and the provincial gang of scribblers gathered around him.—[Amongst these last—Coleridge is not the least notorious & were it not for]." Perhaps the ironic antithesis to so much righteous anger is the mode Byron finally chooses here—silence. Or perhaps it is the heroic tolerance expressed at the end of *The Vision of Judgment* and even in the Dedication, where Southey is finally "duly seated on the immortal hill."

A preface that takes back as much as it gives, that exists as "canceled," that affirms the exuberant beauty of life over both the death-dealing, mind-forged manacles of Southey and the possibly constricted realm of the fictional construct, and that also, as Jerome McGann has argued,[48] celebrates the capacity of the imagination to analyze and thus clarify the nature of human experience, is for Byron's *Don Juan* both beginning and ending. It is an exercise of the romantic-ironic consciousness, an act of self-creation and self-destruction that immediately engages the reader in the ongoing experience of "hovering" that is the poem and the life it metaphorically images.

3

Keats and the Vale
of Soul-Making

Keats, another quintessential romantic ironist, saw life as a process in which no fixed order, no clear "ballance of good and evil,"[1] was discernible. For him, life was a mystery, a mist, a chaos in which pleasure and pain were inextricably entangled. Even on his deathbed Keats did not, could not, escape the ironist's "knowledge of contrast, feeling for light and shade, all that information (primitive sense) necessary for a poem" (II, 360). Thus the poet must hold two opposed ideas in his mind at the same time. To seek to impose a system, a coherent and logical pattern, upon the incomprehensible mystery of life was to reject, with Coleridge and Dilke, the fundamental Keatsian poetic quality of empathic openness to *all* experience, of "negative capability." His letters reveal the romantic ironist's alternation between enthusiasm—"I am certain of nothing but of the holiness of the Heart's affections and the truth of Imagination—What the imagination seizes as Beauty must be truth" (I, 184)—and skepticism —"I am sometimes so very sceptical as to think Poetry itself a mere Jack a lantern to amuse whoever may chance to be struck with its brilliance" (I, 242). Most often, he expresses a delicate hovering between commitment and distrust. Although convinced that "nothing in this world is proveable," he balances this skeptical "nothing" with an enthusiastic "ardour": "probably every mental pursuit takes its reality and worth from the ardour of the pursuer—being in itself a nothing" (I, 242). Consequently, Keats's finest poems are structured as internal debates, in which enthusiastically greeted symbolic objects, ideas, or values are tested against their opposites, qualified, undermined, and finally both rejected and affirmed.

Keats's open embracing of all the contradictions of human experience (of an Iago as well as an Imogen) and his refusal to say that a single moral law or rational order controlled the world were founded on the romantic-ironic perception that life was both creative and de-creative, both beautiful and painful. As he confessed to Fanny Brawne only a year before his death, "If I should die, . . . I have left no immortal work behind me— nothing to make my friends proud of my memory—but I have lov'd the principle of beauty in all things, and if I had had time I would have made myself remember'd" (II, 263). John Middleton Murry rightly emphasized that Keats meant the principle of beauty-in-all-things,[2] the commitment to a vision of the world's chaos as finally life-enhancing, fertile, positive. But this conviction is balanced against Keats's equally certain knowledge that all beautiful things die. This consciousness of mortality was pressed upon Keats almost daily from the early accidental death of his father through the deaths of his mother and grandmother to the lingering con- sumption of his brother Tom and the imminence of his own death. Hov- ering between these extremes, celebration of the beauty of life and a rec- ognition of the certainty of death, Keats's poetry is the "new realism" of romantic irony heralded by Schlegel: "this new realism, since it must be of idealistic origin and must hover as it were over an idealistic ground, will emerge as poetry which indeed is to be based on the harmony of the ideal and the real" (DP, 84). From his early attempt to define for his brothers "what quality went to form a Man of Atchievement especially in literature" to his last attempt to write an epic poem, *The Fall of Hype- rion*, Keats struggled to understand the relationship of the ideal to the real, of beauty to pain-filled mortality, by empathically entering into their contradictory existences.

Keats's best poems are delineations of that struggle, rather than achieved resolutions. As such, they participate in the process of becom- ing that Keats finally came to see as the ultimate human reality, that pro- cess of living and dying, of embracing pain and pleasure always per- plexed, of shaping one's dissolving life into melting patterns, which is the only meaning men and women can find on earth. The Odes and "To Autumn" are affirmations of that process in both human and natural terms; the greatest romances, developing beyond *Endymion*, pose an ideal of perfectly satisfying love against frustrating psychological and circumstantial realities; and *The Fall of Hyperion* fragment commits itself both structurally and thematically to indeterminacy, open-endedness, a process of soul-making.

The terms of the debate so intensely waged in Keats's major poems, while implicit in such early poems as "I stood tiptoe" and "Sleep and Poetry," are made harshly explicit in his March 1818 verse letter to Rey- nolds. Confronted with Reynolds's illness and Tom's wasting consump- tion, Keats posed the supposedly heart-easing beauty of art (in this in-

stance, Claude's *Enchanted Castle*) against his unavoidable consciousness of "an eternal fierce destruction." The poem raises, but does not
answer, the fundamental questions with which Keats would wrestle for
the rest of his short life: can beauty—the beauty of a work of art, of a
natural creature or event, of a fully greeted romantic love, of a noble
mind and heart—can such beauty justify or compensate for the cruel sufferings, the heartache, and the thousand natural shocks that flesh is heir
to? For if the delights of an arcadian bower of sensuous love, together
with the "calm grandeur of a sober line" of poetry, cannot "charm us at
once away from all our troubles," as Keats had enthusiastically and
naively asserted in "I stood tiptoe," then what is the use of poetry? And
more particularly, what is the use of a modern "sentimental" poetry
whose genius, as exemplified by Wordsworth, is committed to a self-conscious exploration of the dark passages of a "Purgatory blind" in which
we wander lost, unable to "refer to any standard law / Of either earth or
heaven"?

For Keats felt keenly the burden of the past and the anxiety of influence, the unreachable heights already scaled by the greatest artists that
he, a sick eagle upon whom "mortality weighs heavily . . . like unwilling
sleep," was too weak to climb. Not only did Keats feel poetically inadequate (six months later he told Woodhouse that he "thought there was
now nothing original to be written in poetry; that its riches were already
exhausted—and all its beauties forestalled"; I, 380). He also feared that
the ironic, self-mirroring poetry he felt compelled to write might destroy
rather than create happiness, might force one "in summer skies to mourn"
and spoil "the singing of the Nightingale." The colors of Titian, the ideal
landscapes of Claude, together with the glories of the Elgin marbles, the
luxuries of Spenser, the grandeur of Milton: these artistic worlds are enthusiastically hailed by Keats as places where "our dreamings all of sleep
or wake . . . their colours from the sunset take: / From something of
material sublime." But Keats himself, in his growing skepticism, cannot
see the world so simplistically: Claude's architectural fantasies seem to
him grotesque ("Then there's a little wing, far from the Sun, / Built by a
Lapland Witch turn'd maudlin Nun"), they can drive a beauteous woman
mad, and at the very least, as the poor herdsman discovers when he tells
his friends of the sweet music and the spot, they are not believable. Keats's
own poetry, if it is to remain true to the explorations and insights of his
own ironic consciousness, must shadow his "own soul's daytime / In the
dark void of night," his own peering "Too far into the sea, where every
maw / The greater on the less feeds evermore." And while Keats would

like to dispell these horrid "moods of one's mind," he cannot honestly take refuge in new romance until reality changes and both Reynolds and Tom are healthy again. And Tom, of course, did not recover health. Keats could not forget what he had written only two weeks earlier: that "there are four seasons in the mind of man," not only lusty Spring and luxuriously ruminating Summer and contented Autumn, but "his Winter too of pale misfeature / Or else he would forego his mortal nature." On account of his "dying day, and because women have Cancers" (I, 292), Keats still wrestled with the question "is there a redeeming beauty or purpose in such suffering?"

Keats's commitment to writing a poetry that included the chaos of the universe and the contradictions of human experience, the "agonies, the strife of human hearts" as well as the "material sublime," is recorded in the first of the great Odes, the "Ode to Psyche." Appropriately, Keats encounters Psyche, his own mind or imagination (that Spirit whose empathic greeting or embracing of the external world alone can make that world "wholly exist"; I, 243), in a Claudian landscape of "hush'd, cool-rooted flowers." In earlier poems his imagination was nourished by luxurious images of arcadian nature and Olympian gods and goddesses and by adolescent fantasies of sensual gratification in a bower of bliss. But Keats now acknowledges that such a "naive" poetry, based on the faded myths of the past and the dreams of his own childhood can no longer suffice. Both the fond believing lyre and the happy pieties of earlier religious systems are inaccessible to the skeptical, modern consciousness. Keats must therefore worship a new kind of imagination, a "sentimental" consciousness that can embrace the chaos, the incomprehensibility, and the finitude of human existence. This new goddess will command a temple in the "untrodden," not yet fully explored, regions of the poet-priest's mind. Her "new grown," self-mirroring poetry will contain the interwoven, "branched" contradictions of "pleasant pain" rather than the naive, intuitive pleasures of "moss-lain Dryads." And from the wise passiveness or fertile indolence of his own mental harvests, in the "wide quietness" of his contemplating mind, the poet will create a sacred sanctuary or poem like a flower-wreathed trellis or dew-glistening spiderweb, that "airy Citadel" or "tapestry empyrean-full of Symbols for [man's] spiritual eye" (I, 232). And the reward of writing such a poem shall be the "soft delight" of "shadowy thought," the knowledge that one has left the Chamber of Maiden-Thought and sharpened "one's vision into the heart and nature of Man," that one has participated in "the general and gregarious advance of intellect" which must include the courageously faced and acute conviction that "the World is full of Misery and Heartbreak, Pain, Sickness and oppression" (I, 281). In addition to the "bright torch" of genuine knowledge, this modern poet shall also experience a powerful and warm love, the love that comes when one can open the casements of one's own mind and feelings, can embrace all life empathically, and erotically. From an exploration of the limits of his own subjective consciousness, the "sentimental" poet can better understand the needs and desires, the frustrations and sufferings, of other human beings, can help them better understand each other, can "let the warm Love in" to human hearts. Thus Psyche, who desired to explore the dark passages of the mind with a no-longer-forbidden torch, can once again be united with Cupid, an abundant, life-engendering love.

The later Odes describe Keats's efforts to explore the dark passages of a chaotic, incomprehensible world. They depict that exploration, but they do not end it. As David Perkins first emphasized, these Odes are internal debates between the inescapable knowledge of human finitude on one side, and the possibly transcendent beauty of nature, art, or the human imagination on the other,[3] or between philosophical irony and romantic enthusiasm. Performing a "greeting of the Spirit," Keats first empathically, enthusiastically seizes a thing of beauty, a symbol of an ideal perfection, explores it, comprehends it. He then skeptically poses this symbol against the equally fully greeted reality of human mutability, of loss, pain and death. The value and utility of the symbol are thus challenged, qualified, and finally rejected *and* reaffirmed. Because the debate is not resolved, because these symbols are and are not truths, these Odes are almost perfect examples of romantic irony.[4]

The nightingale, singing without the poet's self-conscious anxiety, singing gloriously "of summer," is enthusiastically greeted by the poet as a being of perfect happiness. Being so caught up in this empathic apprehension of the bird's song, the poet feels both detached from and yet still imprisoned in his finite self: "My heart aches, and a drowsy numbness pains / My sense." Struggling to cast off the chains of mortality, the poet seeks strategies of self-escape. He calls for a euphoric wine that will deaden his sense of pain and heighten his sensitivity to pleasure, a synaesthetic draught "Tasting of Flora and the country green, / Dance, and Provencal song, and sunburnt mirth!" But his desire to "Fade far away, dissolve and quite forget," like Hamlet's suicidal wish ("O that this too, too sullied flesh would melt, / Thaw and resolve itself into a dew"), only forces back into his consciousness the agony of the human condition, "The weariness, the fever, and the fret . . . Where but to think is to be full of sorrow / And leaden-eyed despairs, / Where beauty cannot keep her lustrous eyes, / Or new love pine at them beyond tomorrow."

After wine has failed to annihilate his skeptical awareness of human limitations, the poet next summons an even more powerful resource, the imagination, whose "viewless wings," like those of the hidden nightingale, might lift him above his perplexed consciousness of the human condition. And the imagination, his greeting Spirit, does and does not perform his will. He empathically joins the bird ("Already with thee!"), but not in that realm of perfect, unchanging beauty which the bird alone can enter ("Already with *thee* tender is the night") and where the Moon and stars perhaps ("haply") always shine. Rather, the poet unites with the mortal bird that is "here," where "there is no light," on earth, "In some melodious plot / Of beechen green, and shadows numberless." For he can unite only with that which he and the bird have *in common*, a shared participation in the natural life cycle. In the central fifth stanza of the poem, the poet empathically explores what it means to be part of this natural process. Beginning in the present with mid-May's blooming white hawthorne and sweet-briar, the poet looks back to April's violets, now fast fading, and forward to June's and July's musk-roses. Thus Keats fills our consciousness with the knowledge that each "seasonable month" brings its own glorious beauties, including the song of the nightingale. But this natural process of abundant creation is also a process of destruction, as each "sweet" dies to make room for the next.

Thus, inexorably, the poet is led to the final form of communion he can share with the bird: "Now more than ever seems it rich to die, / To cease upon the midnight with no pain, / While thou art pouring forth thy soul abroad / In such an ecstasy!" He enthusiastically imagines an ultimate fusion of the two "poured forth" souls; but immediately gives up the image, stopped by the recognition that "death is the great divorcer for ever." His imagination is arrested even more strongly by the perception that, while he like all human beings is aware that he must die, the bird does not share this ironic consciousness. The bird lives and sings, always oblivious to its fate; like the tree and brook "In drear-nighted December," "Thy bubblings n'er remember / Apollo's summer look; / But with a sweet forgetting, / They stay their crystal fretting, / Never, never petting / About the frozen time." It is in this sense that the poet asserts, "Thou wast not born for death, immortal Bird!" Because the nightingale has no self-consciousness, no awareness of its own mortality, because its song is therefore classically "naive" rather than "sentimental" (in Schiller's terms), its melodies are universal and eternally repeatable. Thus the "self-same song" can indeed be heard by emperor and clown, by Ruth and the faeries. But Ruth, weeping, homesick, standing "amid the alien corn," can hear that song in that way only once. Her self-consciousness, and especially her sense of painful alienation, remind the poet and us of the human condition from which we cannot escape: the awareness that we are separated selves who must die. In a world of becoming, every particular individual is transient. In this poem the poet's imagination, rather than evading this truth, intensifies it, while simultaneously celebrating the many delights nature offers us in her passing seasons. And so the poet is left with the sole self with which he began as well as with the recognition that the human imagination, like all things human, is limited. "The fancy cannot cheat so well / As she is fam'd to do, deceiving elf." The imagination cannot lift us forever beyond our awareness of our individual mortality. Thus the bird who does not share the ironic awareness is now as divorced from the poet as the poet is from the bird: the bird's happy song now seems to the melancholy poet a funeral dirge, a "plaintive anthem" that is "buried deep / In the next valley-glades" just as the poet's corpse will one day be buried. "Ode to a Nightingale" is thus a fine example of Socratic irony which, in Schlegel's words, "contains and arouses a feeling of indissoluble antagonism between the absolute and the relative, between the impossibility and the necessity of complete communication" (L, 108). It ends with an open question because the oppositions defined in the poem cannot be honestly reconciled. As Keats once wrote, "A Question is the best beacon towards a little Speculation" (I, 175). The poem thus leads us to speculate: the possibility of a perfectly happy life freed from the burdens of self-consciousness and the past, which the poet glimpsed for an instant before the poem began—is it a vision or a waking dream? And the experience of being so caught up in an abundant natural process that death seems rich and easeful—is that a waking truth or a sleeping delusion?

In "Ode on a Grecian Urn," Keats again poses the romantic delights of an idyllic world, now identified with the deathless realm of art, against the skeptical consciousness of human pain and mortality. Here the debate focuses on the value of art itself rather than on the possibility of unselfconsciousness or lack of irony. Because the urn is static and visible, the poet can greet it directly, fully enter its life, and explore all its dimensions exhaustively. But even as the poet approaches the urn, he is aware of its limitations: it is beautiful, but "unravish'd"—a bride who has not known the ecstasy of sexual consummation. And while the proverb has it that "Truth is the daughter of time," this urn is but a "foster-child" of time, not a direct descendant from truth. The urn is only a "sylvan" historian, a teller of pastoral tales whose knowledge is thus provincial and incomplete. Nonetheless, the urn's beauty is compelling to the poet's empathic capacities;[5] and he eagerly enters into the world depicted on its shape. Asking increasingly urgent questions that record his intensifying involvement in the life of these "men or gods" (who only in the eternal realm of art are indistinguishable), the poet comes to fully apprehend and appreciate the "sweeter" melodies of the pure imagination, uncorrupted by the limitations of human musicians, and the never-ceasing pleasure and beauty of a passionate love "Forever warm and still to be enjoy'd, / For ever panting, and for ever young." But even as he enthusiastically delights in the perfection of ever-green boughs, ever-new songs, and ever-intense, erotic love, he is ironically aware of the distance between such perfect happiness (which is all the more perfect for being anticipated rather than disappointingly realized) and a mortal world where leaves are shed, melodists grow weary, and "breathing human passion . . . leaves a heart high-sorrowful and cloy'd."

Having perplexed his enthusiastic delight in the urn's enduring beauty with his ironic appreciation of a human love that is both consummated and destroyed, the poet turns back to the urn with questions predicated, no longer on the assumption that the figures depicted on the urn are gods, but on the assumption of a shared finite humanity. "Who are these" people? "What little town" did they come from? And now that he sees the urn's figures as human beings rather than as perfect, immortal deities, the poet can see them only as dead, lost in history. "Little town, thy streets for evermore / Will silent be; and not a soul to tell / Why thou art desolate, can e'er return."

And now the urn seems to the poet no longer a living world populated by intensely happy trees, lovers, and musicians but simply an object, an "Attic shape" whose "fair attitude" is as posed and artificial as Lady Emma Hamilton's legendary Attitudes.[6] As Schlegel said, "The play of communicating and approaching is the business and the force of life; absolute perfection exists only in death" (DP, 54). And yet this Cold Pastoral has the capacity, even if only for a single moment, to "tease us out of thought," to do us the service of ultimate good friendship and release us, however briefly, from our ironic consciousness of mortal limits. And because the urn, the masterful work of art, has this power to lift man out of self-consciousness, to make him conscious instead of how it feels to live in a world of perfect beauty, perpetual spring, always passionate love, it has earned the right to display its aphoristic, "leaf-fring'd" legend or inscription. Responding to the poet's questions, the urn at last enters the debate and speaks: "Beauty is Truth,—Truth Beauty,—that is all / Ye know on earth, and all ye need to know." In the realm of art, beauty and truth can fully unite; there, "what the imagination seizes as beauty must be truth," for only what is beautiful has absolute aesthetic validity. And from the point of view of the work of art, aesthetic criteria are all that exist: "That is all / Ye know on earth, and all ye need to know." Since these aesthetic values can bring intense and undeniable pleasure to men and women—the vicarious experience of eternal delight—they are indeed "friends" who must be cherished. But the poem has posed these aesthetic or romantic values of beauty and stasis against another set of values, the ironic truth of a human existence consummated in time. In this realm where death incites the agonies and strife of human hearts, neither love nor beauty lasts; beauty can be only skin-deep; and the truth can be ugly. In this poem's delicate balancing of two opposed realities, the urn's final statement both is and is not true.

Even though the question of whether the beauty of art or nature can justify or compensate for the agonies of human existence remains unresolved, Keats nonetheless affirms in the "Ode on Melancholy" that the ironic or "sentimental" consciousness of loss and death is itself a source of beauty. Rejecting all traditional attempts to evade or dull the experience of grief with drugs or suicide, the poet instead celebrates the heaven-sent melancholic fit, the intense and anguishing awareness that all beautiful things die. This ironic consciousness of mortality in a becoming world is creative as well as painful; it is as nurturing to beauty as an April shower. Rather than avoiding it, one must seek it out and intensify the "wakeful anguish of the soul" by focusing upon the most transient of lovely things: the evanescent rainbow of the salt sand-wave, the full blossom of a peony that lasts only a day, the rich anger of a loving and forgiving mistress that ends as soon as it is spoken. Having thus strenuously burst joy's grape, having experienced with powerful empathy both a glorious beauty and its painfully quick end, one can understand how melancholy fosters joy and beauty. The human consciousness that all beautiful lofty things must go, and quickly too, actually intensifies our appreciation of them during the brief space in which we possess them. Knowing that some lovely thing is rare and soon to be lost makes it all the more precious to us. Thus both its beauty and our delight in it are actually increased by melancholy or irony, by the consciousness that nothing is permanent in an always changing world.

Moreover, the person who even "in the very temple of delight" can "burst Joy's grape" has not only accepted that every beautiful thing will end but has affirmed it as well. One thus retains one's moral freedom by rising from the conditioned to the unconditional, by taking part in one's own self-destruction (bursting the grape) with the enthusiasm of self-creation. One thus embraces Schlegel's romantic irony:

> [It] is necessary to be able to abstract from every single thing, to grasp hoveringly the general, to survey a mass, to seize the totality, to investigate even the most hidden and to combine the most remote things. We must raise ourselves above our own love and be able to annihilate in thought what we worship [that is, "burst Joy's grape"]: otherwise we lack, whatever other capabilities we might have, the faculty for the infinite and with it the sense for the world.[7]

Melancholy thus deserves a sovereign shrine within the temple of Delight.[8] To be vanquished by melancholy or romantic irony is to have known beauty and joy intensely; it is also to have known the agonizing "sadness" of their loss; and finally, it is to have experienced the powerful sense of freedom that comes from devotedly serving rather than resisting that process. But since one remains a "cloudy" rather than a brilliantly shining trophy, Keats's original question—whether intensely appreciated beauty can compensate for or justify the agonies and strife of human hearts—remains open.

Having reached this point in May 1819, Keats in his last Ode of the month, "Ode on Indolence," was content to remain in a state of wise passiveness, of hovering openness to all experience. When the Grecian images of Fame and Love and Poesy appear dreamily before him, he refuses the invitation once again to burn through the fierce dispute between the ideals men imagine and the human impossibility of attaining them. He will immerse himself instead in the richly abundant confusion of life itself, and sustain the romantic ironist's expectant and alert negative capability:

> My soul had been a lawn besprinkled o'er
>   With flowers, and stirring shades, and baffled beams.
> The morn was clouded, but no shower fell,
>   Tho' in her lids hung the sweet tears of May;
>   The open casement press'd a new-leav'd vine,
>   Let in the budding warmth and throstle's lay . . .

His greeting spirit, like Psyche's open casement, will "fret not after knowledge" but welcome instead both the budding warmth and the baffled beams of his perplexed human condition, for as the thrush said, "he's awake who thinks himself asleep."[9]

In the romances, the primary term of Keats's debate shifts from ideal beauty to love: can love, which like poetry requires a greeting of the spirit to exist, compensate for or justify death? We recall that Schlegel considered love to be the desire for permanence, for being as opposed to becoming. For Keats, too, human love seeks an ideal stasis, an eternity of mutually fulfilling pleasure. But Keats, like Schlegel, recognized the existence of powerful opposing forces: the mutability of all living things, the strong human need for freedom and change, the skepticism of human reason. Hence Keats's finest romances, like his Odes, engage in an unresolved debate: the delights and necessity of human love are posed against the inevitability of love's dying and the awareness that all love may be at least partly illusory. For as Shakespeare showed in *A Midsummer Night's Dream*, love like drama demands a willing suspension of disbelief. An act of imagination, in which the lover idealizes or enthusiastically affirms the qualities of the beloved, is essential to the process of falling in love. Whether the resultant love is therefore merely illusion, a fiction of the over-heated fancy, or a self-realizing truth, an authentic relating of the subjective mind to a living object, is the second question of these romances.

In *Endymion* Keats set out to write a long poem detailing the finally successful Neoplatonic quest of a mortal lover for an eternal erotic union with a goddess. But the poem soon developed into a debate (or what Morris Dickstein has called an "urgent dialectic")[10] between the limits of mortality or ironic self-consciousness on the one hand and the seductive pleasure of an ecstatic, sensuous, romantic, but illusive beauty on the other. Endymion's attempt to escape his mortal bonds, to attain the "immortality of passion" promised by the moon-goddess Cynthia, is increasingly called into question as the poem progresses. Endymion's alienation from the Latmians' naive oneness with nature and man and their innocent pagan worship of Pan (the fructifying abundance of nature) is the sign both of his growing self-consciusness and of a kind of death. Withdrawing into the first of the highly symbolic bowers in the poem, Endymion sleeps, dreams of a perfect love with the passionate, beauteous Cynthia, and awakes to despair. Earthly nature has become ugly, and his self has become a barrier to that "fellowship with essence," those "Richer entanglements, enthralments far / More self-destroying, leading, by degrees, / To the chief intensity: the crown of these / Is made of love and friendship" (1.797-801). And the greatest of these two, continues Endymion, is love: "its influence, / Thrown in our eyes, genders a novel sense, / At which we start and fret; till, in the end, / Melting into its radiance, we blend, / Mingle, and so become a part of it" (1.807-811). But the fellowship Endymion seeks in this hidden bower is a sensuous self-absorption, an "ardent listlessness" that would leave him forever cut off from other human endeavors, as solitary as the singing nightingale or Shelley's Alastor.

Endymion's quest, as the poem gradually shifts direction,[11] becomes as much an ironic denunciation of an "enskying" love as a romantic achievement of it. Endymion's ironic awareness of his "habitual" single self is "crude and sore," and includes a painful, even maddening, sense of separation from his desperately desired ideal. On the other hand, the naive, self-annihilating enthrallment that he seeks is increasingly identified with a narcissistic, infantile regression. That other mortal youth beloved by a goddess, Adonis, is found sleeping; his union with Venus must be for half of every year only a dream that leaves a "slumbery pout" upon his lips. Such a bower of love, half dream, half truth, is further undermined in the Glaucus episode in Book III, where Glaucus's succumbing to Circe's beauty in a twilight bower is presented as an imprisonment in a childhood fantasy of symbiosis with the mother.[12] "She took me like a child of suckling time, / And cradled me in roses. Thus condemned, / The current of my former life was stemmed, / And to this arbitrary queen of sense / I bowed a tranced vassal" (3.457-460). Glaucus painfully learns that such erotic consummation is gained at the expense of one's nobler self-consciousness. In thrall to a witch, he is no better than the other human beasts who surround her, begging for death; indeed, he may be worse, since his love for Circe has caused him to abandon and finally destroy his appropriate love, Scylla. Endymion, fulfilling the task of Glaucus's scroll, thus learns that a genuinely beautiful, spiritual love must be humanitarian rather than self-absorbed. It must be grounded on an ironic consciousness of human mortality rather than on a narcissistic and illusory absorption of the other into oneself.

The encounter with the Indian Maiden in the fourth book sharpens Endymion's, and the poem's, division. Having learned that an authentic love must embrace human beings and earthly beauty, Endymion immediately falls in love with the sorrowing girl. But Endymion still feels a conflict between such finite earthly love and the immortal fellowship with heavenly love that he has sought so long. The Indian Maid and Cynthia both appear to him, dividing his love in two. Momentarily deprived of both loves, in the Cave of Quietude, Endymion finally chooses an earthly love over what he now feels was "a nothing, nothing seen / Or felt but a great dream!" Keats has radically reconceived the poem's purpose. Rather than depicting the mortal lover's successful quest, through intense devotion to an ideal, for an "immortality of passion" and an etherealization into godhood, Keats now condemns this romantic quest as a childish fantasy of symbiosis and affirms instead the value of a human love based on finitude and the shared experiences of separate selves. Yet he still attempts to reconcile these two opposed quests by fusing the Indian Maiden and Cynthia into one person and "enskying" Endymion after all. This arbitrary deus ex machina clumsily implies what Keats more skillfully suggests in the image of Endymion's greened tree-carvings: "on the very bark 'gainst which he leant / A crescent he had carved, and round it spent / His skill in little stars. The teeming tree / Had swollen and greened the pious charactery / But not ta'en out" (4.787-791). An organic, natural, earthly love, born out of human fellowship and shared suffering, *is* an ideal, heavenly love. Endymion can find the ideal he has sought only by intensely valuing the real. But this last-minute resolution begs more questions than it answers, for "real" love, as this poem has presented it, is not always ideal. We recall that, even though Glaucus loved Scylla "to the very white of truth," she "would not conceive it" and fled away. Keats's later romances focus more directly upon the problems and contradictions inherent in such "real" love.

The fifteen months that passed between the writing of *Endymion* and the "mawkish" "Isabella" intensified Keats's consciousness of the frailties of human love and human existence. Tom's death weighed heavily upon him. When he turned again to romance, it was with an ironic self-restraint lacking in the earlier poems. "The Eve of St. Agnes" exquisitely balances enthusiasm with skepticism. Everything in the poem is qualified: Keats undercuts his romance with cynicism, his cynicism with romance, his seriousness with comedy, his comedy with seriousness. Ambiguity pervades the poem: nearly every character, every action, can be—and has been—interpreted in opposing ways, and both ways are equally valid. To see the way in which equally intelligent and sensitive critics can respond to the poem in contradictory ways, we need only look at the readings of "The Eve of St. Agnes" proposed by Earl Wasserman and Jack Stillinger. Wasserman subtly argues that Porphyro, by rising up the pleasure thermometer of human sensations and passing through the initial rooms of the Mansion of Many Apartments, is finally etherealized by "miracle" into Madeline's dream of a heaven's bourne where their human love is immortally repeated in a finer, more spiritual tone.[13] We might call this the "romantic" reading of the poem. Stillinger then gives us the "ironic" reading. He argues with equal subtlety that Porphyro is a "peeping Tom and a villainous seducer"; Angela is a panderer; Madeline is "hoodwinked" into losing her virginity; and the poem as a whole is an attack upon the very dream of a heavenly love that Wasserman celebrates.[14] As I shall try to show, both readings of the poem are right and both are wrong—for both fail to allow for the open-endedness, for the ability to hold two opposed ideas in the mind at the same time, that is at the core of "The Eve of St. Agnes" and of Keats's romantic irony.

The contradictions inherent in romantic love inform both the structure and the content of the poem. "The Eve of St. Agnes" utilizes a variety of incongruous conventions: courtly romance, fairy tale, Gothic melodrama, folk legend. Like Schlegel's ideal romantic poem, "this artfully ordered confusion, this charming symmetry of contradictions, this wonderfully perennial alternation of enthusiasm and irony which lives even in the smallest parts of the whole" (DP, 86), is infused with a "transcendental buffoonery" that graces every moment with the lightest comedy. Although the poem does not take its conventions completely seriously, it takes them seriously enough: Madeline's performance of St. Agnes's ritual is a "whim" but it produces its intended result. And while the poem calls the assumptions of romantic love into question, it does not insist on shattering them.[15] Keats allows his readers to make their own guesses about the future of the lovers; he does not commit himself. Yet the comic spirit and open-endedness of the story in no way undermine the very serious questions it raises. Is there a truth, "something of great constancy" as Hippolyta said in A Midsummer Night's Dream, in romantic love? Or is it merely a dream? Does love redeem human suffering? Or merely cause more pain? These questions, which probe a more complex and profound area of human experience than Endymion's yearning for an "immortality of passion," are lightly but deftly debated in "The Eve of St. Agnes."

In deliberate contrast to the springtime abundance of traditional pastoral romances, Keats opens his poem in the "bitter chill" of January and closes it with "cold"; whatever happens within the fairy-tale world of the castle, the lovers must eventually face the "Winter . . . of pale misfeature" outside. But within the castle, love is warm, if not entirely spiritual or rational. In contrast to the Beadsman's numbed fingers and unheard prayers before "the sweet Virgin's picture," Porphyro comes with "warm, unnerved arm" to utter pieties of a highly different sort before a living virgin. Just as the intensity of Porphyro's emotion underscores the sterility of the Beadsman's ascetic ritual, the anchorite's sincere and selfless Christianity undercuts the lover's "pious" language. For Porphyro's religious fantasies—"That he might gaze and worship all unseen"—do not remain quite chaste—"Perchance speak, kneel, touch, kiss." And Madeline, caught up in the superstitious rituals of St. Agnes's Eve, is "hoodwink'd with faery fancy." She naively expects to have her cake and eat it too, to sexually enjoy her lover-husband in her dreams and awake still chaste, "no weeping Magdalen." Aided by Angela, the messenger from heaven and fairy godmother who makes dreams come true (but who takes time out to chuckle like Pandarus), Porphyro gains access to Madeline's bedroom. Like Romeo to Juliet, Dante to Beatrice, Iachimo to Imogen, Merlin to Nimiane, and a bird-hunter to his prey,[16] Porphyro approaches his desire. Madeline comes and virtuous though she is, she is still looking forward to the erotic dreams that sleep will bring. As she enters her bedchamber, a flood of color transforms her chastely white skin to a passionate glow: "Rose-bloom fell on her hands, together prest, / And on her silver cross soft amethyst." To Porphyro she seemed "a splendid angel, newly drest, / Save wings, for heaven"—a lightly ironic description, since her lack of wings will prove crucial and this "newly drest" angel will soon be in precisely the opposite state. As Madeline slowly disrobes, Porphyro grows faint, though hardly from her purity. The comedy increases as Porphyro becomes more and more aroused, but cannot make the slightest movement for fear of betraying his presence. Madeline finally climbs into bed, "But dares not look behind, or all the charm is fled." Of course, if she did look behind she would see Porphyro leering out of the closet at her, enough to guarantee the flight of any charm. But caught up in her impossible dream, "as though a rose should shut and be a bud again," this "mission'd spirit" who is also a "tongueless nightingale" and thus as ravishable as Philomela sleeps deep, deep. Porphyro, rushing around the room in his breathless haste to set up the requisite banquet, wishes for "some drowsy Morphean amulet" (doubtless Keats knew the plot of *Clarissa*). But Madeline does not awake, not even to the combined temptations of sensuous feast and Porphyro's yearning words. Not until he adds music to the pleasures he offers (the highly symbolic "La belle dame sans merci" which threatens his own death if she remains unresponsive; an ironic choice, since Madeline is hardly in a position to play the dame sans merci), does Porphyro's reality begin to approximate the bliss of Madeline's dream. Having thus played Prince Charming to Madeline's Sleeping Beauty, Porphyro sinks to his knees, "pale as smooth-sculptured stone," reminding us of the "sculptured dead" in the Beadsman's chapel. Madeline awakes, not with fear or anger, but with a surprising disappointment—the poem here shifts into a more serious tone. Madeline had been dreaming of an ideal Porphyro, one without "mortal taint," compared to whom the real Porphyro seems "pallid, chill, and drear." The disjunction between dream and reality has been drawn, and Madeline's now self-conscious thoughts fly naturally from love to death: "For if thou diest, my Love, I know not where to go." But her ardent invitation arouses Porphyro, both sexually and emotionally, and he attains a brief moment of dream-like perfection: "Beyond a mortal man impassion'd far / At these voluptuous accents, he arose / Ethereal, flush'd." The lovers then do what is never done in fairy-tale romances: "like a throbbing star . . . Into her dream he melted, as the rose / Blendeth its odour with the violet." Forgetting their separation, they become one, attaining an ecstatic sexual communion in the realm of being. For, as Schlegel said, chaos "waits only for the touch of love to unfold as a harmonious world" (DP, 82).

But such harmonious perfection lasts only a moment: abruptly,

> . . . the frost-wind blows
> Like love's alarum pattering the sharp sleet
> Against the window-panes; St. Agnes' moon hath set.

Winter reigns outside: the dream has ended. Madeline, no longer a virgin, must now deal with the contradictions of reality: she is in love with a "cruel traitor" who nonetheless insists that he will marry and protect her in his home far away on the southern moors. The lovers steal away, past Macbeth's drunken porter who guards the gates of hell, into . . . what? "Aye, ages long ago / These lovers fled away into the storm." Keats places the story back in the realm of "once upon a time," but rather than ending it with the expected "happily ever after," he abruptly shifts to the grim reality with which the poem began. We are never told—and thus must guess—whether the lovers continued to experience the ecstatic delight they both knew in Madeline's waking dream or whether Porphyro abandoned Madeline, a weeping Magdalen indeed, in the storms raging outside the castle. But we are told of that cold night, during which Angela died "palsy-twitch'd" and the Beadsman slept in cold ashes. And thus we are reminded that, whatever else happens to Madeline and Porphyro, ravished angels die and virgin-worshippers must finally sleep in their own cold ashes.

And yet the poem in its delicate balancing has taught us too that an ardent romantic love can create a "paradise" for those capable of feeling it fully, a powerful joy that neither the Beadsman nor Angela knows. As in the Odes, a passionately enjoyed delight does and does not free one from the bonds of mortality. Once again, Keats has shown us how to hold two opposed ideas in our minds at the same time. The poem's treatment of romance has veered no nearer to burlesque than to tragedy. Like Schlegel's ideal artwork, "The Eve of St. Agnes" contains

> something original and inimitable which is absolutely irreducible, and in which after all its transformations its original character and creative energy are still dimly visible, where the naive profundity permits the semblance of the absurd and of madness, of simplicity and foolishness, to shimmer through. For this is the beginning of all poetry, to cancel the progression and laws of rationally thinking reason, and to transplant us once again into the beautiful confusion of imagination, into the original chaos of human nature. (DP, 86).

The question left open at the end of "The Eve of St. Agnes"—can we trust our loving imaginations?—is at the heart of "La Belle Dame sans Merci" as well. Recently, critics have tended to emphasize the belle dame's daemonic qualities and to portray her as the fairy enchantress, Celtic fay, or demonic witch of medieval ballads.[17] In doing so, they have underestimated the very human issues at stake in the poem. The belle dame sans merci of Alain Chartier's Provençal lyric from which Keats took his title, both here and in "The Eve of St. Agnes," was a very real woman, however inaccessible she made herself to her devoted lover.[18] Porphyro, too, was addressing a real woman; and we miss much of the irony of Keats's ballad if we overstress the woman's nonhuman attributes.

The knight or "wretched wight" whom the balladeer encounters in a wintry landscape is alone and dying, despite the abundance of granary and harvest to be found elsewhere. When asked why, the knight tells a richly ambiguous tale whose outline at least is clear: he has fallen in love with and lost a lovely lady, and life for him is now cold, barren, meaningless. But why did he lose her? That is the question the poem leaves open. Many readers have assumed that the lady, Circe-like, enthralled and then (perhaps unwillingly) abandoned him. These readers choose to place their trust in the truth of the knight's "latest" (perhaps obsessively repeated) dream: "I saw pale kings and princes too, / Pale warriors, death-pale were they all; / They cried—'La Belle Dame sans Merci' / Hath thee in thrall!'" In doing so, they forget Keats's frequent—and ironic —insistence that we both trust and distrust dreams. Of course the knight has also chosen to accept this dream as truth. Seeing "their starved lips in the gloom, / With horrid warning gaped wide," he has construed this nightmare as his own reality: "I awoke and found me here, / On the cold hill's side. / And this is why I sojourn here." But perhaps this grotesque dream is a lie, or a merely one-sided version of events. Perhaps the knight, by believing the worst possible interpretation of the lady's behavior (put forth not by himself but by others: "You're in love with a bitch!" say her rejected lovers, in effect), has destroyed the love that they shared and that required a willing suspension of disbelief to survive.

For if we look back at the poem with this possibility in mind, we can see that the lady's behavior, while curious in the knight's eyes, was not overtly hostile or cruel. If we think of her not so much as a fay or "fairy's child" (which is the knight's description, not the poet's) but as, say, a more modern bohemian or "flower child," we may see more of the complexity Keats was presenting. This long-haired, barefoot, wild-eyed lady willingly spent all day long with the knight, fed him (admittedly with unfamiliar, organic foods), sang to him sweetly. "She looked at me as she did love, / And made sweet moan." Keats's delicate balancing between romance and skepticism, between two opposed perspectives or ideas, is nowhere linguistically more deft. The lady looked at him *while* she loved him, making sweet moans of erotic desire and ecstasy; the lady looked at him *as if* she loved him, making sweet moans of sorrow, the sorrow born of the knowledge that she could not remain forever with this mortal whom she did? did not? could not? love. "And sure in language strange she said— / 'I love thee true.' " And it was certain that she said, however strange her unfamiliar accent or foreign tongue sounded, that she loved him truly; it was certain that the language or way in which she proclaimed her love was so strange, so alien, that it was not entirely credible. And why did she weep and sigh full sore? Because she knew her own reputation for being a belle dame sans merci, a rejecting woman, a castrating bitch, would eventually reach the ears of this, her one true love, and destroy his commitment to her? Because she knew that, being a callous woman or a Circe by nature, she would leave this man, whether she loved him or not?

In this open, richly ambiguous and ironic poem, Keats allows his readers to interpret the action as they wish; he does not commit himself. Whether we find truth in the knight's and lady's shared pleasure or in the knight's and death-pale warriors' shared nightmare is our choice. But one thing seems clear: the knight, having chosen to see his lady as a dame sans merci, remains "alone and palely loitering," loveless, and dying. His refusal or emotional inability to give another "greeting of the Spirit" has condemned him to a death-in-life. In "La Belle Dame sans Merci," skepticism outweighs enthusiasm; the result is a plaintive tone, a melancholic coloring, and a ritualistically repeated, grim ending that leaves the reader certain of only one thing: without love, we suffer. But with love? The knight has suffered, but need it have been so? This ironic-skeptical poem does not say.

As Keats matured, poetically and philosophically, he increasingly valued the role of skepticism in self-restraint. Looking back with embarrassment on "Isabella," he called the poem "smokeable" (II, 174) and "mawkish" and said he "could not bear" it (II, 162): "There is too much inexperience of life, and simplicity of knowledge in it . . . There are very few would look to the reality" (II, 174). Keats had introduced a healthy dose of skepticism into "The Eve of St. Agnes," a dose that would have been even stronger had he had his own way in making the love scene more explicit and the ending harsher.[19] But Keats was still unsatisfied: "A good deal" of his objections to "Isabella," he felt, also applied "to St. Agnes Eve—only not so glaring" (II, 174). Keats had gone a step further in "La Belle Dame," and in his final romance, written in the summer of 1819, he pushed his readers even harder to "look to the reality." The result was "Lamia," a poem that approaches pure skepticism as does no other of Keats's major works.

Here, the delicate balancing of romance with disbelief found in "The Eve of St. Agnes" is gone; even the calculated ambiguities of "La Belle Dame" have been forsaken. In "Lamia" we have skepticism without much enthusiasm, ironic self-destruction without much self-creation. Unlike the belle dame, Lamia is presented from the start as a nonhuman figure, a serpent (who may or may not have been a woman once) with suprahuman knowledge: she can see all the comings and goings of gods and mortals, can make a nymph invisible, can even "unperplex bliss from its neighbor pain" (a capacity that Keats in the "Lines Written in the Highlands" a year before had identified as madness, half-idiocy, and beyond mortal grasp). To fall in love with such a creature, however intensely pleasureable that experience may be, is indeed to commit one's life to a demonic, Circe-like power—Lamia's head is "Circean" (1.115), and we remember that Glaucus discovered Circe's bower by following a bewitching flame "like the eye of gordian snake" (3.495). Since Lamia is further associated, as many readers have noticed,[20] with the power to "give to airy nothing a local habitation and a name," to transform the invisible into the visible, to satisfy the desires of gods, and to create the conventions of romance (passionate love, lulling music, a fairy-palace), she can also be associated with poetry or with the imagination itself, the illusion-maker or the greeting Spirit. Keats's grim fears that the imagination and its romances may do more harm than good, especially in an anxious modern age, pervade this poem, unrelieved by any enthusiastic affirma-

tion. The irony of this poem is thus structural: it is a romance that undermines the value and truth of romance.

The poem opens "Upon a time," in a fairy-tale or mythic world that
immediately establishes a contrast between gods and mortals. Keats
again mocks the conventions he uses, just as on another level he satirizes
the bowers of bliss celebrated in his earliest poetry. The realm of immortal pleasure has now passed completely beyond human reach:

> It was no dream; or say a dream it was,
> Real are the dreams of Gods, and smoothly pass
> Their pleasures in a long immortal dream.　　　　　　(1.126-128)

However dependent Hermes may be on Lamia or the human imagination
for the realization of his erotic desires, his "immortality of passion" is a
dream forever inaccessible to mere human beings. But Keats's cynicism
goes further. Not only does he deny the gods' enduring pleasures to mortals, he also undercuts Hermes's passion. Hermes, burning with "a celestial heat . . . from his winged heels to either ear," is a figure of fun, the
perpetual lover or lecher. Like his human predecessor Porphyro, Hermes,
"bent on warm amorous theft," surreptitiously enters the nymph's bower
"to find where this sweet nymph prepar'd her secret bed." Hermes too is a
predator: "Hermes on his pinions lay, / Like a stoop'd falcon ere he takes
his prey." But unlike the ardent and perhaps genuinely self-deceived Porphyro, the "ever-smitten" Hermes has no nobility beyond his handsome-
ness and magical powers. His lust for the nymph is merely a "passion
new." When he and his nymph (who like Madeline is first frightened,
then comforted) finally retire into the "green-recessed woods," their
future contains nothing beyond a purely sexual passion, albeit a lasting
one.

Lamia, first encountered as a grotesque fusion of woman and snake
("Her head was serpent, but . . . she had a woman's mouth with all its
pearls complete"), is changed by Hermes's serpent-rod into "a lady
bright." Her tranformation is a grotesque parody of Apollo's dying into
life in *Hyperion*; for Lamia, too, will now explore the dark passages of
human love, but with an inhuman, "sciential brain" that can "estrange"
pain and pleasure and can order the most "ambiguous atoms" of the "spe-
cious chaos" of the universe "with sure art." Unlike Madeleine in "The
Eve of St. Agnes" who must suffer the actual contradictions and perplexi-
ties of human limits, Lamia can have her cake and eat it too. She is a virgin yet "in the lore of love deep learned to the red heart's core"; here her
wisdom seems sinister as well as admirable. She easily manipulates Ly-

cius into falling in love with her, appearing to him first as a goddess and then as a fragile maiden. Her powers, the powers of romantic love, make the triple league back to Corinth "decrease to a few paces" and invent a paradisiacal palace where none was seen before. Caught up in this dream, Lycius and Lamia enjoy a brief time of ecstatic happiness.

But Keats insists here, as opposed to "The Eve of St. Agnes," that their love is *only* a dream, a dream that must soon end. Lycius becomes dissatisfied with their secluded love and arrogantly wishes to show off his beautiful mistress to his friends at a public wedding. Lamia, her desperate pleas cruelly rebuffed, in a display of feminine masochism "lov'd the tyranny." At that moment, their dream is betrayed "to the dull shade / Of deep sleep." It now needs only the inevitable advent of the cold rationalist, Apollonius, to destroy it openly. Having apportioned the symbolic wreaths (a parody of Keats's own ambitious wearing of Apollo's laurel wreath at Leigh Hunt's party)—Ophelia's weeping willow and ambiguously curative adder's tongue for Lamia, drunken Bacchus' thyrsis for Lycius, cruel spear-grass and the spiteful thistle for Apollonius—Keats moves briskly to the denouement, the confrontation of Lamia, the illusion of love, with the heartless logic of Apollonius. The illusion, of course, is destroyed (Lamia dies or vanishes) by Apollonius's piercing stare. But Keats's view of reality is harsher yet: Lycius, deprived of his dream and bride, loses not only delight but life itself. The point is made: man must either live without rainbows in the cold, objectively catalogued, rational world of Apollonius or succumb to a romantic illusion (of love or poetry) that in its inexorable ending destroys him. Keats had, of course, made this point earlier in the poem, in the grim statement that opens Part II:

> Love in a hut, with water and a crust,
> Is—Love, forgive us!—cinders, ashes, dust;
> Love in a palace is perhaps at last
> More grievous than a hermit's fast:—

Romance does not, cannot last; and the price here exacted for a willing suspension of disbelief on this score is death. Keats's skepticism here finds no comic relief; it is heavy, one-sided, numbing. Stylistically, the poem lacks irony. Schlegel had warned the poet against leaning too far toward the critical side of self-restraint:

> There are only three mistakes to guard against. First: What appears
> to be unlimited free will, and consequently seems and should seem
> to be irrational and supra-rational, nonetheless must still at bottom

be simply necessary and rational; otherwise the whim becomes willful, becomes intolerant, and self-restriction turns into self-destruction. Second: Don't be in too much of a hurry for self-restriction,
but first give rein to self-creation, invention, and inspiration, until
you're ready. Third: Don't exaggerate self-restriction. (L, 37)

Whim, the choice of a lamia as heroine, does turn into willful self-destruction in "Lamia"; no higher principle reveals this arbitrary choice as
absolutely necessary and rational. There is no hope for the lovers: enthusiasm is disallowed from the start. The appropriate genre for Keats's profoundly serious questioning of the value of the constructions of the human imagination is not romance, which requires a willing suspension of
disbelief even to exist, but epic. Keats's last great debate on the uses of
poetry and the value of the imagination rightly takes place in *The Fall of
Hyperion*.

Clearly, *The Fall of Hyperion* is not an example of "transcendental
buffoonery." Its romantic irony is sung in a darker key. Both in structure
and in content, the poem is a rite of passage, a profound exploration of
liminal processualism. It reflects Keats's increasing preoccupation with
change, with the passage from life to death, with self-creation and self-
destruction—and with our human responses to such changes. In the letters and poems of 1818 and 1819, Keats was insisting upon the inevitability of human suffering in a world of change. "Circumstances," he wrote
to George and Georgiana Keats, "are like Clouds continually gathering
and bursting—While we are laughing the seed of some trouble is put into
the wide arable land of events—while we are laughing it sprouts i[t]
grows and suddenly bears a poison fruit which we must pluck" (II, 79).
Sorrow is inherent in a becoming universe, in which everything must
eventually die:

> For instance suppose a rose to have sensation, it blooms on a beauti-
> ful morning it enjoys itself—but there comes a cold wind, a hot sun
> —it cannot escape it, it cannot destroy its annoyances—they are as
> native to the world as itself: no more can man be happy in spite, the
> world[l]y elements will prey upon his nature. (II, 101)

In a world of process, humans must always be conscious of the painful
loss of beauty and love:

> The whole appears to resolve into this—that Man is originally "a
> poor forked creature" subject to the same mischances as the beasts of
> the forest, destined to hardships and disquietude of some kind or
> other. If he improves by degrees his bodily accom[m]odations and
> comforts—at each stage, at each a[s]cent there are waiting for him a

fresh set of annoyances—he is mortal and there is still a heaven with its Stars abov[e] his head. (II, 101)

For humanity does not belong to "the beasts of the forest": we are blessed and cursed with self-consciousness, with the constant ironic awareness of what we have lost and what we have become and what the future may bring. In *The Fall of Hyperion*, Keats explores whether and how this ironic consciousness of process and human finitude can help men and women to live meaningful lives.

But in his first attempt at an epic poem, *Hyperion*, Keats was overshadowed by Milton. He anxiously tried to emulate both Milton's sublime style and his unquestioning confidence in the value and purposefulness of human existence, as expressed in *Paradise Lost*. Yet Keats, like Psyche, was born "too late for the fond believing lyre," in an age when the mythic order of Christian sin, penance, grace, and redemption no longer seemed self-evident. Therefore, the task Keats set himself in *Hyperion* was to discover another system of salvation, a system in which beauty or the powers of the human imagination had the capacity to make "disagreeables evaporate" (evaporate not in the sense of disappear but in the more technical sense of being "sublimed" or vaporized into another, more ethereal and hence less oppressive form).[21]

In *Hyperion*, Keats asserted with Miltonic confidence that beauty could transform, alleviate, or at least justify suffering. In this nonironic epic, Keats planned to celebrate a new order of gods, the Olympians, whose new kind of beauty would justify the fall and sufferings of the older order of gods, the Titans. Keats began negatively, by vividly picturing the immense agony of the fallen Titans, gods whose suffering was equal in magnitude and intensity to the magnificence of the Elgin marbles from which their portraits were drawn. The "realmless" Saturn is conscious only of utter desolation:

> I am gone
> Away from my own bosom: I have left
> My strong identity, my real self.   (1.112-114)

Hyperion, the only Titan still seated upon his throne, is tormented with anxiety and frightened by fearful omens and terrifying nightmares; he foresees for himself nothing "but darkness" (1.242). Indeed, Hyperion has become the very embodiment of the painful human condition, as his father Coelus, the sky, points out:

> Unruffled, like high Gods, ye liv'd and ruled:
> Now I behold in you fear, hope and wrath;

> Actions of rage and passion; even as
> I see them, on the mortal world beneath,
> In men who die.   (1.331-335)

To find out the reason why such immense suffering should occur, Saturn summons the Titans together, and hears from Oceanus the answer Keats is proposing in this poem:

> We fall by course of Nature's law . . .
> . . . as thou wast not the first of powers,
> So art thou not the last; it cannot be:
> Thou art not the beginning nor the end.
> . . . on our heels a fresh perfection treads,
> A power more strong in beauty, born of us
> And fated to excel us, as we pass
> In glory that old Darkness . . .
> . . . for 'tis the eternal law
> That first in beauty should be first in might.   (2.181-229)

Oceanus's solution to the problem of human suffering is a myth of progress, the belief that the greater beauty to come justifies the destruction of former beauties and joys. For such a myth to work poetically, to carry conviction for his readers, and to be proved upon his own pulses, Keats must next depict a god of such beauty and power that we *feel* recompensed for the agony we have empathically suffered with Saturn and Hyperion. And Keats attempts such a sublime resolution. Clymene introduces this new god in her description of the "new blissful golden melody" she recently heard, in which "a voice came sweeter, sweeter than all tune," crying "Apollo! The morning-bright Apollo!" (2.280, 292, 298). And in Book III, we meet Apollo himself, who has left his mother and twin sister and wanders alone beside a stream, weeping. But Keats fails to describe this new god: we are told how Apollo feels but not how he looks. Apollo is then visited by "an awful Goddess" (3.46) who asks the cause of his sadness, and Apollo, gazing on her face (which again is not physically described), is miraculously enlightened. "Knowledge enormous" suddenly pours into his brain, and, simultaneously, tormenting physical pain assails him. Keats implies that this simultaneous consciousness of knowledge and of pain will transform Apollo into a greater god, a being who has transmuted suffering into beauty and thus justified suffering as a direct *cause* of greater beauty.

> Soon wild commotions shook him, and made flush
> All the immortal fairness of his limbs;
> Most like the struggle at the gate of death;
> Or liker still to one who should take leave

Of pale immortal death, and with a pang
As hot as death's is chill, with fierce convulse
Die into life: so young Apollo anguished.   (3.124-130)

But the poem ends here, an incomplete fragment, because Keats has not created a poetic image of Apollo's new "life," of that new kind of beauty that is more than equal to the images of suffering he had already presented in Saturn and Hyperion. Keats tells us that Apollo is a greater god, a god of higher knowledge and self-conscious suffering who has used that consciousness to become more beautiful, but he does not *show* us this Apollo in an image with which we can empathically unite. I think there are at least two reasons for Keats's failure to give us such an image. First, Keats himself had not yet been able to see fully into the "mystery," to discover exactly the kind of poetic image that would suffice. Indeed, the synthesizing image he required, a resolution that would have translated the antithesis "die into life" into an orderly schema, had no precedent in his poetry. In this nonironic epic, Keats attempted an impossible *fusion* of death and life, pain and beauty—and necessarily failed. Secondly, the language of the poem, a deliberate imitation of Milton's prosody, inversions, and epic conventions, was opposed to Keats's developing romantic irony. Milton's style was too assertive and too distanced to include Keats's more self-conscious questionings and urgent debates. In April 1819 Keats set *Hyperion* aside, its questions still open.

Only four months later, he returned to the poem in an anxious attempt to complete a long and complex statement of his maturing ideas before his fatal illness forced him to give up poetry. We notice immediately that *The Fall of Hyperion—A Dream* is a more self-conscious, ironic poem; and the subtitle, "A Dream," directly challenges the poem's accuracy and value. The poem now becomes, like the Odes, a sentimental or self-mirroring work of art, "poetry and the poetry of poetry" (A, 238). It examines not only its subject matter but also its form, its ideals and limitations, its "hindrances and subjects" (A, 255). The poet-narrator now personally poses the question that the poem will debate: is this "dream" the madness of a fanatic or the vision of a true poet? And if the latter, can this "Dream" and the beauty it presents reconcile humanity to its suffering? Can such suffering lead to greater wisdom and delight? Is there value in the chaos and process of life? A partial answer to these questions now comes in the form of a realized image, the face of Moneta or the icon of Wisdom itself.[22] Gazing on this face, empathically uniting with it, the poet learns how the process of life, with all its perplexed pain and beauty, can be affirmed. To understand the implications of this image of Moneta's face, we must first undergo the experiences that schooled the narrator, the dream-experiences or rites of passage that actually led to this image.

Significantly, the poet enters this liminal vision through both an excess of sensual delight—he eats "deliciously" of the remnants of a summer feast seemingly prepared for the angels or Adam and Eve—and an awareness of mortality and death: he drinks the elixir with a pledge to "the dead whose names are in our lips" (1.45). Out of this romantic-ironic consciousness of human self-fulfillment and self-destruction is born the vision of Moneta's face. Having drunk the finite human condition to the full, the poet is suddenly transported to the inner cella of Saturn's temple where he is challenged by the goddess to approach and look directly upon her face. To reach her, he must prove that he is no mere dreamer but a true poet who, although he perplexes pain and joy, nonetheless teaches a redeeming wisdom. Trying to cross the marble pavement to the first step of the altar, the poet, like Apollo, must first destroy his former, limited selfhood. A novice beginning the rituals of initiation, he must pass through a death-agony in order to "die into life," to enter a new self-consciousness. In this liminal phase, he will be able to understand at last the value of poetry which, unlike medicine, venoms pleasure with pain and yet may render that pain bearable. Having crossed this threshold, having suffered all that mortals can, the poet is rewarded with the naked vision of Moneta's face.

> Then saw I a wan face,
> Not pin'd by human sorrows, but bright-blanch'd
> By an immortal sickness which kills not;
> It works a constant change, which happy death
> Can put no end to; deathwards progressing
> To no death was that visage; it had past
> The lilly and the snow; and beyond these
> I must not think now, though I saw that face—
> But for her eyes I should have fled away.
> They held me back, with a benignant light,
> Soft mitigated by divinest lids
> Half-closed, and visionless entire they seem'd
> Of all external things;—they saw me not,
> But in blank splendour, beam'd like the mild moon,
> Who comforts those she sees not, who knows not
> What eyes are upward cast.   (1.256-271)

The poet is simultaneously repelled and attracted by Moneta's face, a face that encompasses all human suffering—not the inhuman suffering that Frank Kermode saw there,[23] but all the agonies of mortal history, all the torments of the humanized Titans in *Hyperion*. Every possible hu-

man loss, grief, sickness, and death has left its ravages upon that blanched
face. But all this suffering is rendered bearable to the poet by the beauty
of Moneta's eyes, by their blank splendour which, like the moon, fills
him with wonder and comfort as he gazes upon it. These eyes so balance
and focus the terrifying whiteness of Moneta's face that the poet can endure the total image: suffering is thus made acceptable because it is u-
nited with a defined image of beauty. Keats's pictorial imagination has
here given us a visual fusion of agonizing pain and intense beauty, of
destruction and creation. Thus this face is an icon of romantic irony. The
glory of Moneta's eyes enables us to bear the ugliness of her face; the hor-
rors of her face intensify the beauty of her eyes. This image, the face of
Moneta, thus becomes Keats's closest approximation to the existentialist
tragedy of *King Lear*, to that "excellence of every Art" which lies in "its
intensity, capable of making all disagreeables evaporate, from their being
in close relationship with Beauty & Truth" (I, 192). We can bear to burn
through *King Lear*, can endure all the unjustifiable agonies of Lear and
Gloucester and Cordelia, only because we *know* it is a play, that in this
shaped form a controlling dramatic intelligence has given to all the confusing and excruciating miseries of human life the "sense of an ending."
Similarly, Moneta's eyes structure, and thus shape, define, and limit, the
horrifying pallor of her face.

The static artistic image—be it a play, a poem, a painted image, or a
sculpted face—thus becomes a spatial analogy for the temporal process
that Keats called "Soul-making." Writing to George and Georgiana Keats
in April 1819, as he struggled with *Hyperion*, Keats groped his way toward a "system of Salvation which does not affront our reason and humanity," the very system which he four months later succeeded in em-
bodying poetically in *The Fall of Hyperion*. Keats's final myth or "system
of Spirit-Creation" is a myth not of progress but of process, of self-becoming, of self-creation. Without Byron's exuberance but with a deeper
compassion for the human suffering involved, Keats here embraces all
the implications of romantic irony. In an abundantly chaotic, always
changing world, a world without absolute orders or meanings, the individual must create his own meaning or self-identity out of his own intense participation in a living and dying universe. As Keats explains,

Call the world if you Please "The vale of Soul-making" Then you
will find out the use of the world . . . I say '*Soul making*' Soul as distinguished from an Intelligence—There may be intelligences or
sparks of the divinity in millions—but they are not Souls till they
acquire identities, till each one is personally itself. I[n]telligences are
atoms of perception—they know and they see and they are pure, in

short they are God—how then are Souls to be made? How then are
these sparks which are God to have identity given them—so as ever
to possess a bliss peculiar to each ones individual existence? How,
but by the medium of a world like this? This point I sincerely wish to
consider because I think it a grander system of salvation than the
chrystain religion—or rather it is a system of Spirit-creation—This is
effected by three grand materials acting the one upon the other for a
series of years—These three Materials are the *Intelligence*—the *human heart* (as distinguished from intelligence or Mind) and the
World or *Elemental space* suited for the proper action of *Mind and
Heart* on each other for the purpose of forming the *Soul* or *Intelligence destined to possess the sense of Identity*. I can scarcely express
what I but dimly perceive—and yet I think I perceive it—that you
may judge the more clearly I will put it in the most homely form possible—I will call the *world* a School instituted for the purpose of
teaching little children to read—I will call the *human heart* the *horn
Book* used in that School—and I will call the *Child able to read, the
Soul* made from that *school* and its *hornbook*. Do you not see how
necessary a World of Pains and troubles is to school an Intelligence
and make it a soul? (II, 102)

To develop a self, a soul, a personal realization of the spark of God
within us all, Keats argues, we must combine our intelligence—our conscious apprehension of the world or knowledge, together with our intellectual capacity to create abstract systems and to shape a purpose or plan
for mankind—with our human heart, our negative capability or empathic participation in both the sufferings and the joys of the elemental
world. By fusing our felt experience of chaos, of pain perplexed with
pleasure, to our conscious knowledge of the nature of human existence in
an always-changing universe, we can grope our way toward a self-
created but psychologically necessary purpose or sense of an ending in
our own lives. In other words, if we as individuals can consciously use
our intelligence or imagination to give to our always changing lives a
sense of direction and meaningful purpose, a purpose that the felt pains
and pleasures of our heart contribute to rather than deny, then we shall
create a soul or identity, a self capable of surviving and developing in a
world of sufferings. In doing so, we shall achieve the romantic ironist's
ideal of self-determination, the self-restraint born out of the constant
alternation of enthusiastic self-creation and skeptical self-destruction that
alone can be called freedom. As Schlegel said in an aphorism that Keats
would have understood, "To become God, to be man, and to educate
oneself, are expressions that are synonymous" (A, 262).

Analogously, if the artist can create a form that includes rather than
omits change and the suffering change entails, and that places such

change in meaningful relation to its own created pattern or purposeful shape (in the sense of Kant's *Zweckmässigkeit ohne Zweck*), this form may aid its audience to accept the inevitable perplexity of beauty and pain. For this inextricable confusion of pleasure and pain was for Keats the bedrock of reality, the unavoidable result of living in a chaotic universe. One must therefore learn to look upon this chaos, not as frightening or absurd, but rather as abundant life: as the potential substance of an always-becoming self and as the content of an always-changing fictional pattern or myth. One must further learn to regard one's own self-images and myths skeptically, as admittedly man-made, and at the same time enthusiastically, as capable of evaporating disagreeables by giving to the agonies and strife of human hearts a significant meaning. This was for Keats the height of both human wisdom and imaginative art; it is also of course the essence of romantic irony and the sublime freedom at which it aims.

Having encountered such romantic irony in the spatial mode of Moneta's face, the poet-narrator now attempts to translate this consciousness into a temporal mode. "I ach'd to see what things the hollow brain / Behind enwombed." By this act of desire and will ("Let me behold . . . What in thy brain so ferments to and fro!"), his consciousness continues to expand:

> there grew
> A power within me of enormous ken
> To see as a god sees.   (1.302-304)

The unvisualized apotheosis of Apollo in the third book of *Hyperion* is replaced in *The Fall of Hyperion* by the secular apotheosis of the poet, a mortal's attainment of sublime wisdom. The poet, unlike Apollo, voluntarily commits himself to a painful and heroic process of self-creation and self-destruction. He continues to see and to struggle:

> Without stay or prop,
> But my own weak mortality, I bore
> The load of this eternal quietude,
> The unchanging gloom, and the three fixed shapes
> Ponderous upon my senses, a whole moon.
>   —Oftentimes I pray'd
> Intense, that Death would take me from the Vale
> And all its burthens—gasping with despair
> Of change, hour after hour I curs'd myself . . . (1.388-392; 396-399)

In choosing to remain and watch, the poet chooses "Wakeful anguish" over "easeful death," the agonizing process of soul-making over a too-easy acceptance of an end-stopped certainty.

Keats's ensuing attempt to reconcile the spatial and romantic-ironic mode of Moneta's face with the temporal and sublime mode of *Hyperion* —the narrative of the fall of the Titans and the creation of a new order of self-conscious gods—necessarily faltered. Keats could not easily recast his earlier assertive Miltonic idiom and myth of progress into a more personal, self-questioning language and myth of process. Although this contradictory poetic effort might have eventually led Keats to an even more complex romantic irony, it demanded too much of him at a time when he was tormented with anxieties about his health, his relationship with Fanny Brawne, and his financial status. In September 1819 he gave up revising *Hyperion* into *The Fall of Hyperion* because, as he explained to Reynolds, "there were too many Miltonic inversions" and "intonation[s]" in it (II, 167). At a deeper level, however, *The Fall of Hyperion* could never have been completed. Like Byron's *Don Juan*, it is a poem celebrating a never-ending process of self-becoming. While we may need a static spatial image to clarify the direction and purpose of our lives, the actual temporal realization of that purpose can end only with our deaths. Keats's developmental imagery—the child learning in school, the mind sucking its identity from the heart's teat, the knowledge "enwombed" in Moneta's brain—emphasizes this life-long temporal process. Thus it is fitting that *The Fall of Hyperion* in its movement from the spatial to the temporal mode remains open-ended, not yet finished. The embodiment of the wholly self-conscious, tragically suffering, transcendently beautiful Apollo can truly take place only in the lives of Keats and his readers. The individual who achieves such conscious selfhood born out of "the anguish of a waking soul" has attained the freedom from physical necessity that both Schiller and Schlegel identified with the positive sublime.[24] As Schiller explained,

> The feeling of the sublime is a mixed feeling. It is a composition of melancholy which at its utmost is manifested in a shudder, and of joyousness which can mount to rapture and, even if it is not actually pleasure, is far preferred by refined souls to all pleasure. This combination of two contradictory perceptions in a single feeling demonstrates our moral independence in an irrefutable manner. For since it is absolutely impossible for the very same object to be related to us in two different ways, it therefore follows that *we ourselves* are related to the object in two different ways; furthermore, two opposed natures must be united in us, each of which is interested in diametrically opposed ways in the perception of the object. By means of the feeling for the sublime, therefore, we discover that the state of our minds is not necessarily determined by the state of our sensations,

that the laws of nature are not necessarily our own, and that we possess a principle proper to ourselves that is independent of all sensuous affects. (OS, 198)

A willed acceptance of the contradictions of human experience, of the chaotic infinity of nature, and of human mortality—together with a rapturous appreciation of the joy and beauty inherent in the terrible—was for Schiller as for Keats the essence of human freedom and nobility.

It is just this acceptance that permeates Keats's last and most completely romantic-ironic poem, "To Autumn." Shakespearean in its fullness, this poem celebrates process: the cycles of nature, the passing of the seasons, the living and dying of men and women. For in that process comes such richness, such ripeness, such abundance that Keats can say "it is enough." Hovering between life and death, between summer and the winter of pale misfeature, autumn swells and sustains such harmonious fulfillment that past and future loss are evaporated into rich present contentment. Temporal process is here spatialized, androgynously personified as the reaper who does not reap, the indolent yet laden gleaner, the loading and blessing bosom-friend of the maturing sun who musically fills the soft-dying day. Caught up, held, filled, in the arms of such mellow warmth, such *Fülle*, our human consciousness freely accepts the subtle movement in the poem from the bees' o'erbrimming summer honey to the stubble-plains' and gathering swallows' intimations of winter. The passage from Indian summer through the ending of the harvest to early November, from late morning to noon to twilight, from tactile to visual to auditory sensations, from vegetal immobility to vegetal mobility to animal vitality (ascending up the evolutionary ladder), from an enclosed space (the cottage garden) to a populated village or farm to the endless openness of sky and horizon[25]—all these movements toward temporal extension, spacial extension, and human enrichment lead the reader to feel, "We have had enough." Significantly, the poet's self-conscious voice is absent from this poem. Addressing autumn, participating in the seasonal processes of life itself, the poet has become the object he addresses. And yet the poem portrays no static synthesis of self and other. The "either-or" syntax of the second stanza leaves the consciousness of the poem—as well as the passage of time—still open to alternative possibilities. In truly ironic fashion, the poem holds together both contradictory extremes[26]—the beauty of becoming and the sorrow of ending, the ecstatic apprehension of perfect pleasure and the certainty that such pleasure is but momentary, the infinite and the finite—refusing to resolve these contradictions because they cannot be resolved. Kant's antinomy, the impossible conjunction of the temporal with the eternal, of the finite with the infinite, has, as Schiller and Schlegel predicted, been proved invalid; for in the processual world of "To Autumn," the temporal and the eternal have embraced.

4

Carlyle's *Sartor Resartus:*
A Self-Consuming Artifact

The young Carlyle, an eager exponent of German transcendental philosophy, shared Schlegel's vision of the universe as a chaotic abundance, a dyamic and incomprehensible process of spiritual becoming. In *Signs of the Times* (1829), Carlyle attacked the prevailing mechanistic conception of man and the universe. Instead, he insisted, "there is a science of *Dynamics* in man's fortune and nature, as well as of *Mechanics*. There is a science which treats of, and practically addresses, the primary, unmodified forces and energies of man, the mysterious springs of Love, and Fear, and Wonder, of Enthusiasm, Poetry, Religion, all which have a truly vital and *infinite* character."[1] Both nature and man are animated by a divine and infinite power, a creative force that overflows any rational system. Carlyle draws on the imagery of oceanic abundance and the immeasurable force of gravity that Byron had also invoked:

> all our systems and theories are but so many froth-eddies or sandbanks, which from time to time [Nature] casts up, and washes away. When we can drain the Ocean into mill-ponds, and bottle up the Force of Gravity to be sold by retail, in gas-jars; then may we hope to comprehend the infinitudes of man's soul under formulas of Profit and Loss; and rule over this too, as over a patent engine, by checks, and valves, and balances.

This "wondrous, unquestionable" nature, this underlying "Moral Force," constantly overthrows old ideas and social institutions to make way for new. But both contraries—the dynamic and the mechanical—are necessary, for, Carlyle argues, "Undue cultivation of the inward or Dynamical province leads to idle, visionary, impracticable courses, and, especially in rude eras, to superstition and Fanaticism, with their long train of baleful and well-known evils." Through the unceasing interaction of these contraries, both nature and man "dimly aim" at a higher, greater freedom. As Carlyle concludes, man's only "reasonable service" is to reform himself, to participate purposefully in the "boundless grinding collision of the New with the Old," and thus to engage in a process of constant self-transcendence that is itself an "emblem" of this "higher, heavenly freedom."[2]

Later essays reaffirm Carlyle's fundamentally romantic-ironic perception of the universe as a dynamic, irrational process. Acted (as opposed to written) history, he argues in "On History" (1830),

> is an ever-living, ever-working Chaos of Being, wherein shape after shape bodies itself forth from innumerable elements. And this Chaos, boundless as the habitation and duration of man, unfathomable as the soul and destiny of man, is what the historian will depict, and scientifically gauge, we may say, by threading it with single lines of a few ells in length! For as all Action is, by its nature, to be figured as extended in breadth and in depth, as well as in length; that is to say, is based on Passion and Mystery, if we investigate its origin; and spreads abroad on all hands, modifying and modified; as well as advances toward completion,—so all Narrative is, by its nature, of only one dimension; only travels forward towards one, or towards successive points: Narrative is *linear*, Action is *solid*.

The role of the spiritually aware man, the "Artist in History," then, is to endeavor to discover and body forth the "Idea of the Whole," knowing always that "the whole meaning lies far beyond our ken."[3]

Confronting this "bottomless, boundless Deep" of nature,[4] this primitive and incomprehensible force, man must acknowledge and yet strive to overcome the limits of his own mind. For Carlyle, as Geoffrey Hartman has shown,[5] consciousness, insofar as it is equated with scientific inquiry based on analysis, "Division, Dismemberment," or even with articulated thoughts, is a disease. Consciously, man can know only "the mechanical, small." Therefore, Carlyle argues in "Characteristics" (1830), man must free himself from the limits of consciousness and participate intuitively, through action rather than thought, in the ongoing life of nature. It is through his work that man reveals "that mysterious Self-impulse of the whole man." Here we see the way in which Carlyle included the Puritan work ethic he learned from his Burgher parents in his Idealist conception of a dynamic universe. Acting, working, man is constantly changing. Insofar as his action seeks to manifest emblematically the Divine Idea of the World, truth "never *is*, always *is a-being*"; truth is never complete, never yet fully revealed. Therefore, as Carlyle began this review of Friedrich Schlegel's *Philosophische Vorlesungen* (1830), "having no system" is best.[6]

Carlyle's fascination with change in human affairs led him to write *The French Revolution* (1837), a history of the most violent social change in contemporary Europe. In *The French Revolution*, Carlyle insists upon the necessity of both anarchy and order in human society. Too little anarchy (that vital "Chaos, primeval Night") causes man's death by inanity, "the fatal condition that results from the atrophy of our taproots into reality," as Philip Rosenberg has put it.[7] But too much anarchy can lead to an explosion of "guilt and criminality."[8] Carlyle can thus defend the Terror as the inevitably violent order created by too long repressed anarchic forces; indeed, he goes further to argue that the Terror is the *only possible institutionalization* of the primal energies of man. Significantly, Carlyle turns to the language of oxymoron to describe the end toward which the French Revolution is tending, "Sansculottism Accoutred." Rosenberg emphasizes,

> For Carlyle the relationship between the revolutionary force of the sansculottes and the new social order they are to help build can be expressed only in terms of paradoxes, just as his ontology of revolution is expressed in the paradoxical postulate that the postrevolutionary order must derive from the anarchic force that destroyed the old order while at the same time it must be—simply by virtue of the fact that it is an order at all—the very antithesis of that anarchic force.[9]

As Carlyle says, the fire-force of sansculottism must be both negated, for it is "a thing *without* order, a thing proceeding from beyond and beneath the region of order," and preserved, for it is "a genuine outburst of Nature, issuing from, or communicating with, the deepest deep of Nature. When so much goes grinning and grimacing as a lifeless Formality, and under the stiff buckram no heart can be felt beating, here once more, if nowhere else, is a Sincerity and Reality."[10]

Between 1829 and 1837, then, Carlyle shared the romantic ironist's perception of the universe as a mysterious, anarchic force that is vitally alive, always moving, changing, making and unmaking. This divine power can be apprehended, not through mechanistic logic, but only intuitively, by actively participating in it (through work), or analogically, by seeing every event as emblematic of a hidden process. Speaking of himself in *The Diamond Necklace* (1837), Carlyle wrote:

> He has witnessed overhead the infinite Deep, with greater and lesser lights, bright-rolling, silent-beaming, hurled forth by the Hand of God: around him and under his feet, the wonderfulest Earth, with her winter snow-storms and her summer spice-airs; and unaccountablest of all, *himself* standing there. He stood in the lapse of Time;

he saw Eternity behind him, and before him. The all-encircling mysterious tide of FORCE, thousand-fold (for from force of Thought to force of Gravitation what an interval!) billowed shoreless on; bore him too along with it,—he too was part of it. From its bosom rose and vanished, in perpetual change, the lordliest Real-Phantasmagory, which men name *Being;* and ever anew rose and vanished; and ever that lordliest many-colored scene was full, another yet the same . . .

Study Reality, he is ever and anon saying to himself; search out deeper and deeper *its* quite endless mystery: see it, know it; then, whether thou wouldst learn from it, and again teach; or weep over it, or laugh over it, or love it, or despise it, or in any way relate thyself to it, thou hast the firmest enduring basis: *that* hieroglyphic page is one thou canst read on forever, find new meaning in forever.[11]

Written during this period, *Sartor Resartus* (1829-31) most fully manifests Carlyle's romantic irony. Both in content and in structure, this is a work of "transcendental buffoonery." It is, first and foremost, a hoax, a book-length review of a book that does not exist. Thus it is a book that is but is not a book. Here Carlyle adapts to his own purposes the familiar wit of *Fraser's Magazine* and *Blackwood's,* the wit of Oliver Yorke and Christopher North, those endearing or irascible editors who also do and do not exist. Carlyle of course expected the more faithful and subtle readers of *Fraser's* to see through his hoax, to penetrate his disguises and recognize *Sartor Resartus* for the jocoserious production that it was. The volume of *Fraser's* immediately preceding the one in which *Sartor Resartus* first appeared included a "literary portrait" (with a photograph) of Thomas Carlyle. The alert reader could not fail to recognize in the opening pages of *Sartor Resartus* the nuances of Carlyle's eccentric style that William Maginn had parodied in that literary portrait:

> Over-set Goethe hath Carlyle, not in the ordinary manner of language-turners, who content themselves with giving, according to the capacity of knowingness or honesty within them, the meaning or the idea (if any there be) of the original book-fashioner, on whom their secondhand-pen-mongery is employed; but with reverential thought, word-worshipping even the articulable clothing wherein the clear and etherial harmony of Goethe is invested, Carlyle hath bestowed upon us the *Wilhelm Meister,* and other works, so Teutonical in raiment, in the structure of sentence, the modulation of phrase, and the round-about, hubble-bubble, rumfustianish (*hübble-bübblen, rümfustianischen*), roly-poly growlery of style, so Germanically set forth, that it is with difficulty we can recognise them to be translations at all.[12]

To help his less knowledgeable readers, Carlyle then included the American and English reviews of *Sartor,* which revealed it for the hoax it was, in its first book-form publication in England in 1838. Furthermore, the inclusion of Jean Paul Friedrich Richter in *Sartor Resartus*, the only man who could make Teufelsdröckh truly laugh (and that only once), acknowledged Carlyle's debt to Richter's buffooning style in the composition of his book. Carlyle himself defined Richter's style as "a wild complicated Arabesque" (using the term Schlegel had advocated), "a boundless, unparalleled imbroglio," a "chaos" which is nonetheless "joined in living union" by Richter's perception of the "Divine Idea of the World."[13]

The content, the structure, and the style of *Sartor Resartus* all present Carlyle's romantic irony. The format of the book review enables Carlyle both to propound Teufelsdröckh's Clothes Philosophy, and at the same time to criticize the limitations of Teufelsdröckh's *articulation* of that philosophy. Through Teufelsdröckh, Carlyle enthusiastically presents a "transcendental" conception of the universe; a conception to which, as we shall see, Carlyle did and did not subscribe. As Carlyle described his manuscript to Mr. Fraser,

> It is put together in the fashion of a kind of Didactic Novel; but indeed properly *like* nothing yet extant. I used to characterise it briefly as a kind of "Satirical Extravaganza on Things in General"; it contains more of my opinions on Art, Politics, Religion, Heaven, Earth and Air, than all the things I have yet written. The Creed promulgated on all these things, as you may judge, is *mine*, and firmly *believed*: . . . The ultimate result, however, I need hardly premise, is a deep religious speculative-radicalism (so I call it for want of a better name), with which you are already well enough acquainted in me.[14]

Simultaneously, through the device of the skeptical Editor, "the main Actor in the business" who "assumes a kind of Conservative (though Anti-Quack) character,"[15] Carlyle's equally sincere "descendentalism" emerges. Always acutely aware of the mortal limits and stultifying systematizing of human thought, Carlyle directs his irony not at Teufelsdröckh's vision of the world as a divine essence or force but at the inevitable failure of human consciousness or language adequately to grasp or articulate such an infinite and chaotic power.

Teufelsdröckh's transcendental vision (which he calls "Natural Supernaturalism")[16] grew out of Carlyle's reading of Kant, Fichte, Schlegel, Goethe, and his native Puritan and Calvinist theologians, especially George Fox.[17] In *Sartor Resartus*, the Editor's numerous and lengthy quotations from Teufelsdröckh's *Die Kleider, ihr Werden und Wirken* and scattered literary and autobiographical documents—which make up half of this "review"—present the Clothes Philosophy in Teufelsdröckh's own enthusiastic terms. As did Carlyle in his contemporary essays, Teu-felsdröckh conceives of the ontological universe as a divine force, which is infinite, incomprehensible, everywhere at work. Animating every activity, every event, in the "mighty, billowy, storm-toss'd Chaos of Life,"[18] this almighty power flows alike through nature and man. As Teufelsdröckh interprets the Hebrew Psalmist,

> knowest thou any corner of the world where at least FORCE is not?
> . . . "That little fire . . . —is it a detached, separated speck, cut-off from the whole Universe; or indissolubly joined to the whole? Thou fool, that smithy-fire was (primarily) kindled at the Sun; is fed by air that circulates from before Noah's Deluge, from beyond the Dog-star; therein, with Iron Force, and Coal Force, and the far stranger Force of Man, are cunning affinities and battles and victories of Force brought about; it is a little ganglion, or nervous centre, in the great vital system of Immensity . . . Detached, separated! I say there is no such separation: nothing hitherto was ever stranded, cast aside; but all, were it only a withered leaf, works together with all; is borne forward on the bottomless, shoreless flood of Action, and lives through perpetual metamorphoses. (52-53)

Further, says Teufelsdröckh, "It is a mathematical fact that the casting of this pebble from my hand alters the centre of gravity of the Universe" (185).

Every element in this universe participates in a process of creation, destruction, and new birth. Surrounded by the chaotic clutter of his apartment at the top of the highest house in Weissnichtwo, the Professor looks down upon a "living flood" of apparitions flowing from eternity to eternity: "Are they not Souls rendered visible: in Bodies, that took shape and will lose it, melting into air?" (15). He calmly accepts the inevitable destruction of all existing things, since from their extinction new forms will arise. He less calmly accepts the monthly destructions or "earthquakes" forced upon him by his devoted Lieschen, whose cleaning expeditions transform the theoretical yet impractical chaos within which the Professor lives to a momentarily functional order, and thus become the "necessary of life" (17). Yet even the triumph of the monster Utilitaria does not worry him, for she will "tread down old ruinous Palaces and Temples with her broad hoof, till the whole were trodden down, that new and better might be built!" (177). Indeed, this destructive power is as essential a part of life as the creative power. What men have variously called witchcraft, spectre-work, demonology, and more recently madness and diseases of the nerves, that power of dark devastation which Carlyle equated with a primeval anarchic force in *The French Revolution*, ever remains the foundation upon which life is built. In Teufelsdröckh's words, this power, call it madness, remains "a mysterious-terrific, altogether *infernal* boiling-up of the Nether Chaotic Deep, through this fair-painted Vision of Creation, which swims thereon, which we name the Real . . . In every the wisest Soul lies a whole world of internal Madness, an authentic Demon Empire; out of which, indeed, his world of Wisdom has been creatively built together, and now rests there, as on its dark foundations does a habitable flowery Earth-rind" (195). Our universe is never fixed on a solid base, but is always shifting: "all things wax, and roll onwards: Arts, Establishments, Opinions, nothing is completed, but ever completing" (186).

For Teufelsdröckh the romantic, this never-ending process is teleological. It is directed, not toward a finite goal, but toward the ever-increasing and infinitely increasable freedom of the human spirit. For "the meaning of Life itself [is] no other than Freedom, than Voluntary Force," directed toward the work of "*Well-doing*" (138). From the smoking ashes of every ruin arises the phoenix of the soul, who immolates herself only that she may "soar the higher and sing the clearer" (186). The Professor assures us that "in that fire-whirlwind, Creation and Destruction proceed together; ever as the ashes of the Old are blown about, do organic filaments of the New mysteriously spin themselves: and amid the rushing and the waving of the Whirlwind-Element come tones of a melodious Deathsong, which end not but in tones of a more melodious Birthsong" (183). Thus, "not Mankind only, but all that Mankind does or beholds, is in continual growth, regenesis and self-perfecting vitality" (29).

On this theoretical level, Teufelsdröckh is ironically aware that the infinite abundance of nature far outstrips the comprehension of any given individual. "To the wisest man, wide as is his vision, Nature remains of quite *infinite* depth, of quite infinite expansion; and all Experience thereof limits itself to some few computed centuries and measured square-miles" (193). Thus, acknowledges Teufelsdröckh, man is but "a Minnow . . . his Creek this Planet Earth; his Ocean the immeasurable All; his Monsoons and periodic Currents the mysterious Course of Providence through AEons and AEons" (193). Man cannot grasp the whole, infinite truth; instead "we sit as in a boundless Phantasmagoria and Dream-grotto; boundless, for the faintest star, the remotest century, lies not even nearer the verge thereof: sounds and many-coloured visions flit round our sense; but Him, the Unslumbering, whose work both Dream and Dreamer are, we see not; except in rare half-waking moments, suspect not" (39). Possibly echoing Schlegel, Teufelsdröckh too invokes the ironic wisdom of Socrates: "They only are wise who know that they know nothing" (40).

But Teufelsdröckh's ironic recognition of human limitations is out-weighed by his romantic enthusiasm for the infinite, albeit incomprehensible, abundance of life, which is for him a source of wonder and gratitude. Teufelsdröckh's calm acceptance of human finitude only baffles the more skeptical, pragmatic Editor, who complains of Teufelsdröckh:

> Gleams of an etherial Love burst from him, soft wailings of infinite pity; he could clasp the whole Universe into his bosom, and keep it warm; it seems as if under that rude exterior there dwelt a very seraph. Then again he is so sly and still, so imperturbably saturnine; shows such indifference, malign coolness towards all that men strive after; and ever with some half-visible wrinkle of a bitter sardonic humour, if indeed it be not mere stolid callousness,—that you look on him almost with a shudder, as on some incarnate Mephistopheles, to whom this great terrestrial and celestial Round, after all, were but some huge foolish Whirligig, where kings and beggars, and angels and demons, and stars and street-sweepings, were chaotically whirled, in which only children could take interest. (23)

For Teufelsdröckh enthusiastically asserts that man is not only a minnow; he is also an active participant in the divine, infinite life that animates the entire universe. For him, man is and is not god. "We start out of Nothingness, take figure, and are Apparitions; . . . These limbs . . . this life-blood . . . are dust and shadow; a Shadow-system gathered round our ME; wherein, through some moments or years, the Divine Essence is to be revealed in the Flesh" (199). Following Fichte and Coleridge, Teufelsdröckh the Discloser affirms the ultimate existence of a divine self or *Me*, what Coleridge called the "infinite I AM," the creative power which animates both man and nature. This "God's-Presence" resides beneath man's clothes, beneath his "Garment of Flesh (or of Senses)" (48), but it can be perceived by the human eye only through the outward manifestation of the human body. Nonetheless, the presence of this divine self can be felt, primarily as a love, which although infinite and free "in its celestial primeval brightness, even here, though but for moments, look[s] through" (49).

It is essential to Teufelsdröckh's doctrine of natural supernaturalism to recognize that the divine essence, the *Me* hidden beneath the material flesh, is not a thing but a force, a power. Thus any individual who could miraculously divest himself of all outward trappings, including his own body, would find not a completed self or being but rather a process, a becoming. Like truth itself, man is always "a-being." He is never completed but always engaged in an activity of self-liberation, of growing freedom, of self-transcendence. The outward man functions most worthily as "a revelation to Sense of the mystic god-given force that is in him; a 'Gospel of Freedom,' which he, the 'Messiah of Nature,' preaches, as he can, by act and word" (165). More than any other man, George Fox's spirit waged that heroic battle to overcome its outward form: "Through long days and nights of silent agony, it struggled and wrestled, with a man's force, to be free" (158).

It follows then that the visible, material, phenomenal world is but a set of Kantian categories or "clothing" imposed by the human mind upon infinite nature (which Teufelsdröckh, like Schlegel, sees as a *Fülle*, a noumenal force rather than a *Ding-an-sich*). For Teufelsdröckh, the visible world is the "emblem" of invisible power. Even space and time and language are but "Thought-forms" or "garments" of this noumenal reality (54, 197). Teufelsdröckh further defines the structures or clothing imposed by the mind on divine chaos as symbols: "In the Symbol proper, what we can call a Symbol, there is ever, more or less distinctly and directly, some embodiment and revelation of the Infinite; the Infinite is made to blend itself with the Finite, to stand visible, and as it were, attainable there" (165).

Teufelsdröckh admits that symbols are only partial manifestations of the divine noumenal force (they "more or less" provide "some" revelation of the infinite). Nonetheless, he argues that only through symbolic language can man even begin to approach an apprehension of the infinite. If the invisible and unknowable can be revealed only emblematically, through visible clothes, then those clothes must be as complicated and imaginative as possible. For, Teufelsdröckh insists, metaphors are the "muscles and tissues and living integuments" of the flesh-garment, language. And among all the phenomenological structures available to the human mind, language is the most powerful in piercing to the noumenal reality beneath: "The WORD," Teufelsdröckh pronounces, "is well said to be omnipotent in this world; man, thereby divine, can create as by a *Fiat*" (156). The verbal symbol, then, can be equated with that love which according to Teufelsdröckh, is "a discerning of the Infinite in the Finite, of the Idea made Real; which discerning again may be either true or false, either seraphic or demoniac, Inspiration or Insanity" (109). If love is a lie, "a Calenture . . . whereby the youth saw green Paradise-groves in the waste Ocean-waters: a lying vision," yet it is "not wholly a lie, for *he* saw it" (113). For Teufelsdröckh the writer-prophet who is "no Adamite" (156), a symbolic language is necessary. Symbols can communicate the hidden mystery of the infinite better than the "faded raiment" of mechanical, discursive, logical prose.

Yet symbols cannot remain the same. Since the divine idea or noumenal power is vital and moving, any outward manifestation or symbol of this power must constantly change. The human faculty with the capacity to make, unmake, and new-make symbols is of course the imagination. For Teufelsdröckh as for other Romantic writers, the creative artist is both Prometheus and Orpheus, the savior of mankind and the unacknowledged legislator of human society (169, 198);[19] and works of art are "the Godlike rendered visible" (168). The more organic and all-embracing the symbol, the better it reveals the divine idea of the whole. Thus Teufelsdröckh calls for poetic prophecy in its most extreme form: the creation of an entire religion or Mythus (146). Carlyle uses the term "mythus" to emphasize that this created religious system must be both devoutly believed (as fervently as primitive peoples believe their myths) and acknowledged as an already "outdated" system, merely a myth or fable.

Thus Teufelsdröckh's philosophy, as the Editor frequently points out, entails a radical politics, the politics of Sansculottism Accoutred. The traditions and institutions of society, its external clothing, must be constantly re-tailored or changed to conform to the dynamic life surging beneath and around them. For Teufelsdröckh, present society, "long pining, diabetic, consumptive, can be regarded as defunct" (174). But from the carcass of this dead society, a new society must be born, phoenix-like; and from that new society, a newer, in a never-ending process of Palingenesia or "perpetual metamorphoses" (177).

To begin this process of new birth, every society—and every individual in society—must first annihilate its old self (*Selbsttödtung*) (141). It must then strive, through a process of conversion (becoming what one had not been), to create a new, more appropriate symbol to express its new, more loving, freer experience. For Teufelsdröckh, such fuller symbols will be increasingly simple and whole; he images them as George Fox's unseamed leather suit or his own childhood "short-cloth . . . one and indivisible" of yellow serge (158, 70). And the society so portrayed will be a "communion of Saints," a universal brotherhood who share a common religious spirit. Such a society will find its emblem or figurehead in a hero who is a true king or wise son of God, a "peasant-saint" who combines the creative powers of the artist with the forceful labor of the craftsman (170-173, 189-191).

Although this classless society could be achieved by human love, courtesy, and self-knowledge, it is more likely to occur, Teufelsdröckh acknowledges, through an outbreak of anarchic power, a class war in which the haves (the dandies) are leveled to the have-nots (the drudges). At the end of *Sartor Resartus*, both Teufelsdröckh and the Editor are anticipating a revolt of the drudges in Ireland and England as well as throughout Europe. Teufelsdröckh's departure for London occurs on the eve of the Paris Revolutions of 1830.

The structure of the book review thus allows Carlyle to put forth in enthusiastic, highly charged, and metaphorically rich language the transcendental vision of Teufelsdröckh. Equally important, this format enables Carlyle, through the device of the skeptical Editor, to keep always before our eyes the perception that Teufelsdröckh's *expression* of that vision is inadequate. Teufelsdröckh's style, as the Editor constantly reminds us, is obscure, chaotic, and often unintelligible (140, 220, 20). *Die Kleider* exhibits "an almost total want of arrangement" (25). In the eyes of the Editor, the book is a "chaos," an "ignoble complexity," and even "mere confusion" (38). The Editor further accuses Teufelsdröckh's book of "bordering on the absurd" and even, on occasion, of plunging into the "Inane" (220, 166).

To these criticisms, Teufelsdröckh might reply that his "piebald, entangled, hyper-metaphorical style of writing" (220) is the appropriate form for his philosophical content. The abundant chaos of the universe must be presented in an abundantly chaotic way. And indeed, Teufelsdröckh's book conveys the impression of an inexhaustible imagination powerfully at work. To the Editor, *Die Kleider* seems "of boundless, almost formless contents, a very Sea of Thought" (5). Once again Carlyle uses the imagery of oceanic immensity to convey the fullness of Teufelsdröckh's mind and the universe it seeks to explore. That the Editor gives us no table of contents for *Die Kleider* further suggests the inexhaustibility of the book.[20] Teufelsdröckh's style intensifies this impression of a dynamic mind energetically pushing against the limits of the conventional and rational. The absence of a sustained argument—together with the use of brief phrases in long, disconnected sentences; lavish punctuation and capitalization; recurrent images of natural forces (for example, fire, electricity, moving water) and abundant life (virtually a zoo of animals); and an extraordinary variety and unexpected sequence of imagery —all this, as John Holloway has shown, forces the reader along at a violent, jarring pace and persuades him that the universe, like Teufelsdröckh's prose, is pulsing with life.[21] And Teufelsdröckh's syntax, which relies on assertion, inversion, repetition, and imbalance, parallels his revolutionary ideas, as Carlyle implied in his defense of *Sartor* to John Sterling.[22] This convoluted and unfamiliar syntax manifests the dynamic activity of a mind always seeking to confront an ever-changing, ever-developing truth. In particular, Teufelsdröckh frequently uses a "this? nay, that" rhetorical form (*correctio*) to articulate the mind's struggle to release itself from dead metaphors, outworn concepts, unchallenged assumptions.[23]

Throughout, Teufelsdröckh is striving to find a language more suited to his radical perceptions, a new syntax and a new vocabulary for his new ontology. Names, new names for new concepts, are thus all-important to Teufelsdröckh: "Could I unfold the influence of Names, which are the most important of all Clothings, I were a second greater Trismegistus. Not only all common Speech, but Science, Poetry itself is no other, if thou consider it, than a right *Naming*" (66). The obsessive use of German foregrounding (the inclusion of the German original with its English translation) throughout *Sartor Resartus* accentuates the book's fundamental concern with finding the right name, the perfect word. Finally, the structure of *Sartor Resartus* as a whole, the book review of a nonexistent book, is, as Leonard Deen suggests, deliberately irrational. This format functions as Carlyle's calculated attack on his era's compulsive and sterile reliance on logic and mechanics.[24] Teufelsdröckh's revitalized and ever-shifting metaphors suggest that there are more things in heaven and earth than are dreamt of in a rationally systematic philosophy.

Of course, the Editor's criticisms of Teufelsdröckh's stylistic excesses also function rhetorically. They help both the real and the created "British Reader" to overcome his initial discomfort and even hostility to Teufelsdröckh's neologisms, teutonisms, and hyperboles.[25] By providing an ally in the conservative, British, "anti-quack" Editor who shares the reader's resentments at such unfamiliar language and concepts, Carlyle encourages his audience to "stay with" Teufelsdröckh's speculative radicalism longer than they might otherwise have done. The reader is thus engaged in a suspension of disbelief that enables him to participate in the learning process or "consciousness raising" that is at the core of Carlyle's epistemology.

On a more personal level, the eccentricities of Teufelsdröckh's style together with the Editor's criticisms reflect Carlyle's private sense of linguistic inadequacy. As George Levine has commented, Carlyle turned to fiction with an exuberance born of desperation, not knowing or even being able to guess, as he wrote to Mill, "what or who my audience is, or whether I have any audience."[26] A fierce conviction of his principles and a powerful self-deprecation come together in Carlyle's convoluted, Germanic syntax, nonsequential organization, obsessively developed metaphors, and editorial self-mockery. Carlyle reveals his personal frustration with the limitations of language in one of the Editor's concluding observations on Teufelsdröckh's style: "Our conjecture has sometimes been, that perhaps Necessity as well as Choice was concerned in it. Seems it not conceivable that, in a Life like our Professor's, where so much bountifully given by Nature had in Practice failed and misgone, Literature also would never rightly prosper: that striving to paint this and the other Picture, and ever without success, he at last desperately dashes his sponge, full of all colours, against the canvas, to try whether it will paint Foam?" (221).[27]

Most important, however, the Editor's criticisms of Teufelsdröckh's style—together with his own failure to build a firm bridge of logic over the chaotic floods of Teufelsdröckh's thought—establish the primary ironic tension in the book. Teufelsdröckh battles heroically to expand the syntax and tropes of conventional figural language in order to articulate accurately the chaos of the universe—and necessarily fails. The Editor tries to force Teufelsdröckh's thoughts and expressions into a coherent, logical system—and necessarily fails. Carlyle thus shows us simultaneously the mind's rage for order; the need for a more vital metaphorical language; the failure of all human attempts to fit the infinite abundance of life into a single system; and especially the ultimate inability of even the most richly symbolic language to comprehend life or to express accurately the nature of its incomprehensibility.

Thus Carlyle drives his readers to acknowledge the incapacity of *all* semiotic systems fully to contain or express the divine or infinite. By substituting clothing for language as the primary semiotic system in this book, by making clothing the epistemological metaphor for the entire phenomenal world, Carlyle has forced us to confront the limitations of language itself. If clothes are the primary unit of human meaning, as Teufelsdröckh asserts ("Church-clothes are, in our vocabulary, the Forms, the *Vestures*, under which men have at various periods embodied and represented for themselves the Religious Principle; that is to say, invested The Divine Idea of the World with a sensible and practically active Body, so that it might dwell among them as a living and life-giving WORD"; 161), then words make up a secondary semiotic code whose meaning depends on clothes. Language is thus absorbed by clothes, just as the Editor's "English purity" has been absorbed by Teufelsdröckh's German exuberance: "Even as the smaller whirlpool is sucked into the

larger, and made to whirl along with it, so has the lesser mind, in this instance, been forced to become portion of the greater, and like it, see all
things figuratively" (220). By substituting one semiotic system (clothing)
for another (language), Carlyle has revealed the merely relative authority
of *all* semiotic systems.[28]

But it is necessary to distinguish Carlyle's linguistic theory from that of
modern structuralists. For Ferdinand de Saussure, all signs are arbitrary,
unmotivated;[29] for Carlyle certain kinds of signs (namely, symbols) are
at least partially motivated. For Carlyle the romantic ironist, language
both exists independently of and points to a noumenal reality, just as
clothes both hide and reveal the outlines of the naked body beneath. As
Teufelsdröckh insists, in the symbol "there is ever, *more or less* distinctly
and directly, *some* embodiment and revelation of the Infinite" (165; italics added). Or as the Editor's summary of chapter 8, "The World out of
Clothes," more tersely states: "A deeper meditation has always taught,
here and there an individual, that all visible things are appearances only;
but also emblems and revelations of God" (232).

To the extent that Carlyle acknowledges that words cannot *fully* grasp
the divine essence or be equated with ontological reality, he sees words as
unmotivated signs, as the arbitrary creations of men. To this degree,
Carlyle anticipates current structuralist arguments that language has no
literal integrity, no pointing referent, no solidity; and hence that all signs
are merely figures. As Teufelsdröckh extends the implications of his
metaphor, it is not only clothes and words that must be seen figuratively,
but also social institutions, nature (the "Volume . . . whose Author and
Writer is God"; 194), space and time (mere "Thought-forms" both). All
these semiotic systems are intrareferential; their meaning resides in their
synchronic and diachronic relationships.

It follows from Carlyle's protostructural linguistics that "facts" (insofar as they are embodied in language) are "fictions." Carlyle draws our
attention to this in the second book of *Sartor Resartus*, where the Editor
attempts to write the biography of Teufelsdröckh. This endeavor grows
out of the Romantic poets' insistence that truth is grounded in personal,
subjective experience, rather than in universal, objective axioms. As the
Editor asks, "to state the Philosophy of Clothes without the Philosopher,
the ideas of Teufelsdröckh without something of his personality, was it
not to insure both of entire misapprehension?" (6). But the factual accuracy of the Editor's biography is called into question from the very beginning of his attempt, when he is presented not with the historical chronicle
based on objective evidence that he had naively expected from Herr

Heuschrecke, but with six large paper bags, marked with the zodiac signs of the winter months, containing "miscellaneous masses of Sheets, and oftener Shreds and Snips" in Teufelsdröckh's almost illegible Fraktur script. Simultaneously with the Editor's sense that these fragments present a confusion worse compounded, we might recall Schlegel's celebration of the fragment as the necessarily partial but nonetheless solely viable insight into the abundant chaos of the universe. Yet the authenticity of even these fragments—these dreams, philosophical disquisitions, anecdotes, autobiographical reminiscences—is put in doubt. The Editor suspects that not only the bags' contents but even Herr Heuschrecke's covering letter are "some trick" of Teufelsdröckh (56), a hoax within a hoax, so to speak.

Moreover, the Editor's attempt to impose a chronological or rational order upon Teufelsdröckh's life—which is imaged throughout *Sartor* as flowing water, unstable, immeasurable—commits the error Carlyle had just defined in "On History." One falsifies human history whenever one writes a merely "linear Narrative" and thus threads the boundless and unfathomable solid action of the past "with single lines of a few ells in length."[30] And indeed, the biography the Editor selects and arranges is clearly a "fictional" life. Teufelsdröckh's experiences follow the familiar typology of the medieval saint's life, expanded to include the fairy-tale origins of the folk heroes of German *Märchen*. More closely still, his life fulfills the typology of Romantic crisis autobiography first defined by Wordsworth's *Prelude*: the child of innocence who falls into self-consciousness and alienation but who regains paradise through a renewed consciousness of his participation in divine powers.[31] Or, as the Editor himself defines the pattern of Teufelsdröckh's life, "Thus have we . . . followed Teufelsdröckh through the various successive states and stages of Growth, Entanglement, Unbelief, and almost Reprobation, into a certain clearer state of what he himself seems to consider as Conversion" (149).

In Teufelsdröckh's case, the typology of innocence, fall into experience, and circuitous journey back to paradise is given in a particularly extreme form. As a baby, Teufelsdröckh is abandoned by an exotic stranger from the East[32] to the nurturing, good-hearted, upright peasant couple: "Cincinnatus" Andreas Futteral and his devoted "Desdemona" Gretchen. Left like Oedipus, the heroes of the Greek romances, and Shakespeare's Perdita on the slopes of a pastoral arcadia, Teufelsdröckh trails "clouds of glory" through his happy childhood on the banks of the Kuhbach. But this innocent child inevitably becomes frustrated by an academic education (at the Hinterschlag Gymnasium) that stresses the mechanics of science and the pedantry of rote memory but ignores or even actively smothers the moral and imaginative spirit. The disillusionment, alienation, and spiritual doubt engendered by Teufelsdröckh's intellectually sterile university are further intensified by the prevailing spiritual desolation of the mechanical age in which he lives and by his inability to find work in a society committed to a free-trade economy. Teufelsdröckh's doubt is transformed into active despair by the failure of romantic love (the force toward being and unity that Schlegel celebrated). With the loss of Blumine, the flower-goddess, Teufelsdröckh sees no purpose for himself in a "Steam-engine Universe." Like the world-weary Childe Harold of the "Satanic School" (114) or the Wandering Jew,[33] he travels aimlessly across the face of the earth, finding no comfort in his birthplace, in the sublimities of nature, or in human companionship. Cut off from his divine father, he is filled with a self-hatred born of paranoic anxiety; he is trapped in the everlasting No. "I lived in a continual, indefinite, pining fear; tremulous, pusillanimous, apprehensive of I knew not what: it seemed as if all things in the Heavens above and the Earth beneath would hurt me; as if the Heavens and the Earth were but boundless jaws of a devouring monster, wherein I, palpitating, waited to be devoured" (127).

Then suddenly, miraculously, in the paradoxical Rue Saint-Thomas de l'Enfer, this self-destroying fear gives way to a conviction of personal strength and value. " 'Let [Death] come, then; I will meet it and defy it!' And as I so thought, there rushed like a stream of fire over my whole soul; and I shook base Fear away from me forever. I was strong, of unknown strength; a spirit, almost a god" (127). This baphometic fire-baptism, this oxymoronic conversion (through the union of fire and water), leads Teufelsdröckh out of the world of being (where one fears for the preservation of the "self") into a world of becoming, of freedom. Teufelsdröckh successfully annihilates his self (*Selbsttödtung*), renounces all desire for self-fulfillment, and commits his life to service or work. In Teufelsdröckh's case, this work or participation in becoming is an unending struggle to create, through a revitalized language, a new mythus or religion. "I too could now say to myself: 'Be no longer a Chaos, but a World, or even Worldkin. Produce! Produce! Were it but the pitifullest infinitesimal fraction of a Product, produce it, in God's name! 'Tis the utmost thou hast in thee: out with it, then. Up, up! Whatsoever thy hand findeth to do, do it with thy whole might. Work while it is called Today; for the Night cometh, wherein no man can work' " (148-149). To call such a stance "suicidal," as Philip Rosenberg does,[34] is to seriously underestimate the strength that Carlyle himself derived from the Puritan work ethic and its attendant emphasis on self-denial and to ignore the sense of transcendent freedom that both Carlyle and other romantic ironists derived from the consciousness of actively participating in an ongoing process, a condition of becoming that aggressively seeks to annihilate by surpassing the limits of individual being or selfhood. Teufelsdröckh has given up selfhood-as-entity to become selfhood-as-act.

That Teufelsdröckh's life is in itself a mythus, a fabrication of the imagination, is acknowledged by the Editor. The bags of "autobiographical documents" may have been created by Teufelsdröckh, a product of his "humoristico-satirical tendency" that was erroneously taken literally by the foolish, self-deceived, and innocently deceiving Hofrath Nose-of-Wax (152). Moreover, these documents, even if literally true, are so imbedded in "needless obscurity, by omission and commission" (140), that they manifest no clear pattern. The Editor is thus forced to recognize that all his biographical facts are at best but hieroglyphs or "engraved Hierograms" (153). They are symbols which reveal as well as conceal the "spirit" of the man. Indeed, Teufelsdröckh's life as a whole is but a symbol, a "transit out of Invisibility into Visibility" (61). Or, to put it the other way round, Teufelsdröckh's life is but "spiritualised, vaporised Fact" (118). The "hieroglyphic" character of Teufelsdröckh remains an enigma, despite the Editor's first-hand acquaintance and relentless probings. Teufelsdröckh speaks rarely, laughs but once; and his eyes contradictorily emit "gleams of an etherial or else a diabolic fire" that create in the Editor the impression of "the rest of infinite motion, the sleep of a spinning top" (11). Teufelsdröckh is thus a paradox embodied. Both angel and devil, in motion yet in stasis, he is and is not the Professor of Things in General.

Just as Teufelsdröckh is an oxymoron, an impossible yet living contradiction, so the world that he inhabits unites opposites. Insofar as language has no pointing reference, no solidity, it follows that linguistic distinctions cannot be maintained. When words are arbitrary and unmotivated, they can be changed—and have been changed, diachronically by the collective human will, and synchronically by the *parole* of the individual language-user. More important, in a world predicated on flux, on becoming rather than on being, stable separations cannot be sustained. As the Editor concludes, "We stand in a region of conjectures, where substance has melted into shadow, and one cannot be distinguished from the other" (223). At both the ontological and the linguistic level, distinctions break down in *Sartor Resartus*.

This is most clearly seen, perhaps, in the structuring relationship between the Editor and Teufelsdröckh. At first sight, Teufelsdröckh and the Editor seem to represent the two sides of romantic irony: Teufelsdröckh the enthusiastic creator of a new vision versus the skeptically pragmatic Editor.[35] Teufelsdröckh's life and writings manifest an abundant chaos, which the Editor tries valiantly but unsuccessfully to order into a coherent, rational pattern (he imposes a "linear Narrative" upon the imbroglio of fragments contained in the six paper bags; he "reviews" *Die Kleider* in a syllogistic, tripartite structure).[36] The Editor introduces himself as a man opposed in personality and opinions to Teufelsdröckh. The Editor is British, conservative, speculative, discursive, and skeptical of German abstract thought and "misdirected industry" (3). Teufelsdröckh is German, radical, and mystical.

But such a division is too simplistic a reduction of Carlyle's romantic irony. In the ontological and linguistic universe of *Sartor Resartus*, such rational and semantic distinctions are blurred even as they are made. The Editor can be as enthusiastic as Teufelsdröckh, as the opening paragraphs of *Sartor* suggest, with their metaphoric extravagance (especially the image of the world as an apple dumpling), their attack on scientific analysis and the cramping "practical tendency" of English thought (4), and their approval of abstract speculation. Admittedly, the Editor ironically implies that the discoveries of "learned, indefatigable, deep-thinking" Germany may be only the blasts of a cowhorn (2-3). Still, as we discover, in character the Editor and Teufelsdröckh are more similar than dissimilar. Both are "speculative," the Editor seeking new ideas while Teufelsdröckh radically annihilates the old to make way for the new (4-5, 187). Both are "discursive": the book is divided evenly between Teufelsdröckh's writings and the Editor's commentary. Both are mysterious: Oliver Yorke tells us that the Editor is "masked" and bears a "feigned name" (8n); while Teufelsdröckh remains "enigmatic" (7, 58). By the end of the book, Teufelsdröckh the speculative radical is *editing* the Dandy manuscript, while the conservative, skeptical Editor is actively proselytizing for Teufelsdröckh's revolutionary Clothes Philosophy.[37] In method, too, Teufelsdröckh and Editor proceed alike: Teufelsdröckh gives us the origin and influence of clothes (*ihr Werden und Wirken*); the Editor gives us the *Werden und Wirken* of Teufelsdröckh. Both Editor and Teufelsdröckh rely heavily on metaphors, on the dash and the parenthesis, on the rhetorical device of *correctio*. Teufelsdröckh begins by dividing the world into the tailors and the tailored while the Editor instead attempts to build a logical bridge over the chaotic medley of Teufelsdröckh's book by uniting like with like; but such divisions break down in the fusing metaphors employed alike by Teufelsdröckh and the Editor. And both endorse the idea that man must act, produce, work (60, 149). Throughout *Sartor Resartus*, despite the Editor's anxious insistence upon his mingled astonishment, gratitude, and disapproval of Teufelsdröckh's work, for all practical purposes the Editor's ironic voice and demurring opinions are swept up in the larger whirlpool of Teufelsdröckh's Clothes Philosophy. At the end of his review, the Editor finds the doctrine of natural supernaturalism "all-illuminating" (191); and he himself describes the dandy in Teufelsdröckhian terms as the embodied perversion of a religious symbol (205). Moreover, the Editor, in the chapter on dandies and drudges, reveals through his calculated Swiftian or rhetorical irony a personal commitment to the necessity for a class war. As the very title suggests, the Editor is retailored by Teufelsdröckh every bit as much as Teufelsdröckh and *Die Kleider* are retailored by the Editor.

That Carlyle wished to emphasize the ways in which enthusiasm and skepticism can fuse in a becoming world is indicated by his decision to change the title of his hoax from *Teufelsdreck* or *Thoughts on Clothes* to *Sartor Resartus*, the Tailor Retailored/Tailoring. That Teufelsdröckh and the Editor can be seen as virtually the same person at the end of the book is further suggested internally by the fact that the Editor can speak of Teufelsdröckh's presence in London with a "conjecture, now amounting almost to certainty" (223-224). Externally and more circumstantially, Carlyle publicly identified himself *both* with the Editor-as-book-reviewer —by continuing his literary quarrels with his own editor, William Maginn (Oliver Yorke) of *Fraser's*—and with Diogenes Teufelsdröckh (whose initials appear as the author of Carlyle's "On History Again" in 1833). Finally, both Editor and Teufelsdröckh *are* Thomas Carlyle, fusing his own religious faith in the tenets of natural supernaturalism with his personal self-doubt and his awareness of the inevitable limitations of language.

This blurring of opposites, together with the inadequacy of language, forms the basis of Carlyle's transcendental buffoonery. The humor of *Sartor Resartus* grows out of the Editor's inability to distinguish between metaphor and reality, the same impossibility that is the essence of Teufelsdröckh's metaphysics. The Editor frequently amuses us by taking Teufelsdröckh's metaphors literally, as in his response to Teufelsdröckh's advocacy of George Fox's unseamed leather suit:

Will Majesty lay aside its robes of state, and Beauty its frills and train-gowns, for a second-skin of tanned hide? By which change Huddersfield and Manchester, and Coventry and Paisley, and the Fancy-Bazaar, were reduced to hungry solitudes; and only Day and

Martin could profit. For neither would Teufelsdröckh's mad daydream, here as we presume covertly intended, of levelling Society
(*levelling* it indeed with a vengeance, into one huge drowned
marsh!), and so attaining the political effects of Nudity without its
frigorific or other consequences,—be thereby realised. Would not
the rich man purchase a water-proof suit of Russian Leather; and the
highborn Belle step-forth in red or azure morocco, lined with sha-
moy: the black cowhide being left to the Drudges and Gibeonites of
the world; and so all the old Distinctions be re-established? (160)

Teufelsdröckh himself practices this brand of humor in his frequent jux-
tapositions of the apparently trivial and the spiritual. In his buffooning
chapter on aprons, Teufelsdröckh hails aprons as the ultimate guardians
against not only dirt but also injury, lust, and sin, while he particularly
celebrates the invention of paper aprons as a new "vent" for literature.
By constantly playing on the proverb "Clothes make the man," a proverb
that is of course the foundation of a phenomenological universe in which
clothing is the basic semiotic system, Teufelsdröckh can jocoseriously
proclaim that the scarecrow is a first-class citizen entitled to all civil
rights (46); while the now dead, and therefore naked, Count Zahndarm is
nothing more than a defunct eating and shitting machine (100).

    Despite his play with metaphors and his commitment to symbols, Teu-
felsdröckh is acutely aware that language is an "imperfect organ" (211).
Since language, like any semiotic system, is synchronically static, it necessarily falsifies by expressing in fixed terms the dynamic, ever-changing
force that *is* universal life and by creating distinctions and divisions that
do not exist. To overcome these limitations of a fixed semiotic system,
Teufelsdröckh attempts to "motivate" language. Recalling his closest
youthful friendship, he introduces us to his comrade "Herr Towgood, or,
as it is perhaps better written, Herr Toughgut" (88). Towgood/Toughgut
shares that same paradoxical, oxymoronic quality—he is both friend and
(as Blumine's husband) enemy to Teufelsdröckh—that characterizes Teufelsdröckh's own character and name. Diogenes Teufelsdröckh combines
the "god-born" with "Devil's dung." His name invokes both Diogenes
the Cynic who sought truth with a single lamp and Diogenes Laertius,
the biographer of philosophers whose style, like Teufelsdröckh's, was
fragmentary and anecdotal, as well as *Teufelsdreck,* the German word
for asafoetida, a powerful emetic with a strong aloetic smell, brought
from the East (the home of astrology and mysticism), to cure constipated
England.[38] For Teufelsdröckh is painfully aware of the paradox inherent
in an unmotivated language: "strangely in this so solid-seeming World,
which nevertheless is in continual restless flux, it is appointed that *Sound,*

to appearance the most fleeting, should be the most continuing of all things" (150).

But Teufelsdröckh fails to create a language as fluid as the universe it attempts to manifest; just as the Editor fails to impose a stable order upon the chaotic flux of Teufelsdröckh's life and work (59, 157, 201-202). As Teufelsdröckh acknowledges, in a symbol there is both concealment and revelation (165). While the process of palingenesia constantly creates new and fuller symbols, these signs will nevertheless fail, as all man-made—and thus necessarily finite—semiotic systems must fail, to contain and reveal completely the infinite. Such systems, like Teufelsdröckh's book itself, no matter how abundantly chaotic, must "like all works of genius" finally resemble the sun itself, "which, though the highest published creation, or work of genius, has nevertheless black spots and troubled nebulosities amid its effulgence,—a mixture of insight, inspiration, with dulness, double-vision, and even utter blindness" (20). Thus the ultimate consequence of Teufelsdröckh's vision and of the Editor's attempt to render it intelligible to the British Reader is to force that reader to face head-on the inevitable failure of a merely human attempt to understand the divine. Confronted with this awareness of the limits of language, and even of symbols, the person who still desires to be free, to live in touch with his divine *Me*, must abandon language. One must give up the attempt to communicate through deceptive and limited signs, "for in what words, known to these profane times," asks Teufelsdröckh, can one "speak even afar-off of the unspeakable?" (140).

Instead, one must act. The clutter of Teufelsdröckh's abstract, impractical thought and messy words must finally give way to the silent, energetic, and pragmatic house-cleanings of the faithful Lieschen, who communicates, if at all, "chiefly by signs" (17). Like the British Reader who has been shown the new gold-country of Teufelsdröckh's abundantly chaotic and inexhaustibly wealthy universe, each person must "dig for his own behoof, and enrich himself" (156). This, as Philip Rosenberg has persuasively argued, is the conclusion to which Teufelsdröckh (and Carlyle) comes.[39] Having published his book, Teufelsdröckh ceases to speak. His final recorded words, on the eve of the Paris Revolutions of 1830, indicate his commitment to a new way of living, to a life of action "out of doors" (17) rather than a life of writing and speech within doors: "Es geht an" (223).

The only other appropriate response to Teufelsdröckh's simultaneous vision of an infinitely abundant universe and of the limits of language is silence and wonder. "Speech is of Time, Silence is of Eternity," proclaims Teufelsdröckh, acknowledging that silence is pregnant with ever-

new creations; indeed, silence is "the element in which great things fashion themselves together; that at length they may emerge, full-formed and
majestic, into the daylight of Life, which they are thenceforth to rule"
(164).[40] Significantly, Teufelsdröckh's own written work, *Die Kleider*, is
"published" or made manifest by Stillschweigen and Co^{gnie}, by "Ever-
silent and Company." Overwhelmed by the immensity of the becoming
universe, man must fall down and worship, for wonder is "the only reasonable temper for the denizen of so singular a Planet as ours," holds
Teufelsdröckh. "Wonder," he continues, "is the basis of Worship; the
reign of wonder is perennial, indestructible in Man" (50). In a state of
wonder, man willingly suspends disbelief; he gives up his small, rational,
mechanical systems and prepares to participate actively in the paradoxical flux of becoming.

This is the point to which the Editor finally comes. Having been affected by Teufelsdröckh's book, having experienced "changes in [his]
way of thought" (20) as a consequence of reading it, the Editor feels compelled first to communicate its meaning as best he can. In the process, the
Editor, as we have seen, is closely associated with Teufelsdröckh. His
own more literal, judgmental, syntactically regular prose style alternates
with his use of Teufelsdröckhian charged metaphors, "with which mode
of utterance Teufelsdröckh unhappily has somewhat infected" him (202).
Further, the Editor comes closer to Teufelsdröckh both spatially (both
are in London) and philosophically (both share a conviction of the necessity of radical social reform based on the acknowledged value of every
individual divine *Me*). But the Editor's language or "bridge-building" has
failed him, just as Teufelsdröckh's symbolism has finally failed him. The
Editor has therefore come to feel uneasy about his own writing career.
He remains "in a state of quarrel" with Oliver Yorke and the world of literary magazines, just as he continues to "disapprove" of Teufelsdröckh's
style. He is at odds with the world of language because he too has been
"moved" to the realm of wonder, silence, and action.

The Editor thus serves to show us that *Sartor Resartus* is, in Stanley
Fish's useful term, a self-consuming artifact. It is a book designed to
"cure" the reader's ills, to force the British Reader to undergo a painful
experience of self-destruction in order to participate in a healthier process
of self-development or becoming. As the Editor responds to the British
Reader's exasperated questioning of the purpose of Teufelsdröckh's
work, "In the way of replenishing thy purse, or otherwise aiding thy di-
gestive faculty, O British Reader, it leads to nothing, and there is no use
in it; but rather the reverse, for it costs thee somewhat" (202).

Stanley Fish has defined the self-consuming artifact in the context of seventeenth-century English prose as a literary work that utilizes a dialectical (as opposed to a rhetorical) presentation that disturbs rather than satisfies the reader. "It requires of its readers a searching and rigorous scrutiny of everything they believe in and live by. It is didactic in a special sense; it does not preach the truth, but asks that its readers discover the truth for themselves, and this discovery is often made at the expense not only of a reader's opinions and values but of his self-esteem." Reading such a work is, for the reader, a humiliating experience whose end result "is (or should be) nothing less than a *conversion,* not only a changing, but an exchanging of minds." This experience, though painful, is nonetheless a beneficial one, much like the process whereby a sick patient (the reader) is cured by a good physician (the author, who in this respect is somewhat like God, the Great Physician). The cure prescribed by the physician characteristically consists of a movement from rational understanding (whose "characteristic motion is one of distinguishing, and the world it delivers is one of separable and discrete entities where everything is in its proper place") to an antidiscursive and antirational way of seeing the world ("rather than distinguishing, it resolves, and in the world it delivers the lines of demarcation between places and things fade in the light of an all-embracing unity"). The moment of conversion from rationalism to antirationalism is marked, Fish tells us, "by the transformation of the visible and segmented world into an emblem of its creator's indwelling presence." Fish then concludes that "a dialectical presentation succeeds at its own expense; for by conveying those who experience it to a point where they are beyond the aid that discursive or rational forms can offer, it becomes the vehicle of its own abandonment." Such a work is self-consuming in two respects: first, "the reader's self (or at least his inferior self) is consumed as he responds to the medicinal purging of the dialectician's art," and second, "that art, like other medicines, is consumed in the workings of its own best effects." The aesthetic theory of the good physician-author, then, is "anti-aesthetic, for it disallows to its productions the claims usually made for verbal art—that they reflect, or contain or express Truth—and transfers the pressure and attention from the work to its effects, from what is happening on the page to what is happening in the reader."[41]

That *Sartor Resartus* is a self-consuming artifact may, by now, scarcely need saying. The clues are perhaps all too obvious. Teufelsdröckh, whose very name is a German homonym for a strong laxative, has proven to be for his British Readers "an uneasy interruption to their ways of thought and digestion" (224) (in just the way that Teufelsdröckh had earlier, in a reversal of the curative process, been made nauseous by reading a fashionable novel; 208). The experience of conversion is of course central to the book. Both the physician Teufelsdröckh and his first patient, the Editor, have undergone a painful process of *Selbsttödtung,* Teufelsdröckh from the everlasting No to the everlasting Yea and the Editor from an approving skepticism to a skeptical approval of Teufelsdröckh's Clothes Philosophy. Throughout the book, the British Reader has been invited, even dared, to follow the tortuous path of Teufelsdröckh's thought. As the Editor comments on the section entitled "Natural Supernaturalism," "This stupendous section we, after long painful meditation, have found not to be unintelligible; but on the contrary, to grow clear, nay radiant, and all-illuminating. Let the reader, turning on it what utmost force of speculative intellect is in him, do his part; as we, by judicious selection and adjustment, shall study to do ours" (191). This desire to involve the reader actively in the experience of conversion explains why both the Editor and Teufelsdröckh so often use the rhetorical figure of *correctio*: this device forces the reader to reconsider, to give up an idea as soon as it is grasped in order to make way for a qualification, an extension, or more likely a new idea. For instance, the Editor, having denied that the British Reader can find "use" in Teufelsdröckh's writings, immediately corrects himself:

> *Nevertheless,* if through this unpromising Horn-gate, Teufelsdröckh, and we by means of him, have led thee into the true Land of Dreams, and through the Clothes-screen, as through a magical Pierre-Pertuis, thou lookest, even for moments, into the region of the Wonderful, and seest and feelest that thy daily life is girt with Wonder, and based on Wonder, and thy very blankets and breeches are Miracles, —then art thou profited beyond money's worth; and hath a thankfulness towards our Professor; *nay,* perhaps in many a literary Tea-circle wilt open thy kind lips, and audibly express the same.
>
> *Nay,* farther, art not thou too perhaps by this time made aware that all Symbols are properly Clothes. (201-202; italics added)

Through a process of self-correction (self-destruction and self-creation or *Selbstbeschränkung*), Teufelsdröckh, the Editor, and the attentive British Reader have all moved from a rational, mechanical conception of the universe as a complex machine to an antirational, non-Aristotelian perception of the universe as a dynamic becoming which impossibly unites opposites, just as Diogenes Teufelsdröckh impossibly unites in name and character the "satanic" and the "angelic."

And yet there is one distinction we must make between Carlyle's self-consuming artifact and those seventeenth-century English prose tracts Stanley Fish describes. *Sartor Resartus,* in true romantic-ironic fashion, is both an antiaesthetic and an aesthetic work. Throughout the book, Carlyle insists simultaneously upon the necessity of a symbolic or fictional discourse to tell the truth and upon the inadequacy of all language ever to tell the whole truth. Even as the Editor pledges himself to worship only "our divinity" Truth, to wage "internecine war" with the Prince of Lies and Darkness, and writes *"No cheating here"* on his doorstep (9), he enters into the "lie" of reviewing a book that does not exist. The irrational, mysterious truth of a chaotically becoming universe can be approached *only* through an irrational, fictive discourse. But even as he romantically celebrates the power of a poetic language, Carlyle ironically concedes the necessary failure of such a language. Thus *Sartor Resartus* is a fictional work designed to consume itself by revealing the limitations both of its own symbolic language and of language as such. It is intended not as a monument of truth but as a goad to action. Therefore it cannot be wholly satisfying to the British Reader, just as it has not been completely satisfying to the Editor. While astonished and grateful, the Editor still disapproves of Teufelsdröckh's work. It has caused him pain and effort as well as brought him wonder and illumination, and it has left him, like his "irritated" readers, in "a state of quarrel" with Oliver Yorke (224), and out of harmony with the semiotic universe in which he lives. *Sartor Resartus* ends, not in a pleasant, harmonious unity, but in unresolved—and irresoluble—conflict. This "capricious, inexpressible" book (156) has taught us that what is and what we are able to comprehend or express are not—and can never be—the same.

Faced with these inexorable limits of human language, Ludwig Wittgenstein later ended his *Tractatus Logico-Philosophicus* on a skeptical note: "Whereof one cannot speak, thereof one must be silent."[42] For Wittgenstein such silence embodies the failure of the human mind to attain any meaningful knowledge beyond what can be articulated in language. But for Carlyle that same silence was filled with mystery and abundant life. Carlyle's romantic irony must therefore be distinguished from Byron's, as Teufelsdröckh himself insisted: "Close thy *Byron;* open thy *Goethe*" (145). Byron exuberantly calls into question every system, every self-conception, every affirmation of an absolute truth:

If people contradict themselves, can I
　Help contradicting them, and every body,

Even my veracious self?—But that's a lie:
I never did so, never will—how should I?
He who doubts all things nothing can deny.   (*Don Juan*, 15.88)

But Carlyle never doubts that the world is improving; for him, the dynamic chaos of the universe is teleologically directed. Despite the Editor's ironic demurrer ("For us, who happen to live while the World-Phoenix is burning herself, and burning so slowly that, as Teufelsdröckh calculates, it were a handsome bargain would she engage to have done 'within two centuries,' there seems to lie but an ashy prospect"; 183), Teufelsdröckh's myth of progress is never sincerely challenged in *Sartor Resartus*. As Teufelsdröckh proclaims, "Find Mankind where thou wilt, thou findest it in living movement, in progress faster or slower" (186). For Carlyle, process and change are equated with progress, as the Editor's summary description of chapter 7, "Organic Filaments," states: "Destruction and Creation ever proceed together . . . Sequence and progress of all human work, whether of creation or destruction, from age to age" (235). Carlyle's skepticism is directed, not at the assumption that the dynamic chaos of the universe is a life-force carrying men onward and upward, but at man's inevitably doomed attempts fully to perceive, comprehend, or express this force, even in the most powerful forms of fictional or symbolic discourse. *Sartor Resartus* masterfully embodies, in structure and content, this ironic attack upon the limits of language. Yet Carlyle completed the book leaving at least one term uncriticized: Teufelsdröckh's "Baphometic Fire-Baptism" (128) is never demystified, its expressive adequacy never questioned.[43] This instance, in which Carlyle's commitment to a perfectly balanced, romantic-ironic "hovering" is incomplete, paves the way to Carlyle's future career. Like Teufelsdröckh, Carlyle only laughed once. After *Sartor Resartus*, Carlyle abandoned the difficult process of constant self-criticism (*Selbsttödtung*). In later works, this increasingly sublime egotist shed the motley of the buffooning romantic ironist and donned instead the sombre robes of the Victorian sage.

PART TWO

The Perimeters of Romantic Irony

5

Guilt and
Samuel Taylor Coleridge

The authentic romantic ironist embraces with enthusiasm and hope a vision of the universe as dynamic becoming. But other ways of emotionally responding to this ontological vision are possible. Two negative responses to romantic irony paradigmatically define the psychological as well as the historical boundaries of the concept. At the beginning of the nineteenth century, Samuel Taylor Coleridge confronted his perception of a chaotic universe with a guilt-ridden ambivalence; seventy years later, as I shall show in the next chapter, Lewis Carroll and Søren Kierkegaard were filled with fear and trembling by the vision of a chaos underlying reality and strove to control it through words, games, or a leap of faith.

Coleridge's major poems reveal his awareness of the existence of a dynamic, unconscious, amoral, and abundantly creative force, a force he later defined in the *Biographia Literaria* as the fundamental principle of the "Free Life." But these poems simultaneously convey Coleridge's insistence that a contradictory and equally fundamental principle also exists, what he later called the "Confining Form."[1] For the religiously devout Coleridge, the existence of an ordered, moral, Christian universe was a psychological necessity. His finest poems embody romantic irony's unresolved tension between a vision of an always-becoming universe and a demand for coherent meaning. Coleridge found this tension deeply painful. He desperately wanted to believe in the absolute validity of an ordered Christian universe but *could not*, could not because his own acute intelligence perceived the existence of an underlying chaos. Coleridge thus shared Schlegel's view of ontological reality and the unconscious will as a chaotic *Fülle* or dynamic creativity, but rather than exulting in life's potential fertility, Coleridge regarded an enthusiastic indulgence of this free creativity as blasphemous, even evil.[2] In this sense, Coleridge's poems mark the point, historically and psychologically, at which a traditional Judaeo-Christian theology confronts a revolutionary vision of ontological chaos.

"The Rime of the Ancient Mariner" presents this unresolved tension most sharply. As Coleridge has told us, his original intention in preparing the poem for the 1798 *Lyrical Ballads* was to depict a disordered universe: "the incidents and agents were to be, in part at least, supernatural; and the excellence aimed at was to consist in the interesting of the affections by the dramatic truth of such emotions, as would naturally accompany such situations, supposing them real."[3] By "supernatural" Coleridge meant events or powers which defy the ordered and stable "laws of nature," laws of physical causality, laws of reason and logic. These are the "strange things" promised in the original Argument: "How a Ship having passed the Line was driven by storms to the cold Country towards the South Pole; and how from thence she made her course to the tropical Latitude of the Great Pacific Ocean; and of the strange things that befell; and in what manner the Ancyent Marinere came back to his own Country."

Both the reader and the Mariner enter a chaotic universe of unpredictable "strange things." The reader is immediately plunged into a world that defies systematic logic and common sense. The Mariner "stoppeth one of three" wedding guests and "holds him with his glittering eye" (ll. 2-3). Why does the Mariner stop only one guest? Why not all three? And how can he hold a grown man eager to attend his closest kinsman's wedding with only one bright eye? Coleridge's fast-paced ballad meter rushes the reader along, arousing his curiosity and seducing him into a willing suspension of disbelief. As Coleridge knew from his own childhood obsession with the tales of the Arabian Nights, the exotic display of strange powers can enthrall even the rational mind.

The Mariner too sails into a realm where all events and actions are arbitrary. Having dropped "below the kirk, . . . below the lighthouse top," below the realm of conventional morality and religious ritual, below the light of common sense and rational understanding, his ship is adventitiously trapped in an ice-floe. Suddenly an albatross arrives and is hailed by Mariner and crew "in God's name"; the ice splits; the ship sails south through mists and clouds. Equally suddenly and arbitrarily, the Mariner kills the albatross. The crew, being men of common sense, reason from effect to cause and conclude that the Mariner "had killed the bird / That made the breeze to blow" (ll. 93-94). But in this chaotic world, deductions based on laws of logic and the scientific method are not valid. The sun shines gloriously, "like God's own head," and the crew are forced to change their hypothesis: the bird brought not the good south wind but the fog and mist, and therefore *should* have been killed. But this deduction is no more valid than the first. Shortly afterwards, the ship bursts onto a completely uncharted sea, a realm far beyond the conventional assumptions of logic and morality. Yet the crew still attempt to impose a familiar pattern upon their experience. Becalmed, dying of thirst, some "in dreams" (which express their own subconscious desires) are "assured" of what they want to believe, that a Spirit controls their destiny and is intent upon avenging the death of the albatross. Eager to relieve their consciences of any moral complicity incurred by justifying the albatross's death, they throw the whole burden of guilt upon the Mariner and hang the enormous bird about his neck, marking him as their scapegoat. It is important to realize that up to this point in the poem, all the logical and moral judgments concerning the causes, effects, and justice of the Mariner's action have been made by the crew (or by the reader); neither the Mariner nor the narrator has judged or tried to explain his behavior or the ship's situation.

The spectre ship's appearance upon the horizon is as sudden and arbitrary as the appearance and killing of the albatross. Again the crew, and now the Mariner as well (who has cannibalistically sucked his own blood in order to summon the ship), judge incorrectly that the ship will bring them weal. But on the spectre-ship, two monstrous figures—a black and charnel-crusted skeleton and a leprously white-skinned, vampirish woman called Life-in-Death—are casting dice and by the arbitrary luck of the throw, Death wins the crew and Life-in-Death wins the Mariner. The crew die, cursing the Mariner, but whether they have gained salvation, whether their lot is better or worse than the Mariner's, whether their souls fled "to bliss or woe," the poem does not say. It is crucial to recognize that the fate of both Mariner and crew have been decided *wholly by chance*; they are neither a logical nor a moral consequence of the preceding events.

Left alone in this arbitrary, chaotic universe, the Mariner is controlled only by his own irrational moods. At first he feels abandoned both by man and by God: "And Christ would take no pity on / My soul in agony" (*Lyrical Ballads*, 1798, ll. 234-235). The Mariner experiences what was for Coleridge the ultimate pain, a never-ending separation from love in utter solitude.[4] With great psychological insight, Coleridge records the Mariner's reaction, superbly achieving his goal of presenting "the dramatic truth of such emotions, as would naturally accompany such [supernatural] situations, supposing them real." The Mariner, undergoing the agonizing isolation one feels in moments of extreme depression or suicidal despair,[5] yearns to join the "beautiful" dead and escape all "slimy," "rotting" living things, escape too the guilt aroused in his living soul by the cursing eyes of the dead. He sees his environment as totally alien; even the "softly" moving moon, bringer of comfort and consolation to many, only seems to mock the sultry water with her frosting beams. Suddenly, the Mariner's eye is caught by the "rich attire" and "golden fire" of the coiling water snakes, and his mood changes. As arbitrarily as he killed the albatross, he now blesses the snakes, suddenly seeing them as beautiful and feeling an inexplicable "spring of love" for them. His blessing of the snakes is as unpremeditated, as "unaware," as his killing of the albatross; and a sense of joyful communion with an abundant life now replaces his previous sense of isolation. He prays, the burden of the albatross slips away, sleep and rain refresh his body, and sounds like the notes of musical instruments or the songs of birds and angels fill the skies.

But whereas the Mariner's conviction of isolation had been complete ("Alone, alone, all, all alone, / Alone on a wide, wide sea!"), his new-found communion with life is less so. The poem refuses to endorse the Mariner's conviction that a coherent moral meaning resides in his experiences. A devout medieval Catholic sailor, the Mariner assumes a traditional Christian conception of the universe in which man sins, feels guilt, does penance, and is finally pardoned and redeemed, a universe in which the albatross is rightly hailed "in God's name." But the "two voices in the air" which the Mariner heard and in his soul discerned (saying "the man hath penance done, / And penance more will do") do not articulate a conception of the universe that Coleridge or the poem as a whole supports. These voices occur in the Mariner's "soul" and express his subconscious conviction of guilt and hope for redemption through penance.[6] But these voices are not able to explain the workings of the universe: "why drives on that ship so fast, / Without or wave or wind?" (ll. 422-423). To this question, the second voice can give, not an answer, but only a description: "The air is cut away before / And closes from behind." These voices have no access to ontological truth; they are restricted to the limits of the Mariner's own consciousness.

Furthermore, the Mariner's "redemption" into a human community of joy, prayer, and meaningful activity is at best only partial. Although the spell of the curse in the eyes of the crew, which endured through the Mariner's blessing of the watersnakes, has finally snapped, the Mariner finds that he is still terrifying, even hateful, to the eyes of men. The Pilot's boy, who like the crew judges inductively and thus invalidly, sees the Mariner as the Devil and goes crazy with shock. The Hermit who has always welcomed returned sailors looks upon the ancient Mariner with horror. The wedding guest has throughout the tale been frightened and hostile. And the Mariner himself, while insisting that he has wisdom to "teach" to those men capable of understanding him, also acknowledges that he is forever denied the pleasures of ordinary social relationships. Neither husband nor father, he confesses, "O sweeter than the marriage-feast, / 'Tis sweeter far to me, / To walk together to the kirk, / With a goodly company!" (ll. 601-604). Worse yet, the Mariner is repeatedly forced to relive his terrible experiences, "ten thousand times" in fifty years, said Coleridge.[7] Allotted to "life-in-death," he must constantly veer between the goodly company in the church where he can confidently assert that "the dear God who loveth us, / He made and loveth all" and the painful solitude of a chaotic world where his "soul hath been / Alone on a wide, wide sea: / So lonely 'twas, that God himself / Scarce seemed there to be."

The final analysis of the Mariner's experience is made by the narrator whose voice frames the Mariner's tale. The narrator initiates the poem by introducing the Mariner and confirming that the wedding guest cannot choose but hear his tale. He concludes the poem by stating that the wedding guest has become "a sadder and a wiser man." If we take this framing voice as the closest to an authorial judgment within the poem, we may see here Coleridge's own painful acknowledgment of the existence of an irrational, amoral reality lying beneath the too-simple certainties of Christian theology. For the sad wisdom the guest learns is this: once one has entered the "supernatural" world, the chaotic reality that lies beneath the consoling assumptions and conventions of social morality and systematic logic, one can never go back. Insofar as Coleridge's readers have vicariously experienced this supernatural world, they—like the Mariner who is eternally separated from the pleasures of normal social intercourse—are left "stunn'd" and "of sense forlorn." The vision of the 1798 "Rime of the Ancyent Marinere" is a dreamlike, even nightmarish, vision of a world dominated by arbitrary tackings and veerings between communion and isolation, between life and death, rather than an orthodox view of a world controlled by a comprehensible rational order or moral theology. In 1797, as Coleridge later wrote in *Biographia Literaria*, he was undergoing a period of intense religious and philosophical questioning in which he doubted the very existence of a moral universe or a God:[8]

"So lonely 'twas that God himself / Scarce seemed there to be." In "The Rime," the Mariner's simple pious credo—"the dear God who loveth us, / He made and loveth all"—stands in unresolved opposition to his fate: to pass from land to land, like the eternally cursed, Wandering Jew,[9] constantly reliving almost unendurable agonies for no rational or acceptably Christian moral reason. For could a God who "made and loveth all" condemn a penitent sinner—and a man whose only sin was to kill a single bird without premeditation or hope of gain—to an eternity of torment and isolation? Thus "The Rime of the Ancyent Marinere" brilliantly depicts a chaotic, dynamic universe in which "supernatural events and agents" seem completely real and in which neither logic nor Christian morality has ontological validity.[10]

How did Coleridge feel about this ironic vision? His original reaction to the existence of a chaotic universe, as seen in his depiction of the Mariner's experiences, was an intense empathy with the *pain* that the Mariner felt at his separation from the human community and his subsequent alienation from all living things. Later revisions of the poem, however, reveal Coleridge's profound sense of guilt that, in telling the truth as he had once known it, he had deprived his audience of the certainties they (and he as well) needed to make living possible. We can trace Coleridge's increasing discomfort with—and guilt-ridden denial of—his philosophical irony in the later versions of "The Rime."

We must remember that "The Rime of the Ancyent Marinere" was not a success with its original public. Wordsworth, in an ungracious but critically perceptive note added to the 1800 edition of *Lyrical Ballads*, asserted that the poem "has indeed great defects; first, that the principal person has no distinct character . . . ; secondly, that he does not act, but is continually acted upon; thirdly, that the events having no necessary connection do not produce each other; and lastly, that the imagery is somewhat too laboriously accumulated."[11] Wordsworth, who was anxiously committed to the linear, apocalyptic plot of a secularized Christianity or "natural supernaturalism," felt uncomfortable with the uncertainties and irresolutions of romantic irony. Wordsworth moved "The Rime" from its original place of honor at the beginning of the volume to the penultimate position and, having signed himself as the author of the 1800 *Lyrical Ballads*, noted that this was the work of an anonymous "Friend." Coleridge was probably aware too of the dismay expressed by Wordsworth in a letter to Cottle on 24 June 1799: "From what I can gather it seems that The Ancyent Marinere has upon the whole been an injury to the volume, I mean that the old words and the strangeness of it have deterred readers from going on."[12] Certainly the poem's supernatural elements had alienated Robert Southey, who denounced "The Ancyent Marinere" in *The Critical Review* as "a Dutch attempt at German sublimity."[13] Coleridge was always acutely sensitive to any criticism of his work. Walter Jackson Bate has rightly stressed his excessive and neurotic need for the approbation and love of his elders and respected peers.[14] Coleridge's greatest fear, as "The Rime" itself so vividly conveys, was to be isolated from a loving human community. As he later described the only antidote to his frequent and terrifying nightmares in "The Pains of Sleep,"

> To be beloved is all I need,
> And whom I love, I love indeed.

Perhaps because he hoped to overcome Wordsworth's objections and thus win approval both for his poem and for himself, perhaps because in later years he emerged from his religious crisis with a Christian faith strong enough to survive amidst the continuing intellectual doubts and painful depressions of his troubled life, Coleridge added a new and conflicting dimension to later editions of "The Rime of the Ancient Mariner." The philosophical irony of the original poem, its presentation of an alogical, amoral, dynamic universe, remained unchanged. But in later editions, this philosophical irony is guiltily denied by either the prefaces or the presentation of the poem. The prefatory material Coleridge added proclaims the existence of a universe diametrically opposed to the nonmoral, nonlogical, supernatural world of the poem itself.

In the 1800 edition of *Lyrical Ballads*, Coleridge introduced a subtitle and new language into the Argument which present a very different version of ontological reality than that given by its original narrator. "The Rime of the Ancient Mariner" is now subtitled "A Poet's Revery." Although we know that for Coleridge the reverie or daydream could be a valuable means of access to the subconscious mind, the introduction of the term in his subtitle rhetorically operates as a public evasion or apology.[15] A reverie need not be taken seriously by rational men; it is a mere fancy, a toy, a wanton pastime which may give some fleeting pleasure. Thus Coleridge warded off Wordsworth's criticism that the poem had too much supernatural machinery (is this not common in fanciful daydreams?) and too "laboriously accumulated" imagery (for is not a reverie by nature undisciplined and self-indulgent?). Coleridge thus undermines the serious intentions of his original poem (to explore the operation of human emotions in a "supernatural" or chaotic world) by defining the poem as a mere "revery" or time-wasting daydream.

More effectively, Coleridge altered the Argument for the 1800 edition:

"How a Ship, having first sailed to the Equator, was driven by Storms to the cold Country towards the South Pole; how the Ancient Mariner cruelly and in contempt of the laws of hospitality killed a Seabird and how he was followed by many and strange Judgments: and in what manner he came back to his own Country." The Argument now imposes upon the arbitrary events of the poem both a rational and a moral order. No longer are we to read of "strange things that befell" (by chance, by the throw of a die); now the Mariner is "followed." An orderly law of cause and effect is now imposed upon the Mariner's universe. Despite Hume's skepticism, Coleridge's Argument imposes a causal relationship upon a mere sequence of events; despite Kant's anthropology, the Argument implies that this order is not merely man-made (by an individual "argument-maker") but is inherent in the noumenal universe.

The 1800 Argument also imposes a moral order upon the world of the poem: the Mariner now acts "cruelly and in contempt of the laws of hospitality" and is therefore punished "by many and strange Judgments." We are now told to see his actions, not as inexplicably arbitrary, but as sins. And the events of the poem, to ward off Wordsworth's shrewd criticism, no longer have "no necessary connection . . . [and hence] do not produce each other." On the contrary, asserts the Argument, they have a necessary moral connection and fall into the traditional Christian plot of sin and punishment. It is important to remember that this Argument *preceded* the poem; thus Coleridge's readers encountered the poem with a prejudiced conception of its plot and meaning. But this moralizing, rationalizing Argument was omitted from both the 1802 and 1805 editions of *Lyrical Ballads*, perhaps because so heavy-handed an imposition upon the poem of a diametrically opposed view of the Mariner's universe made Coleridge uneasy.

Eliminating the Argument brought back the force of Wordsworth's and others' disapproval, however, and for his 1817 *Sibylline Leaves* Coleridge produced an extremely complicated piece of romantic irony. Guiltily unwilling to affirm or completely to deny his earlier philosophical irony (his vision of the "supernatural" universe as a dynamic chaos), Coleridge now juxtaposed the Mariner's experiences with an antithetical view of reality. The poem itself remained a powerful testament to the arbitrary, irrational nature of reality and of man's emotional and intellectual life. But in an effort to rationalize this irrational vision, Coleridge now added a Latin epigraph, which was taken with additions and omissions from the 1692 edition of Thomas Burnet's *Archeologiae Philosophicae*. This epigraph is a learned affirmation of the existence of unknown, invisible, or supernatural forces or elements in a Christian world.[16] Replacing the now omitted subtitle, the epigraph defends the credibility and moral value of Coleridge's poetic enterprise: to explore the workings and effects of "supernatural" circumstances or invisible agents upon the human mind. Supported by the authority of Burnet, Coleridge now asks rational men to take his poem seriously.

More important, Coleridge now added a long prose gloss to the poem, similar to the glosses accompanying the texts of seventeenth-century travel books. This prose gloss, like the Argument of the 1800 edition of "The Rime," insistently imposes a logical and moral order upon the Mariner's experiences. The gloss, however, does not precede the text and thus need not prejudice the reader's responses completely. Rather, in the *Sibylline Leaves* edition of 1817, the gloss runs *beside* the text. It is printed in the outside margin and would thus normally be read before the text of left-hand pages, after the text on right-hand pages. This scrupulous spatial balancing of text and gloss is a visual emblem of Coleridge's anxious guilt: that his irrational, chaotic universe *not* be seen as true and that it *must* be seen as true.

For Coleridge has carefully insured that the gloss, unlike the 1800 Argument, is not presented as the authorial voice of the poet. The gloss is clearly a dramatic monologue or interpretation provided by a distinctly individuated persona. Specifically, the gloss-maker is a highly educated seventeenth-century English Christian. As George Watson emphasized, the prose style of the gloss is "richly, even extravagantly, Jacobean-Caroline."[17] The gloss-maker's massings of adjectival clauses, frequent parallel constructions, paired nouns and verbs, and extended similes and metaphors are all characteristic of the elaborate prose style of the early seventeenth century practiced by Jeremy Taylor, John Donne, Izaak Walton, the travel-book writers from whom Coleridge derived specific verbal echoes,[18] and later by Thomas Burnet. For example, "In his loneliness and fixedness he yearneth towards the journeying Moon, and the stars that still sojourn, yet still move onward; and everywhere the blue sky belongs to them, and is their appointed rest, and their native country and their own natural homes, which they enter unannounced, as lords that are certainly expected and yet there is a silent joy at their arrival" (l. 263f.). At another point, the gloss gives what is very nearly an English translation of a passage in Burnet that Coleridge omitted from his epigraph. Burnet included this discussion of invisible spirits: "Theologi Ethnici multa philosophantur circa mundum invisibilem, Animarum, Geniorum, Manium, Daemonum, Herorum, Mentium, Numinumque &

Deorum. Ut videre est apud Jamblichum de mysteriis Aegyptorum, apud Psellum & Plethonem in Chaldaicis, & passim apud Authores Platonicos."[19] Abbreviating because of space limitations, substituting Josephus (one of Burnet's favorite authorities)[20] for Jamblichus, and conflating Psellus and the Platonists, the gloss says this: "A Spirit had followed them; one of the invisible inhabitants of this planet, neither departed souls nor angels; concerning whom the learned Jew, Josephus, and the Platonic Constantinopolitan, Michael Psellus, may be consulted" (l. 132f.). In content as well as style, the glosses impersonate a seventeenth-century Anglican scholar-divine such as Thomas Burnet.

The content of the glosses defines the specific philosophical assumptions and psychological attitudes held by this seventeenth-century gloss-maker. He is a very sensible person, with a tendency to reduce the supernatural or highly metaphorical images and events in the Mariner's narrative to their most common-sense, literal equivalents. The Mariner's "The Sun came up upon the left, / . . . and on the right / Went down into the sea" becomes the glosser's "The ship sailed southward" (l. 25f.). The Mariner's striking image of the wind as an anthropomorphized persecuting Storm-Blast who "struck with his o'ertaking wings, / And chased us south along" is reduced to "The ship driven by a storm toward the south pole" (l. 41f.). The Mariner's vivid description of the upper air bursting into life where "a hundred fire-flags" fly, the "wan stars" dance, the wind roars, and the sails sigh is brushed aside with "He heareth sounds and seeth strange sights and commotions in the sky and element" (l. 310f.). And the ominous image of the sun glaring through the rigging of the spectre ship "As if through a dungeon-grate he peered / With broad and burning face" collapses into the glosser's down-to-earth "It seemeth him but a skeleton of a ship, / And its ribs are seen as bars on the face of the setting sun" (l. 177f.).

The gloss-maker is clearly a rationalist. He supplies logical connections between events that the Mariner's narrative presents only sequentially. He thus, like the crew, falls into the trap that David Hume defined so brilliantly, of attributing to a mere sequence of events a necessary causal connection which is neither observed nor proven. The Albatross's arrival, which is followed by "a good south wind," is presented as a causal relationship by the glosser: "And lo! the Albatross proveth a bird of good omen" (l. 71f.). And when the First Spirit asks the Second Spirit why the Mariner's ship is moving so swiftly, "without or wave or wind," and the Second Spirit responds with a description of the event rather than an explanation, the gloss-maker immediately supplies the missing causal link:

"The Mariner hath been cast into a trance; for the angelic power causeth the vessel to drive northward faster than human life could endure" (l. 422f.).

Whenever the supernatural dominates the Mariner's account, the gloss-maker offers pseudoscientific explanations that rationalize away the existence of chaotic or irrational beings or events. The appearance of the Polar Spirit (whose existence defies the assumptions of both empirical science and natural reason) is legitimized by the weight of scholarly opinion: "A Spirit had followed them; one of the invisible inhabitants of this planet, neither departed souls nor angels; concerning whom the learned Jew, Josephus, and the Platonic Constantinopolitan, Michael Psellus, may be consulted. They are very numerous, and there is no climate or element without one or more" (l. 131f.). With a precision that creates the illusion of scientific certainty, the glosser carefully explains that the dead crew were "inspired" or brought to life again "not by the souls of the men, nor by daemons of earth or middle air, but by a blessed troop of angelic spirits, sent down by the invocation of the guardian saint" (l. 346f.).

In addition to being a rationalist, the gloss-maker is a moralist. Whenever scientific laws fail to establish a necessary relation between the occurrences related by the Mariner, the gloss-maker assigns a moral causation to them. The Mariner's arbitrary killing of the Albatross is immediately condemned by the glosser as "inhospitable" (l. 80f.). The crew who justify the Mariner's act become "accomplices in the crime" (l. 97f.). The Mariner must therefore undergo a "horrible penance" (l. 230f.), from which he is redeemed only "by grace of the holy Mother" (l. 297f.). From the glosser's moral stance, the Mariner's sudden, inexplicable perception of the beauty of the water snakes is not arbitrary but rather a divinely ordained revelation. After all, the snakes *are* "God's creatures of the great calm" (l. 271f.).

The gloss-maker's underlying religious conviction that the universe is a cosmic harmony ruled benevolently by a merciful and loving God is vividly revealed in his eloquent description of the moon and stars. Although the text asserts that the moon and stars "no where did abide" in the constantly changing skies, the glosser contradictorally insists that the stars "still sojourn, yet still move onward" (l. 262f.) and further affirms that "everywhere the blue sky belongs to them [the moon and stars], and is their appointed rest, and their native country, and their own natural homes, which they enter unannounced, as lords that are certainly expected and yet there is a silent joy at their arrival" (l. 269f). From the glosser's Christian viewpoint, the Mariner's experience clearly demonstrates the existence of a universal moral law, which all men must obey or suffer the consequences. Having sinned against one of God's creatures, a "pious bird of good omen" (l. 79f.), the Mariner must do penance "long and heavy" to the Polar Spirit (l. 393f.) until the "curse is finally expiated" (l. 442f.) by the blessing of the snakes and the forgiveness of the crew. The Mariner is thus redeemed and, as a sign of his return to holy grace, he now teaches, "by his own example, love and reverence to all things that God made and loveth" (l. 610f.). It is true that the Mariner still suffers "the penance of life"—"ever and anon throughout his future life an agony constraineth him to travel from land to land" (l. 574f.) retelling his tale—but according to the glosser, he is once again a participant in the One Life and lives in harmony and love with God and man and beast.

One other characteristic response of the glosser to the Mariner's narrative should be mentioned. Whenever the Mariner is suffering most horribly, whenever his account becomes almost too painful for the sympathetic listener to bear, the gloss-maker distances himself from the Mariner's agony and seizes instead upon more lyrical, comforting images. At the moment when the Mariner's excruciating solitude, self-disgust, and suicidal despair reach their peak: "Seven days, seven nights, I saw that curse, / And yet I could not die" (ll. 261-262), the gloss-maker responds, not to this *cri de coeur*, but rather to the Mariner's brief description of the "softly" rising, unabiding moon. The beautiful gloss on the moon and stars quoted above creates a stable and comforting world from which the Mariner feels permanently alienated. Later editions of the gloss accentuate this emotional distance between glosser and Mariner. The lovely metaphor "No twilight within the courts of the Sun" (l. 199f.) which fills the skies with an aura of power, security, and peace, is introduced immediately after the Mariner has lost control over *his* only kingdom, his life. He has just been won in the dice game by the leprous nightmare Life-in-Death. But this seventeenth-century Christian gloss-maker, secure in his widely shared belief in a just and omnipotent moral law, can soften and even escape such agony by invoking God's ever-present mercy and love.

By placing this sensible, rational, moral, and deeply Christian vision of an ordered and just universe beside his 1798 narration of the Mariner's inexplicable, agonizing, joyful experience of a chaotic world, Coleridge has created a powerful expression of romantic irony: "an artfully ordered confusion," a "symmetry of contradictions." He has indulged his imaginative exploration of a chaotic universe and articulated man's deepest

and most contradictory emotional experiences; and he has simultaneously satisfied his conscious rage for order and his guilt-charged sense of
Christian responsibility. For we must acknowledge that Coleridge is
equally committed to these two antithetical visions of an amoral universe
and of a Christian theology. Coleridge has thus sustained the intrinsic
polarity of the universe, the conflict between the "free life" and the "confining form."

Yet this polarity remains a painful tension in "The Rime of the Ancient
Mariner," rather than an exuberant transcendental buffoonery. Coleridge's response to his romantic-ironic view of reality is finally tragic
rather than comic. Neither the wedding guest nor the narrator takes joy
in the Mariner's experiences. And the Mariner's own sense of "redemption" has seemed unconvincing to some of Coleridge's most sensitive
readers.[21] Much as Coleridge was attracted by the serene vision of a cosmic order embodied in the tradition of the great Anglican apologists from
Richard Hooker to Thomas Burnet, the tradition that Coleridge evokes
both conceptually and stylistically in the gloss, the poem and gloss together continue to manifest Coleridge's painful recognition that a Christian theology fails to explain every aspect of the observable or psychological world. Coleridge's later, rather testy (and guiltily defensive?)
response to Anna Barbauld's criticisms of "The Ancient Mariner" confirms that he remained aware of the disjunction between the Mariner's
experiences and a Christian conception of the universe:

> Mrs. Barbauld once told me that she admired the "Ancient Mariner"
> very much, but that there were two faults in it; it was improbable,
> and had no moral. As for the probability, I owned that there might
> admit some question; but as to the want of a moral, I told her that in
> my own judgment the poem had too much; and that the only, or
> chief fault, if I may say so, was the obtrusion of moral sentiment so
> openly on the reader as a principle or cause of action in a work of
> such pure imagination. It ought to have had no more moral than the
> Arabian Night's tale of the merchant's sitting down to eat dates by
> the side of a well, and throwing the shells inside, and Lo! a genie
> starts up, and says he *must* kill the aforesaid merchant, *because* one
> of the date shells had, it seems, put out the eye of the genie's son.[22]

The "obtrusion of moral sentiment" which Coleridge here describes
sounds like either the gloss of 1817 or the Mariner's own pious and rhetorically weak credo: "He prayeth best who loveth best, / All things
both great and small." It seems that Coleridge continued to feel deeply
uncomfortable with the unresolved romantic-ironic juxtaposition of a
chaotic, dynamic world with a Christian system.

However painful his romantic irony was to the guilt-ridden Coleridge, "The Rime of the Ancient Mariner" as it now stands, poem and gloss, accurately reflects the deepest ambivalences in Coleridge's most important poetry. Like "The Ancient Mariner," these poems manifest a profound conflict between the claims of "pure imagination" and the claims of orthodox belief, whether embodied in Christian doctrine, Aristotelian logic, or pragmatic common sense. Characteristically, Coleridge affirms the existence of a dynamically creative but irrational and amoral world of "pure imagination" and at the same time guiltily rejects this world as blasphemous and evil. For Coleridge, the world of pure imagination *is* arbitrary, amoral, and emotionally charged: it embraces polarities and contradictions without choosing between them, as do dreams; and it brings to man some of his most intensely felt moments of pain and joy. What I have been calling the world of "pure imagination" was equated by Coleridge, as Laurence Lockridge has suggested, with the unconscious will, that reservoir of libidinal energy that actively sought to do evil but that could be channeled by reason into the creation of a healthy, productive self.[23]

If we look ahead for a moment to Coleridge's most famous description of the nature and effects of the imagination, we can see him struggling— and finally failing—to reconcile this freely creative impulse with a moral universe:

> The IMAGINATION then, I consider either as primary, or secondary. The primary IMAGINATION I hold to be the living Power and prime Agent of all human Perception, and as a repetition in the finite mind of the eternal act of creation in the infinite I AM. The secondary Imagination I consider as an echo of the former, co-existing with the conscious will, yet still as identical with the primary in the *kind* of its agency, and differing only in *degree*, and in the *mode* of its operation. It dissolves, diffuses, dissipates, in order to recreate; or where this process is rendered impossible, yet still at all events it struggles to idealize and unify. It is essentially *vital* even as all objects (*as* objects) are essentially fixed and dead.[24]

Owen Barfield and J. R. de J. Jackson have taught us what Coleridge meant.[25] The primary imagination is the power of life itself, which resides both in nature and in the human unconscious. In Nature, this life force manifests itself simultaneously as natura naturata, the forms of the phenomenal world, and also as natura naturans, the productive power or constitutive laws in accord with which the phenomenal world and, by extension, a moral Christian universe, is formed. Thus, the life force seeks simultaneously to generate an infinity of external forms for itself and to maintain within those multiple forms a coherent selfhood: the unity in multeity which is life. In the human unconscious, this life-force or primary imagination again operates as a productive power or "constitutive intelligence" which both energizes and determines the forms taken by human perception. Coleridge thus follows Kant in suggesting that perception is grounded on an a priori shaping process. The primary imagination is the act of perceiving, which logically precedes the conscious apprehension of the product of that act, the perception. It is also an act that creates simultaneously a perceiving subject and a perceived object. In this sense, it is an act that renews life by projecting both a constituting self and the multiple objects of the phenomenal world.

The primary imagination thus repeats the divine act of life itself, the act of self-creation, "the infinite I AM." Coleridge's capitalization of "I AM" implicitly suggests that this "I" can be identified with Jahweh, the Hebraic-Christian God. When man becomes conscious of his participation in the primary imagination, when he becomes aware not only of his perceptions or thoughts but of the underlying activity of perceiving or thinking, he can then choose by an act of "conscious will" to perform those acts of self-creation or "separative projection"[26] by which the individual mind simultaneously discovers its unity with all living things and its own individuality or separate identity. This conscious or "secondary" imagination "dissolves, diffuses, dissipates" both its own selfhood (as an isolated object) and the detached, isolated object-hood of other things in order to reveal the power that animates all living things. Or where this process of self-expansion into a communal life is rendered impossible, either by the failure of the individual will or by the unyielding objectivity, stubborn individuality, or rockhard "otherness" of the world around one, still the secondary imagination struggles to unify external objects by making them realize their origin in a single spiritual power or energy. The primary imagination is the power of divine life operating in man and nature; the secondary or "poetic" imagination is the attempt to bring that power into consciousness, to articulate the authentic relationship that all living things share, to manifest the "unity in multeity" of being. Coleridge thus attempts to absolve the secondary or artistic imagination from a purely "wilful"—or heretical—dissolution or destruction of God's created world.[27]

But insofar as the unifying primary imagination does blur the fundamental moral distinction between God and man and between good and evil, it comes into conflict with Coleridge's more orthodox and traditional beliefs. As Owen Barfield has shown,[28] the demand that the universe "fit into" a clearly rational and moral pattern is identified by Coleridge with what he called the "understanding" or "judgment." At its best, when most in harmony with the conscious imagination, the understanding helps man to analyze and thus become more accurately aware of the minute relationships that link all things. Divorced from the productive power of life, the understanding can operate only upon perceptions of the external world associated by laws of causality and contiguity. Because it deals with the givens of perception rather than generating new perceptions, the understanding regards the universe as a collection of fixed ("dead") bodies or objects, which must be categorized according to scientific hypotheses, moral laws, or "fancied" models. In opposition to the imagination, the understanding seeks—not to discover the constitutive ideas or pervasive power that unifies the multiplicity of the perceived universe—but to impose upon these myriad perceptions an order or system that seems rational or moral.

Coleridge's celebration of the imagination in *Biographia Literaria* suggests that it is both superior to Fancy or understanding and also capable of perceiving and creating an orderly and hence potentially Christian universe. But it is clear both from the context of this passage and in Coleridge's earlier poems that he felt a great deal of uncertainty about whether the fundamental polarity of the unconscious imagination's free life and the understanding's confining forms could be reconciled in an acceptably Christian way. Coleridge's enthusiastic affirmation of the primary and secondary imagination is itself introduced by a long and apologetic letter, supposedly from an unnamed "friend" but actually written by Coleridge himself, which insists upon the obscurity, incoherence (resulting from an insufficiently developed argument), and excessive length of Coleridge's treatment of "ideal Realism" or the nature of the imagination.[29] Coleridge thus protects himself from the criticism of the "Public" by giving only a very short, condensed (yet complete) analysis of the workings of the imagination and by rationalizing away ahead of time any confusion or religious objections his readers might have. While this "letter" is an effective rhetorical device to excuse any shortcomings in his description of the secondary and primary imagination, it also reveals Coleridge's own uncertainties and guilt concerning the truth and intelligibility of his own ideas. And long before the *Biographia* was written, this pattern of guilty self-doubt dominated many of Coleridge's poems, where it was most often expressed as a conflict between the demands of pure imagination and the demands of judgment.

Such guilt-ridden tension between the imagination and conventional wisdom or the understanding surfaces in one of Coleridge's earliest poems, "To the Muse" (1789):

> Tho' no bold flights to thee belong;
> And tho' thy lays with conscious fear,
> Shrink from Judgment's eye severe,
> Yet much I thank thee, Spirit of my song!
> For, lovely Muse! thy sweet employ
> Exalts my soul, refines my breast,
> Gives each pure pleasure keener zest,
> And softens sorrow into pensive Joy.
> From thee I learn'd the wish to bless,
> From thee to commune with my heart;
> From thee, dear Muse! the gayer part,
> To laugh with pity at the crowds that press
> Where Fashion flaunts her robes by Folly spun,
> Whose hues gay-varying wanton in the sun.

Even though "judgment's eye severe" would condemn both the versification and the content of his poem, Coleridge defiantly exalts the gifts to be won from the conscious exercise of the poetic imagination: a more profound and sensitive awareness of his emotions and spiritual desires, an expanded vision that transmutes sorrow into joy, a greater desire to love and bless others, and the ability to laugh at and dismiss the trivial occupations and limited fashions (of dress and thought) of the crowd.

The claims of the severe eye of judgment press harder in "The Eolian Harp" (1795). The poem begins in utmost decorum, with the newly wed couple relaxing beside their cottage in an idyll of bourgeois domestic bliss. But soon the happily married husband's imagination begins to stray, led by the sight and music of the Eolian harp into sexual fantasies. Projecting himself as the Eolian harp, the poet-husband enters a realm where sexual polarities are androgynously unified. The harp, like the man stretching his limbs on the midway slope of yonder hill, is "placed length-ways in the clasping casement" which thus delicately suggests a woman's body; and then, Tiresias-like, metamorphoses into "some coy maid half yielding to her lover," the caressing breeze. So the poet half yields to the "wild and various" fantasies caressing his effeminate "indolent and passive brain," fantasies that implicitly tempt his judgment or understanding to do "wrong." Finally, pure imagination successfully seduces his mind and generates from the harp's elfin "witchery" of melody a vision of "all of animated nature" as "organic Harps diversely fram'd, / That tremble into thought, as o'er them sweeps / Plastic and vast, one intellectual breeze, / At once the Soul of each, and God of all." But this

pantheistic vision of a single life force energizing all living beings is immediately rejected by the "more serious eye" of Sara, the voice of logic,
understanding, conventional morality, and Coleridge's own uneasy conscience. And here the eye of judgment successfully holds the poetic imagination against its will. The poet grants authorial allegiance to this voice
of hallowed humility. Adopting Sara's rather priggish tones, he rejects
his "shapings of the unregenerate mind; / Bubbles that glitter as they rise
and break / On vain Philosophy's aye-babbling spring" and condemns
himself as a "sinful and most miserable man, / Wilder'd and dark." To
the eye of rational judgment and moral certainty, the poetic imagination
appears either frivolous or evil.

"To the Muse" and "The Eolian Harp" define the extremes of Coleridge's responses. Between them lie poems that attempt to reconcile conventional morality and rational judgment with poetic imagination.
"Pantisocracy" images a utopian "cottag'd dell / Where Virtue calm with
careless step may stray, / And dancing to the moon light roundelay, /
The wizard Passions weave an holy spell." Here the tension between a
virtue "calm" but carelessly dancing to a brisk roundelay and passions
simultaneously bewitching and "holy" is so strong as to break into oxymoron. Nor is the invocation "To the Rev. W. J. Hort" to bid his young
female pupil to accompany his flute song with "the Poet's kindred strain
/ In soft impassion'd voice, *correctly* wild" (italics added) easily realized.
Coleridge's effort to domesticate his imagination is imaged more successfully in "To the Nightingale." After hailing the "sad" and "pity-pleading"
strains of the nightingale, sweeter even "than the delicious airs / That
vibrate from a white-arm'd Lady's harp, / What time the languishment
of lonely love / Melts in her eye, and heaves her breast of snow," the
poet turns from this intensely erotic vision to the sweetest voice of all—
"My Sara—best beloved of human kind" who, "breathing the pure soul
of tenderness," thrills "me with the Husband's promised name!" Yet even
here, I sense a strain between the erotic/poetic and the domestic—the
mere "name" of husband seems inadequate recompense for abandoning a
white-breasted, languishing, deliciously singing lady. And "Lines, composed while climbing the left ascent of Brockley Coomb," in so vividly
describing this "enchanting spot" which blends "wild-wood" melodies,
white blossoms, green boughs, and a magnificent prospect of luxurious
landscape; and in wishing so climactically that "my Sara" were here;
only draws attention to the painful but inescapable fact that Sara—the
wife, the mother, the embodiment of social respectability—is not there.
Coleridge's efforts to reconcile imagination with judgment, intellectual

freedom with conventional thought, fail in these poems, just as his marriage to Sara Fricker failed.

Coleridge's inability to reconcile these conflicting visions—together with his inability finally and whole-heartedly to choose between them—constitute the romantic-ironic structures of "Kubla Khan," "Christabel," and several other major poems. "Kubla Khan" poses the enduring vision of a unifying imagination against the antithetical forces of mortality, self-doubt, social respectability, and rational understanding—and leaves them unreconciled. Kubla Khan personifies the powers of the imagination. Like his ancestor Jenghis Khan, Kublai Khan was a mighty ruler who brought the alphabet and hence a written language and the foundation of civilization to his people.[30] He thus has the ability to raise the primary imagination into human consciousness and to preserve its visions within a lasting artistic structure. Like the secondary imagination that cooperates with the "conscious will," Kubla Khan "decrees" the creation of a residence both pleasing and stately, both sensually and intellectually satisfying. In this single coherent structure, Kubla Khan miraculously unites polar opposites—a "sunny" dome rests upon "caves of ice," caressed by the "mingled" music of life ("the fountain" that gives birth to the river Alph) and death ("the lifeless ocean"). The architectural neoclassicism of the rounded dome finds metrical parallel in the iambic regularity of the lines describing the dome and gardens (ll. 1-11, 26-36). In both pleasure-house and walled estate, Kubla's poetic imagination creates unity in multeity, "girdling round" and thus chastely domesticating a fertile ground of sun and shadow, water and earth, cultivated gardens and ancient forests.

Beyond this conscious reconciliation of polar opposites lies the realm of the unconscious, primary imagination—the realm of life itself. "But oh! that deep romantic chasm which slanted / Down the green hill athwart a cedarn cover!" This savage place, a *mons veneris* where libidinal sexual and poetic passions are released, gives birth in "fast thick" orgasmic pants to a mighty fountain of life. In this place both "holy" and "enchanted" occurs a process simultaneously temporal and eternal, creative and destructive. The mighty fountain is born both "at once" and "ever"; and in its burst rebound huge fragments as destructive as hail and as nourishing as chaffy grain. The pressure of this mighty fountain against any rational system or structure is manifested in strikingly irregular metrics (ll. 12-25). Beginning beyond or beneath Kubla's coherently landscaped gardens and moving past or under his kingdom to the "caverns measureless to man," the fountain-river flows like the primary imagination, like dynamic life, beneath and beyond the temporal orderings of the secondary imagination or any consciously willed structure.

Because the creative and destructive impulses of chaotic life overwhelm the constructions of the conscious mind, the "tumult" of the river's fall into the "lifeless ocean" carries to Kubla's ears "Ancestral voices prophesying war." Any structure built in wood and stone is subject to the devastations of time and hostile men. Coleridge's later remarks in *Biographia Literaria* clarify the implications of this "tumult." He there distinguishes between "poets of absolute *Genius*" and "men of *commanding genius*":

> While the former rest content between thought and reality, as it were in an intermundium of which their own living spirit supplies the *substance*, and their imagination the ever-varying *form*; the latter must impress their preconceptions on the world without, in order to present them back to their own view with the satisfying degree of clearness, distinctness, and individuality. These in tranquil times are formed to exhibit a perfect poem in palace, or temple, or landscape-garden . . . But alas! in times of tumult they are the men destined to come forth as the shaping spirit of Ruin, to destroy the wisdom of ages in order to substitute the fancies of a day, and to change kings and kingdoms, as the wind shifts and shapes the clouds.[31]

Kubla Khan seems to be such a man of commanding genius, a man whose creations, because built in stone and mortar, become inflexible and lead to the ruinous war prophesied by his ancestors midst the "tumult," a war which destroys his domes and gardens.

Other, more destructive enemies of the miraculously unifying visions of the imagination invade the poem. The poet's inspiration can desert him. He may lose his creative ability, cease to perceive the underlying workings of life, or fail to find a language that expresses clearly what has been revealed to him. The tentative tone and subjunctive mood in which the poet speaks of his muse, an Abyssinian maid playing upon a dulcimer, reveals Coleridge's lack of confidence in his own poetic powers: "Could I revive within me / Her symphony and song, / To such a deep delight 'twould win me / That . . ." Since in the previous stanza the "sunny dome" with "caves of ice" has in fact been built "in air," in the words and music of poetry, Coleridge's introduction of this hypothetical situation, this qualification, is strictly speaking a contradiction and certainly poetically unnecessary. Philosophically and psychologically, however, these lines give powerful voice to a central element of romantic irony: the poet's recognition of his own limitations, his dependence on forces beyond his control.

If and when the poet of genius succeeds in creating his dome "in air," he runs the greater and more painful risk of cutting himself off from the human community. His audience, so aroused by the power of his words that they can "see" the sunny dome with caves of ice, will become so awed and frightened by this logically impossible miracle that they will react with hostility rather than love. "And all should cry, Beware! Beware! / His flashing eyes! His floating hair! / Weave a circle round him thrice, / And close your eyes with holy dread." They would exorcise the poet as though he were a demon, come like the Ancient Mariner with a vision their limited intelligences and conventional assumptions cannot accept. Coleridge understood well what Dostoyevsky's Grand Inquisitor later argued so powerfully: that if Christ were to come on earth again, he would again be crucified. Even though the poet has fed on honey-dew and "drunk the milk of paradise," his listeners would insist that it is "holier" to fear and ostracize than to welcome him. To his more conventional audience, the visionary poet will seem a blasphemer, a fearful revolutionary, a "demon-lover" who abandons his "wailing" wife and family responsibilities.

Within "Kubla Khan," then, the artistic product of pure imagination, the sunny dome with caves of ice, is ironically posed against the poet's limitations, either of creative ability or of self-control (he may impose his poem on nature, thus subjecting it to the ruins of war and time); against the hostility of its audience; and against the greater powers of dynamic life (which continually transforms even an "immortal" poem in the minds of its readers). Surrounding "Kubla Khan" is yet another ironic structure, the preface and the subtitle. Coleridge here, as in the gloss for "The Ancient Mariner," adds on a rational voice that significantly differs from the authorial voice of the poem. Although "Kubla Khan" clearly satisfies the genre conventions of the Romantic odal hymn in which a divine power (here the imagination) is invoked, its capacities enumerated, and a commitment to its service made by the poet-priest, despite whatever obstacles and hardships may attend that service,[32] the subtitle and preface both identify the poem as merely a fragment. The preface further says that somewhere between 150 and 250 lines of the original poem are missing, though critics may well wonder what more Coleridge could have had to say, and at such length, on this subject! By calling the poem a "fragment," Coleridge guiltily protects himself against the charge of blasphemy, of committing himself personally to the creation of such a miraculous dome in air. Hostile readers are hereby invited to assume that in the additional lines Coleridge himself would have rejected his vision as irrational or even immoral and affirmed instead their communally shared values of logic and morality. The subtitle, "A Vision in a Dream," further assures readers that the poem need not be taken too seriously. The poem is only a dream, an idle playing of the mind; the miraculous dome is only a "vision," a mere figment of the imagination, within that dream. Coleridge thus carefully twice distances his demonstration and celebration of the creative powers of the imagination from the realm of rational discourse. In so doing, he further protects himself from critical analysis and condemnation. Sympathetic readers might note in passing, however, that calling "Kubla Khan" a "vision in a dream" places the poem squarely within the traditional genre of the "dream-vision," the form used by medieval allegorists to convey the deepest moral and spiritual truths.

The preface undermines the poem in an even more profound way. Its voice of rational judgment and humble modesty dismisses the poem as a mere "psychological curiosity," which the author publishes only at the insistence of a famous anonymous poet (perhaps unnamed because Coleridge feared alienating those readers who disapproved of Byron), and for which the author himself hastily disclaims all "poetic merits." Coleridge then creates another fiction every bit as famous as the poem itself—the tale of the poem's composition in the summer of 1797, at a lonely farmhouse between Porlock and Linton, under the influence of opium, inspired by the reading of Purchas's *Pilgrimage*; and its interruption, leaving over 150 lines unwritten, "by a person on business from Porlock." It is possible that Coleridge's story is true, although the weight of evidence seems to lie against it.[33] But even if Coleridge did compose "Kubla Khan" in the fall of 1797 under the mutual stimulation of opium and Purchas's volumes, the most significant detail—the fatal interruption of the creative process by the visitor from Porlock—is still likely to be false. On thematic and stylistic grounds, the poem is complete. The poem describes the creative process: the created product (the dome) is evoked, the sources of creativity celebrated, the consequences of the creative act examined. Metrically, the poem moves full circle from the regular prosody of the opening lines through the irregular prosody of the lines describing the source and ending of life itself, back to the metrically regular lines of the closing description of the poet's impact on his audience. What the (literal or symbolic) visitor from Porlock, from the realm of conventional morality and mundane business affairs, destroyed was not the ending of the poem but Coleridge's confidence in the value, significance, and truth of his poem. The preface, together with the eighteen-year delay in publishing "Kubla Khan," testifies to Coleridge's pervasive guilt toward his own creative production. His poem celebrates the divine capacity of the human imagination to recreate life, to reconcile the eternally opposed forces of life and death in a never-ending dynamic polarity, while the framing preface and subtitle simultaneously denounce that reconciliation as incomplete, frivolous, a drugged trifling with the laws of logic and morality which cannot and should not be taken seriously by the rational reader.

A similar tension between the laws of logic and morality and the law of the imagination occurs in "Christabel." The imaginative union of polar opposites begins in the opening lines of the poem where midnight and dawn are joined: " 'Tis the middle of night by the castle clock, / And the owls have awakened the crowing cock." This union of contraries then extends to the major characters, images, and concerns of the poem, merging Christabel and Geraldine, dove and snake, innocence and evil. Venturing beyond the castle gates at the witching hour of midnight, Christabel like the Ancient Mariner encounters a realm beyond logic and conventional morality. The lovely lady she finds behind the maternally "broad-breasted" oak and literally carries back into the castle is both exceedingly beautiful and possessed of a bosom and side that are "lean and old and foul of hue."[34] Geraldine is both a protecting mother and a corrupting demon-lover, usurping Christabel's place at her father's side, seducing Christabel into the experience of guilt (" 'Sure I have sinn'd!' said Christabel," l. 381), yet claiming on heavenly authority that "Even I in my degree will try, / Fair maiden, to requite you well" (ll. 231-232). Overwhelmed by the force of Geraldine's presence, Christabel unconsciously and involuntarily but nonetheless completely absorbs Geraldine's small snake-like eyes and "look of dull and treacherous hate." Bard Bracy's dream becomes doubly ambivalent: the green serpent coiling round and choking the helpless white dove is both Geraldine corrupting Christabel and Christabel attempting to get rid of Geraldine, "Lord Roland's beauteous dove." The poem explores the "supernatural" or imaginative fusion of good and evil in life.[35] Geraldine is mother, witch, lesbian, and even, in one account of how Coleridge meant to end the poem, Christabel's beloved knight.[36] Christabel is innocent Abel, martyred Christ, and perpetrator of hatred. Leoline is a devoted yet rejecting father and a loyal yet betraying friend.

These psychological and moral confusions, emblemed in the ambiguously interpreted dream of Bard Bracy, are extended in the important Conclusion to Part II to the realm of language as such. Here another father rejects another innocent child, but this rejection arises not from conflicting loyalties to daughter and friend, but from the nature of language itself:

> And pleasures flow in so thick and fast
> Upon his heart, that he at last
> Must needs express his love's excess
> With words of unmeant bitterness.
> Perhaps 'tis pretty to force together
> Thoughts so all unlike each other;
> To mutter and mock a broken charm,
> To dally with wrong that does no harm.
> Perhaps 'tis tender too and pretty
> At each wild word to feel within
> A sweet recoil of love and pity,
> And what, if in a world of sin
> (O sorrow and shame should this be true!)
> Such giddiness of heart and brain
> Comes seldom save from rage and pain
> So talks as it's most used to do.

Coleridge first suggests that it is an aesthetic impulse or act of imaginative wit that "forces together / Thoughts so all unlike each other." He acknowledges the subtle pleasure the human psyche finds in expressing a hostility it does not feel, in muttering and mocking a broken charm. Thus, a father can simultaneously express a hostility to his child that he may feel now or have felt in the past and defuse that hostility with joking self-mockery. Moreover, he may intensify his awareness of his affection and empathy with his child, feeling "a sweet recoil of love and pity" for the child's sorrow at his father's cruel, wild words. But the final lines, in a philosophical movement characteristic of Coleridge's mind and poetry, go beyond the psychological to the ontological realm. Coleridge speculates that man's most intense feelings ("Such giddiness of heart and brain") are normally emotions not of joy but of anger or pain, and "So talks as it's most used to do." If the language used to express intense feeling is a language born of anger or pain, then in a very real sense man has no language for extreme joy. If one must use "words of unmeant bitterness" to express intense joy, then language (like the imagination) fuses polarities and defies the distinctions of logic and morality. Interestingly, even in this brief conclusion, Coleridge includes a note of conventional horror and guilt at such linguistic or imaginative conflations. A failure to divide moral good from evil, to distinguish love from hatred, occurs only "in a world of sin," and if true, must cause us "sorrow and shame." "Christabel" ends where "The Ancient Mariner" ended. The reader, made vividly aware that we live in a world where clear moral, logical, psychological, and linguistic divisions between good and evil or truth and falsehood do not exist, is left "sadder and wiser"—and also innocently guilty (" 'Sure I have sinn'd!' said Christabel").

Coleridge's personal sense of guilt for having written "Christabel" cries out in the disguised voice of the preface. Perhaps because the poem is so obviously unfinished and the Conclusion to Part II so clearly a structural excrescence (whatever its thematic relevance), Coleridge apparently felt no psychological need to undermine its poetic claims. Instead, Coleridge's preface raises a quite different moral issue. Rather than apologizing for the moral ambiguities or supernatural elements in the poem, Coleridge attempts to vindicate himself of a possible charge of plagiarizing "Christabel" from Scott or Byron. Since Scott had publicly acknowledged the indebtedness of his *Lay of the Last Minstrel* to "Christabel" and Byron had praised "Christabel" as a "wild and singularly original and beautiful poem" in a note to *The Siege of Corinth* (1816), Coleridge's self-justification seems unnecessary. Not even Norman Fruman's lengthy recataloging of Coleridge's proved or suspected plagiarisms suggests that "Christabel" was derived from other authors.[37] The gratuitousness of the apology makes its appearance all the more significant. It clearly manifests Coleridge's obsession, well documented by Fruman, with the moral issue of plagiarism. There is no doubt that on many occasions Coleridge allowed the work of others to be taken for his own. The preface to "Christabel" thus articulates his general consciousness of wrongdoing even as it rightly defends his innocence in this particular case. Here a voice of conventional morality is set beside an imaginative vision that denies the very foundation of that morality (the assumption that right and wrong, good and evil, yours and mine, can be distinguished). This prefatory voice of conventional propriety extends, moreover, to blaming the author's "own indolence" and even to justifying the meter. "The meter of *Christabel* is not, properly speaking, irregular, though it may seem so from its being founded on a new principle: namely, that of counting in each line the accents, not the syllables." The preface to "Christabel," like the gloss for "The Ancient Mariner" and the preface to "Kubla Khan," ironically places a language of poetic decorum beside a language of pure imagination that must needs express love's excess in words of unmeant bitterness. Christabel *is* Geraldine, but Coleridge (clearly identifying himself with Christabel, as Walter Jackson Bate has shrewdly noted)[38] is the soul of propriety.

In "Dejection: An Ode," Coleridge again sets two opposed visions of the world side by side without reconciling them, but here he blames himself for their irreconcilability. On the one side is a universe created by the power of joy as it flows through and energizes the "shaping spirit" of the primary imagination. Such joy, which is readily accessible to Sara Hutchinson and Wordsworth (whose own "Ode: Intimations of Immortality" demonstrated joy's positive powers and inspired this poem), enables one to see the natural world as beloved, and in thus "wedding" nature to us, creates around us "a new Earth and new Heaven," a harmonious one life in which even sounds and colors fuse in Newtonian waves.[39]

Opposed to this redemptive vision of universal beauty, harmony, and pleasure is Coleridge himself, isolated by his inability to feel such joy. Imprisoned in his dejection, his "grief without a pang, void, dark, and drear," Coleridge not only does not feel pleasure; he feels nothing at all. He can see the beautiful stars, moon, and peculiar yellow-green tint of the western sky, can see but not "feel how beautiful they are!" This emotional depression or impotence has been caused, he guiltily admits, wholly by himself. In an effort to escape the pain of his life—his failed marriage and career, his frustrated love-affair with Sara Hutchinson, his opium addiction—he has taught himself to feel nothing, to "not think of what I needs must feel," to be stoically "still and patient," to sublimate all his emotions into "abstruse research" (ll. 87-89). The result has been the loss of all feeling, of the passions that both make one human and arouse one's secondary imagination to create meaningful mythic structures.

After establishing this polarity, the poem moves, not to a reconciliation, but to an intensified awareness of the distance between these two human conditions. The winter storm arouses the "dull sobbing" Aeolian poet to an act of secondary, poetic imagination: he creates a poem whose images are shaped by his own pain. The howling wind becomes a "Mad Lutanist," singing the Devil's song; a tragic actor; a mighty poet who can tell only of epic destruction ("an host in rout") or lyric suffering (a small child lost in the woods, screaming in terror for her absent mother). Roused to a "mountain-birth," to poetic speech, by the storm, Coleridge can voice, first discursively and then passionately, only his own emotions of loss and pain. His primary imagination can receive but what it gives, can provide for the secondary act of willed creation only images of separation, alienation, self-destruction, and pain.

Sara, the pure of heart, remains apart, hidden on the far side of the insurmountable mountain. Able to feel joy, she can respond to the storm as a different kind of "mountain-birth," as a fructifying arrival of health and beauty. The poem ends with a powerful image of the very polarity it has structurally developed:

> To her may all things live, from pole to pole,
> Their life the eddying of her living soul!   (ll. 135-136)

But even as Coleridge images a life in which opposed centrifugal and centripetal forces fertilely interact, he ironically detaches himself from participation in such "eddying" life. He ushers Sara into a blessed health and joy that he himself can never directly experience: "Thus mayest thou ever, evermore rejoice" (l. 139). In contrast to "The Rime of the Ancient Mariner," Coleridge here suggests that a chaotic world of positively and negatively charged forces produces merrily multiplying life. But it is a life from which he excludes himself. And yet, in romantic-ironic fashion, his own dejection has in the course of the poem eddied through both intense pain and vicarious pleasure in the joy experienced by his "Dear Lady! friend devoutest of my choice." While always ostracizing the guilty Coleridge from participation in joy, the poem has nonetheless swept him up in a powerful whirlpool of celebrated joy and acute dejection, of eddying pain and pleasure. Thus Coleridge does and does not experience "this beautiful and beauty-making power," "Life, and Life's effluence," Joy itself.

Both structurally and thematically, the romantic irony in Coleridge's poetry is energized by guilt rather than by a Schlegelian enthusiasm. Intellectually dismissive subtitles—"A Poet's Revery," a "Fragment," even "A Conversation Poem"—apologetically disclaim the visionary truths of the imagination in such poems as "The Rime of the Ancient Mariner," "Kubla Khan," "The Three Graves," "The Ballad of the Dark Ladie," and "The Nightingale." Self-condemning prefaces establish standards of propriety which the accompanying poems fail to meet, as in "Christabel" or "Fire, Famine, and Slaughter." Or these prefaces invoke traditional criteria of logic and common sense in terms of which the accompanying material can be condemned as a mere psychological curiosity ("Kubla Khan," "The Three Graves") or as clearly inadequate treatments of the subject (Coleridge's letter preceding his description of the imagination in *Biographia Literaria*, chap. 13). The Nehemiah Higginbottom self-parodies further testify to Coleridge's pervasive insecurity with his own poetic diction, metrical experiments, and subject-matter. All these apologies and self-parodies, like the Christianizing gloss for "The Ancient Mariner," establish a profoundly ironic opposition between Coleridge's imaginative visions and his religious beliefs. And for Coleridge, such an oppo-

sition could arouse only anxiety and guilt, an obsessive self-condemna-
tion as "a sinful and most miserable man." For Coleridge was neurotically
afraid of offending others, excessively dependent upon approbation even
from people whose opinions he did not respect, obsessed with the need to
justify his life in the face of the failure of his career and marriage—and on
a more pragmatic level, acutely aware that his financial survival depended on earning and keeping the interest and admiration of wealthy
patrons or a wide public. All these factors help to explain, on a psychological level, why Coleridge could respond to the ontology of romantic
irony, to a vision of the universe as alternating between chaotic abundance and limited, man-made systems, only with anxiety. Guiltily, he
feared that he would be blamed for the truths he saw, and guiltily he responded with a set of defensive, self-justifying rhetorical strategies that
effectively deny his responsibility for these truths and even on occasion
their very accuracy.

6

Fear and Trembling:
From Lewis Carroll to Existentialism

Like the other romantic ironists I have been considering, Lewis Carroll conceived the ontological universe as uncontrolled flux. But unlike the others, this Victorian don was frightened by this vision. Lewis Carroll shared his upper-class contemporaries' anxiety that change was change for the worse, not the better. The Reform Bill of 1832 had initiated a political leveling of English society; the Industrial Revolution had created a society whose highest priority was materialistic prosperity rather than spiritual growth and freedom; the new Higher Criticism of the Bible propounded by David Friedrich Strauss and Joseph Ernst Renan had undermined the fundamentalist Christian belief in the divinity of Christ; and Darwin's *Origin of Species* (1859) had argued that "progress" could be equated with a brutal warfare resulting in the survival of the fittest. Lewis Carroll responded to these changes with the strategies of romantic irony. Eagerly, he tried to impose man-made systems onto this flux. At the same time, he forthrightly acknowledged the limitations of such systems as language, logic, and games. But unlike the romantic ironist who engages enthusiastically in a never-ending process of creation and decreation, Lewis Carroll felt, and felt intensely, that one must commit oneself wholly to one's created systems. Giving up such heuristic systems, he believed, is tantamount to sacrificing both rational thought and moral behavior—and plunges one into bestial violence.

Personally, Charles Dodgson (Lewis Carroll) was a withdrawn, shy, obsessively neat man, a man who felt alienated from society in general, a man who apparently had very few close friends and no lovers, a man who was afraid of intense emotional relationships. His sense of his own inability to cope with the world—and of the necessity therefore to learn methods of controlling his environment—had probably been acutely intensified by his excruciating boyhood years at the Rugby School, where this stuttering, scholarly child was generally ostracized. Only at Oxford, where Dodgson could live a retired life as a confirmed bachelor and a mathematics don, did he feel comfortable. His closest friendships, as we know, were with prepubescent girls who could threaten him neither intellectually nor sexually.[1]

Frightened by the shifting sands both of the sociopolitical world and of adult, passionate relationships, Dodgson tried desperately to deny the chaotic flow of life by transforming all human realities into a structured game, a game whose rules he alone understood and that he alone could win.[2] Even as a child, Dodgson had relished creating complicated games for his sisters that are remarkable for their ruthlessness, as in the Railway Game in which "All passengers when upset are requested to lie still until picked up—as it is requisite that at least three trains should go over them, to entitle them to the attention of the doctor and assistants."[3] As a mathematician, he delighted in constructing mathematical puzzles (*Pillow Problems*) which he alone could solve; and he spent years developing a symbolic logic which strictly divided all statements into real versus imaginary, and into assertions of existence versus assertions of nonexistence. By reducing the complexities of human interactions to a set of statements which could then be equated with grey and red checkers on a two-dimensional chart of circumscribed squares (what he called "the game of Logic"), Carroll could successfully force a rigidly closed and completely rational system upon the world.[4] Dodgson/Carroll then taught these puzzles and logic-games in girls' schools. At such times, the introverted don lost his stutter and became eloquently and emotionally involved in logical arguments. Apparently, Dodgson channeled most of his repressed emotional and sexual energies into creating and then authoritatively imposing his logical or mathematical systems (games) upon his obedient female students. Significantly, in the published *Symbolic Logic*, Carroll explicitly refers to the Problem-poser as the "Inquisitor" and to the Problem-solver as the "Victim."[5] Carroll's fierce desire to control his students' minds, by painful force if necessary, is revealed both in his metaphor and again in his refusal to guest-teach in any but girls' schools. He naturally preferred to educate young girls, who were, on the whole, more submissive, deferential, and easily manipulated—as well as more sexually appealing to Carroll—than young boys. As the Duchess tells Alice, one must "speak roughly to your little boy"[6]—and *her* boy promptly turns into a pig.

Carroll's obsession with photography, a hobby to which he devoted thousands of hours between May 1856 and July 1880, again reveals his compulsion to force his own order upon the chaotic flux of time. Photography is an attempt to seize and fix a passing moment in a static, spatial image. Significantly, as Helmut Gernsheim comments, Carroll's real talent as a photographer lay in his sense of arrangement: he was a "master of composition" who "did not aim at characterisation, but at an attractive design."[7] By forcing his models—generally either famous men or, more often, little girls—to stand still and pose while he photographed them, Carroll could capture and preserve the past (time would thus stand still, forever frozen on his collodion plate). And he could force the present moment into the shape he wished it to take for eternity. He preferred to photograph his young female subjects either in costume (and thus metamorphose them into the figures of his own imagination—see, for example, his photographs of Agnes Grace Weld as "Little Red Riding Hood" and of Xie Kitchin as "A Chinaman") or in the nude (and thus preserve for all time their innocent, unconscious sexuality, uncorrupted by mature female anatomy, desire, or experience). Art thus functions, for Carroll, to deny the passage of time, to deny flux, to deny chaos. (Appropriately, in order to persuade his very young models to remain absolutely still during the two-to-three-minute exposures of collodion-plate photography, Carroll would tell them stories, again using art to control the normal flux of motion in time. That this control was felt to be painful is documented both by his models' recorded resentment and by Carroll's reference to them as his "photographic victims.")[8] The photographic image calculatedly selects a single arrangement of human experience, a single expression upon a child's face, and defines that image as the truth for all time. As Carroll's poem accompanying his photograph of Alice Murdoch insists, photography is an attempt to seize the glorious "celestial benizon" of her childish innocence and to preserve it forever, despite the ravages of the future, "those realms of love and hate, / . . . that darkness blank and drear."[9]

Dodgson's lust for order extended to every aspect of his compulsively regulated life. As Michael Holquist tells us,

> when he had packages to be wrapped, he drew diagrams so precise that they showed to a fraction of an inch just where the knots should be tied; he kept congeries of thermometers in his apartments and never let the temperature rise above or fall below a specific point. He worked out a system for betting on horses which eliminated disorderly chance. He wrote the Director of Covent Garden telling him how to clear up the traffic jam which plagued the theatre; to the post office on how to make its regulations more efficient. And after hav-

ing written all these letters (more than 98,000 before he died), he
then made an abstract of each, and entered it into a register with
notes and cross-references.[10]

By transforming every aspect of his daily life into a rigidly ordered system or game, Carroll could gain the psychological security of living in a
totally controlled world; in Elizabeth Sewell's phrase, he could play at
being God.[11] For in his own games, Carroll alone knew the rules; he
alone determined the winner; he was all-powerful. Derek Hudson has
traced Carroll's obsession with using the imagination to control a disorderly universe back to his father's equally egotistical and comically
sadistic fantasies. Commissioned by his son to purchase an iron file, a
screwdriver, and a ring, the Rev. Charles Dodgson wrote to the nine-
year-old Carroll:

> . . . I will not forget your commission. As soon as I get to Leeds I
> shall scream out in the middle of the street, *Ironmongers, Ironmon-*
> *gers.* Six hundred men will rush out of their shops in a moment—fly,
> fly, in all directions—ring the bells, call the constables, set the Town
> on fire. I WILL have a file and a screwdriver, and a ring, and if they
> are not brought directly, in forty seconds, I will leave nothing but
> one small cat alive in the whole Town of Leeds, and I shall only leave
> that, because I am afraid I shall not have time to kill it. Then what a
> bawling and a tearing of hair there will be! Pigs and babies, camels
> and butterflies, rolling in the gutter together—old women rushing
> up the chimneys and cows after them—ducks hiding themselves in
> coffee-cups, and fat geese trying to squeeze themselves into pencil
> cases. At last the Mayor of Leeds will be found in a soup plate
> covered up with custard, and stuck full of almonds to make him
> look like a sponge cake that he may escape the dreadful destruction
> of the Town.[12]

Carroll's most famous attempts to force a system of his own making
upon the chaos of the universe are his two nonsense books, *Alice in*
Wonderland and *Through the Looking-Glass.* Nonsense is of course a
kind of game with its own rules, "a carefully ordered world, controlled
and directed by reason, a construction subject to its own laws," in Elizabeth Sewell's definition.[13] Wonderland, then, is a game played with
words. In this book, the professional mathematician Charles Dodgson
builds a closed system, not out of numbers, but out of words. It is a linguistic structure, which, although it denies or distorts customary vocabu-
laries, grammar, syntax, and the usual order of events, nonetheless maintains an absolute control over the relation of order to disorder. Like all of
Lewis Carroll's games, the game of Wonderland attempts to impose an

overtly man-made, rational system upon a chaotic universe. In the process, Carroll draws attention both to the underlying disorder of the noumenal world and to the irrationality of other men's systems, most notably language itself. By undermining the logical and hence the moral authority of previous game-systems and hence destroying his readers' faith in the objective reality of their belief-systems, Lewis Carroll tries to construct a game—or nonsense—world in which he alone is the master.

The game of Wonderland is based on a rigorously logical and systematic reversal of normal human assumptions. Here Carroll, like Schlegel before him, conceives the universe in terms of a non-Aristotelian logic, in which p = not-p.[14] But unlike Schlegel, Carroll's protagonist Alice— with Carroll himself—responds to this world of irrational becoming with more anxiety and fear than unmitigated wonder and delight. As Donald Rackin has argued, the book originally entitled *Alice's Adventures under Ground* "embodies a comic horror-vision of the chaotic land beneath the man-made groundwork of Western thought and convention."[15]

In the non-Aristotelian logic of Wonderland, p is not p. Alice has no permanent identity; she gets big or little at will or in accord with what she eats; and in the external world, things constantly metamorphose. Inanimate objects move of their own accord (a tea tray flies through the sky, a deck of cards plays croquet); animate objects function as inanimate objects (hedgehogs are used as croquet balls, flamingoes as mallets); and babies turn into pigs (87). Space and time, two a priori Kantian categories of phenomenological experience, are systematically distorted. Alice cannot maintain stable geographical relationships ("London is the capital of Paris, and Paris is the capital of Rome," she murmurs; 38); places change unpredictably; and the characters inhabit a systematically displaced space (Pat, the White Rabbit's gardener, is "digging for apples"; 60). Time is experienced not as duration or an orderly chronological sequence of events but as a naughty young person who has had to be "beaten" and subsequently "murdered" by the Mad Hatter.

Mathematical and social systems are turned upside down in Wonderland. Alice can't count to twenty because, as Alexander Taylor points out, she changes the scales of notation at differing intervals: "the scale of notation was increasing by three at each step and the product by only one."[16] Social relationships defy conventional expectations. In Wonderland, animals rule over human beings (the White Rabbit orders Alice/ Mary Ann—all little girls look alike to a rabbit—to fetch his gloves) and fathers behave like children (70-71). Political systems based on a distinctly differentiated hierarchy of power and on earned rewards are re-

placed in Wonderland with a contradictory caucus-race in which everyone runs in circles and everyone must have prizes (49).[17] The legal system
is similarly inverted: Fury eats the mouse after a trial that has had neither
judge nor jury, while at the Knave of Hearts's trial the sentence is pro-
nounced before the verdict. And the moral codes that prevail, however
tenuously, in Alice's English society are overturned. The sentimental
notion that animals are loving and lovable is undone by the Darwinian
Lobster Quadrille, while genuine feelings of compassion and love are reduced to mere sentimentality in the Mock Turtle's love song to "Beau—
ootiful Soo-oop" (141). The very concept of morality is rendered ludi-
crous by the Duchess's meaningless maxims: "Everything's got a moral, if
only you can find it" (120).

Most disturbing to Alice, however, is the fact that even rational
thought processes are distorted in Wonderland. There are no logical connections between events. The law of causality becomes an absurdity in
Alice's meditation: " 'Maybe it's always pepper that makes people hot-
tempered,' she went on, very much pleased at having found out a new
kind of rule, 'and vinegar that makes them sour—and camomile that
makes them bitter—and—and barley-sugar and such things that make
children sweet-tempered' " (119-120). Communication can take place in
Wonderland without the use of objective signs: the Caterpillar responds
to Alice's unspoken thoughts with extrasensory perception.

> Then it [the Caterpillar] got down off the mushroom, and crawled
> away into the grass, merely remarking, as it went, "One side will
> make you grow taller, and the other side will make you grow
> shorter."
> "One side of *what*? The other side of *what*?" thought Alice to her-
> self.
> "Of the mushroom," said the Caterpillar, just as if she had asked it
> aloud; and in another moment it was out of sight. (73)

In *Alice in Wonderland*, Carroll does more than create a systematically
coherent nonsense world based on non-Aristotelian logic. He also demonstrates the illogicality of the most important game we play, the game
of language. Carroll shows that both the grammatical structures and the
lexical content of the English language are often irrational. He further
denies that any necessary relationship exists between words and things;
well before Ferdinand de Saussure, Carroll insisted upon the arbitrary
motivation of words and upon the role of cultural tradition and agreed-
upon convention in determining the *langue*. As he wrote in 1880 in an
article for *The Theatre*, "The Stage and the Spirit of Reverence,"

... no word has a meaning *inseparably* attached to it; a word means what the speaker intends by it [Saussure's *parole*], and what the hearer understands by it [Saussure's *langue*], and that is all.

I meet a friend and say "Good morning!" Harmless words enough, one would think. Yet possibly, in some language he and I have never heard, these words may convey utterly horrid and loathsome ideas. But are *we* responsible for this? This thought may serve to lessen the horror of some of the language used by the lower classes, which, it is a comfort to remember, is often a mere collection of unmeaning *sounds*, so far as speaker and hearer are concerned.[18]

And again, in the "Appendix, Addressed to Teachers" that concludes his *Symbolic Logic*, Carroll insists upon the arbitrary nature of word-meanings, particularly when used by individual language-speakers:

... I maintain that any writer of a book is fully authorised in attaching any meaning he likes to any word or phrase he intends to use. If I find an author saying, at the beginning of his book, "Let it be understood that by the word 'black' I shall always mean 'white,' and that by the word 'white' I shall always mean 'black,' " I meekly accept his ruling, however injudicious I may think it.[19]

Many of Carroll's wittiest jokes play on the irrationality of the English language. He exploits the confusions inherent in homonyms (the Mouse's tail/tale) and in the fact that a single word can have very different meanings (dry is the antonym both of wet and of exciting). His frequent use of puns and portmanteau words challenges the notion that one word can signify only one thing and draws attention to the ambiguity of the English language. He emphasizes the arbitrary nature of syntax: a change in word order can effect a change in meaning, since the converse of a statement does not necessarily share its truth value (as in Alice's famous and erroneous insistence that "I mean what I say" is the same as "I say what I mean"; 95). Moreover, syntax itself can be ambiguous, as in the Mouse's dry tale, where

"Edwin and Morcar, the earls of Mercia and Northumbria, declared for him; and even Stigand, the patriotic archbishop of Canterbury, found it advisable—"

"Found *what*?" said the Duck.

"Found *it*," the Mouse replied rather crossly; "of course you know what 'it' means." (47)

The Duck's inability to determine what "it" means results from the syntactic ambiguity caused by his interruption (the subordinate clause to which "it" refers has not yet been uttered), as well as from the potentially confusing capacity of a pronoun to refer to a multiplicity of things. More often, Carroll's wordplay focuses on the disjunction between words and meanings, between the signifier and the signified. Language-speakers can use signifiers that have no meaning for them, as when Alice, in falling down the rabbit-hole, expects to arrive at the "Antipathies" (28); or when the Dodo tells Alice he can't "explain" or define a Caucus-race, he can only do it (48). Anticipating the logical positivists, Carroll asserts that questions that cannot be answered are meaningless:[20] "Alice began to get rather sleepy, and went on saying to herself, in a dreamy sort of way, 'Do cats eat bats? Do cats eat bats?' and sometimes, 'Do bats eat cats?' for, you see, as she couldn't answer either question, it didn't much matter which way she put it" (28).

Increasingly, in *Alice in Wonderland*, Carroll insists that there are no necessary connections between words and things-in-themselves. The traditional realist assumption that words "point at" things is thus drawn into question. In Wonderland, for instance, attributes can exist without a subject to which they refer: Alice sees "a grin without a cat" (91). Labels, or signs, have no fixed relationship to the things they purportedly designate; they are "empty symbols."[21] When Alice opens a jar labeled "orange marmalade," she finds nothing in it (27); when she tastes the contents of a bottle, which has no "poison" label on it, it almost destroys her by shrinking her down so far that she wonders nervously whether she might not be going out altogether, "like a candle" (32). Furthermore, in Wonderland the sum of a subject's attributes do not necessarily constitute the thing itself. The pigeon who deduces from Alice's long neck that she must be a serpent makes the same error we make when we assume that an attribute defines a thing.[22]

Finally, then, when Alice exchanges Wonderland for the above-ground world, she is only exchanging one nonsense-world for another. She is only replacing one language-game, the Queen of Hearts's "Off with her head," with another language-game, "You're nothing but a pack of cards" (161). Carroll forces us to recognize that both Wonderland and our conventional "reality" are arbitrary game-systems created by the human imagination and imposed on other minds by mental will or physical force. Alice's language-game prevails at the end of the story only because she literally *grows bigger*; her will can therefore master the Queen's will and her arbitrary definitions of signs or *parole* can triumph.[23] But Carroll subtly insists upon the linguistic relativity of Alice's language-game even as he ends the tale with a comforting description of the future. Alice's sister's dream of present and future time is as much a narrative based on fantasy and unmotivated signs as the nonsense of Wonderland:

> So she sat on, with closed eyes, and half believed herself in Won-
> derland, though she knew she had but to open them again, and all
> would change to dull reality—the grass would be only rustling in the
> wind, and the pool rippling to the waving of the reeds—the rattling
> teacups would change to tinkling sheep-bells, and the Queen's shrill
> cries to the voice of the shepherd boy—and the sneeze of the baby,
> shriek of the Gryphon, and all the other queer noises, would change
> (she knew) to the confused clamour of the busy farm-yard—while
> the lowing of the cattle in the distance would take the place of the
> Mock Turtle's heavy sobs. (163-164)

Alice's sister's definition of "dull reality" is as arbitrary and fictional as
Carroll's description of Wonderland. Her description of the "real world"
is a sentimental pastoral idyll culled from literary tradition ("tinkling
sheep bells," "the voice of the shepherd boy," "the busy farm-yard," "the
lowing of the cattle"). As such, it is as much a denial of the chaos of noumenal becoming as is Wonderland. She attempts to control the flux of
future time with a narrative structure or language-game:

> Lastly, she pictured to herself how this same little sister of hers
> would, in the after-time, be herself a grown woman; and how she
> would keep, through all her riper years, the simple and loving heart
> of her childhood; and how she would gather about her other little
> children, and make *their* eyes bright and eager with many a strange
> tale, perhaps even with the dream of Wonderland of long ago; and
> how she would feel with all their simple sorrows, and find a pleasure
> in all their simple joys, remembering her own child-life, and the
> happy summer days. (164)

But her narrative is as doomed to linguistic relativity as Carroll's own attempt to reshape the past into the arrangement he preferred. Despite his
emphatic assertion that the tale of *Alice's Adventures under Ground* was
composed "all in a golden afternoon" on July 4, 1862, we know from the
British Meteorological Office that the weather was "cool and rather wet"
in Oxford that day.[24]

Alice in Wonderland thus embodies Carroll's recognition that the apparently well-ordered and meaningful reality we take for granted is not
absolute and that all linguistic and moral systems are but arbitrary games
whose authority rests solely upon tradition and convention. Carroll, of
course, uses comedy to distance himself and his audience from the frightening implications of this ontological chaos. But his fear of living in such
a disorderly world pokes its ugly head through his best comic defenses.
Alice never knows who she is (is she Mabel? or a serpent?); she is frequently left alone in a hostile world (the Mouse swims away from her,

while the Queen of Hearts wants to chop off her head); and she responds to the aggressive chaos of her environment with an equally violent aggression, sometimes directed at others (she kicks Bill the lizard out the chimney) and sometimes at herself (on several occasions, she almost kills herself, as when she drinks the "poison," holds the fan too long, and almost drowns in her own tears). Despite the charming wit of Carroll's nonsense, Alice's bland response to the violence and cruelty of the chaotic world she has experienced—to dismiss it as a "wonderful dream" (162)—is a patently inadequate psychological and rhetorical response to the uncertainties and anxieties, the "scream, half of fright and half of anger" (162), she has endured. The overt sentimentality and self-conscious "fictiveness" of Carroll's concluding fantasy of Alice's future only draws attention to his own inability to live comfortably with the illogical, chaotic universe that he discovered lying just under the linguistic and social games men call reality.

In *Through the Looking-Glass and What Alice Found There,* Carroll takes Alice directly into this noumenal realm. When Alice climbs through the looking-glass, she enters a world where things and relationships are mirror images of the normal world. She also enters a house of mirrors where signs or words only reflect or refer to each other. Here things are only words, words are things, and things behave as arbitrarily as words. In the Looking-Glass world, the connections between words and things are broken; and order and meaning necessarily dissolve.

The question that *Through the Looking-Glass* poses is no longer which game shall we play, but rather, what is reality? What does lie beneath the social conventions, the logical systems, and the linguistic structures that we perceive as reality? Carroll offers two possible answers to these questions. Beneath the phenomenological realm of structured experience may lie an ultimate harmony of things coexisting in a loving peace. When Alice enters the forest where things have no names, where no nouns are spoken and hence no divisions made between one thing and another, she and the fawn can unite in perfect friendship. "So they walked on together through the wood, Alice with her arms clasped lovingly round the soft neck of the Fawn" (227). But this idyllic communion is abruptly destroyed by the return of names or linguistic signs: "they came out into another open field, and here the Fawn gave a sudden bound into the air, and shook itself free from Alice's arm. 'I'm a Fawn!' it cried out in a voice of delight. 'And, dear me! you're a human child!' A sudden look of alarm came into its beautiful brown eyes, and in another moment it had darted away at full speed" (227). Not only do linguistic classifications break up this noumenal harmony, but Carroll seems not to believe it exists. He places this vision at the beginning of the book where it is overwhelmed by the nightmare vision that follows it and concludes the story.

For Carroll, like Schlegel, finally conceives of noumenal reality as pure chaos. But in contrast to Schlegel, Carroll sees this chaos as wholly self-destructive; it is a predatory jungle where "Nature, red in tooth and claw / With ravine, shriek'd." In *Through the Looking-Glass*, Carroll takes us deep into this violent chaos in an attempt to convince us that if we do *not* play his games we will be eaten up.

On first entering the Looking-Glass world, Alice finds a seemingly orderly world, a predictable mirror image of conventional reality. True, the clock has a face, but it is smiling—no danger there. And while the Jabberwocky poem has an unfamiliar vocabulary, it can be translated into English and it does obey normal syntax—Alice is sure at any rate that "somebody killed something" (197). It is when Alice steps outside the house that life becomes difficult. Certain rules of reversal still pertain: to go forward, you must move backward; to stand still, you must run as fast as you can; and time moves backward (the White Queen screams first, and is pricked second). A more fundamental rule of the Looking-Glass world is that signs are completely motivated: words are things; phrases are real situations; poems are events. The trees "bark" with a "bough-wough" (202); the flowers are awake and talking because their beds are hard (203); and Alice sees the substantive "nobody" on the road (179). Alice's word-play, "I love my love with an H," becomes a phenomenological reality: the Haigha ("Hare") is hideous, eats ham sandwiches and hay, and lives on the hill. The people Alice meets are nursery-rhyme characters; their lives are determined by the narrative plots of their respective poems. Tweedledee and Tweedledum fight over a rattle and are frightened by a black crow, while the unicorn and the lion fight for the crown, eat plum-cake, and are drummed out of town. In this universe of motivated linguistic discourse, whatever words one invents become existing things—for example, Alice's "Bread-and-butter fly." But since these things are only words, *they* cannot invent words—the "weak tea with cream" they need to survive—and hence they die (223). As the Red Queen tells Alice, "when you've once said a thing, that fixes it, and you must take the consequences" (323).

If words are things and linguistic structures are actual events, then what are things-in-themselves? In the nominalist universe of the Looking-Glass world, the answer is obvious: things without words or names are no-things, nonidentities, part of a constantly metamorphosing flux. Alice begins to experience the chaos upon which all man-made systems are so precariously constructed as soon as she begins to play her second game, the chessgame. To play two games simultaneously (chess and looking-glass) is to be caught between two conflicting systems and thus forced to recognize the merely relative authority of each set of rules. At this point, logic begins to break down in the book and pure metamorphosis to prevail. Having jumped over the brook, Alice suddenly finds herself in a railway carriage without a ticket, with insects who "think in chorus"; equally suddenly and illogically, the carriage leaps into the air and Alice finds herself sitting quietly under a tree (221). Frightened by the crow that flies overhead during Tweedledee and Tweedledum's battle, Alice hides under a large tree and catches the shawl that flies by her. After a-dressing the White Queen in her shawl, Alice suddenly realizes that the Queen is a sheep and that she is in a shop. Asked to buy something, Alice notices that the shelves, although filled, are never static: "Things flow about so in here," she complains (253). The sheep's shop, the book's climactic image of noumenal reality, is in constant flux, never in shipshape order. No "thing" exists long enough in one shape to be named or identified; every thing is in a process of becoming, changing, and vanishing, even right through the ceiling. Alice's own identity becomes unstable: "Are you a child or a tee-totum?" demands the Sheep. Alice suddenly finds herself rowing through a sticky river, picking rushes, catching crabs; only to be back again in the shop buying an egg.

The egg is of course a person, Humpty Dumpty, who plays his own games with linguistic signs, forcing words to mean just what he chooses them to mean, neither more nor less (269). Humpty Dumpty is the *auteur*, a persona for Lewis Carroll himself, writing and translating Jabberwocky/nonsense. As an author and game-creator, Humpty Dumpty shows us one way to deal with a frightening chaos (and it is perhaps the only way that Carroll himself could imagine): to force signs to mean what you stipulate they mean, to impose a self-referential linguistic system upon a resisting chaos. And there's the rub: "The question is, which is to be master" (269), as Humpty Dumpty himself acknowledges. For Humpty Dumpty is clearly *not* the master of his game. His arrogance leads only to a fall from which all the King's men cannot rescue him. For Humpty Dumpty, like all signs, is trapped in the linguistic system that alone assigns him significance and power. His attempts to assert control over that system fail ("But 'glory' doesn't mean 'a nice knock-down argument,' " Alice objected; 269), for the *langue* is always more powerful than the *parole*. Moreover, his attempt to move from motivated to unmotivated signs only renders his own existence (as a completely motivated sign) arbitrary. Both linguistically, then, as a member of an established and self-enclosed system of signs (the nursery rhyme "Humpty Dumpty sat on a wall"), and ontologically, as a newly "arbitrarily motivated" signifier, Humpty Dumpty must cease to exist as a noumenal thing-in-itself; he must fall off his wall into chaos.[26]

The last character Alice meets, the White Knight, also attempts to impose order on chaos, to invent practical ways of coping with a disorderly reality. But his attempts (to stop his hair from falling out by making it grow up a stick; to invent a pudding made of blotting-paper, gunpowder, and sealing wax) are manifestly futile. Alice leaves him still tumbling off his horse; while the White Knight leaves her with a song that denies any hope for a moral meaning or coherent rational pattern in life. The Knight's song is a vicious parody of Wordsworth's "Resolution and Independence." It ironically undercuts Wordsworth's romantic moral code, which Carroll sees as an overly naive faith in man's ability to endure hardships and old age with courage and generosity in an ultimately benevolent nature. More important, Carroll's parody denies the very existence of an absolute moral order. The White Knight's song reduces the old leech-gatherer to a blathering fool and all moral or religious systems to absurdity. The narrator achieves not a self-affirming "apocalypse by imagination"[27] but merely a "design / To keep the Menai bridge from rust / By boiling it in wine" (313). And the old man becomes not a heroic figure of solitary dignity and humanistic courage but a "mumbling crow" with a mouth "full of dough" (313).

Immediately after Alice encounters this vision of moral codes as arbitrary and of noumenal reality as pure chaos, she wins the game and becomes queen; the pawn is now the most powerful piece on the chessboard. But Alice soon realizes that she still has no control over reality: the other queens arrange her dinner-party, the footman won't let her in to attend her own party, and most frightening of all, the mutton and pudding refuse to be eaten. Alice suddenly finds herself in the midst of a nightmarish world in which she is unaccountably rising into the air, the candles are growing up into the ceiling, and the bottles are becoming dinner-birds.

> At this moment she heard a hoarse laugh at her side, and turned to see what was the matter with the White Queen; but, instead of the Queen, there was the leg of mutton sitting in the chair. "Here I am!" cried a voice from the soup-tureen, and Alice turned again, just in time to see the Queen's broad good-natured face grinning at her for a moment over the edge of the tureen, before she disappeared into the soup. (335)

In this world of total confusion, of aggressive chaos ("Already several of the guests were lying down in the dishes, and the soup-ladle was walking up the table towards Alice's chair, and beckoning to her impatiently to get out of its way"; 336), words are no longer sufficient to establish order. Alice must act, and quickly. And, for Lewis Carroll, the only possible action left to Alice is an act of sudden, destructive violence. Alice pulls the cloth out from under the creature-dishes, throwing them in a crashing heap upon the floor, and then turns "fiercely" upon the Red Queen in order to shake this now-diminutive doll-like creature into a harmless kitten. Alice, the innocent child, has apparently become an uncivilized savage who reacts to the inherent chaos of reality with a primitive violence. Carroll here implies that if we refuse to play games, to submit to the logical and linguistic systems that our human reason and imagination construct, we shall turn into vicious, brutal panthers, wholly possessed by the murderous impulses of our primal passions—those very emotions that terrified the repressed bachelor don.

"Which Dreamed It?" Alice certainly hopes that her frightening vision is her own dream. Much better that this nightmare be her own, that the Red King be a creation of her own mind, than that she be a figment of *his* imagination. But Alice can get no confirmation: the kitten refuses to answer her, just as earlier Tweedledee and Tweedledum refused to believe she was "real" (238-239). And Carroll, too, refuses to answer; he ends the book with the open question, "Which do *you* think it was?" (344). In a noumenally chaotic world, all signs and systems, all answers are arbitrary; hence all questions must remain open.

The concluding poem, "A boat, beneath a sunny sky," restates Carroll's view that everything we call reality (the entire phenomenal world) is only a dream, a construct of the fictionalizing and rationalizing mind:

> Ever drifting down the stream—
> Lingering in the golden gleam—
> Life, what is it but a dream?   (345)

Carroll thus leaves us with his private horror: a vision of a world without order, reason, or meaning, a world that he can endure only if he can transform it into a game of which he is the sole master.

Psychologically, Carroll needed to invent games that he alone could win in order to control his changing environment. He wanted to master time itself and thus be able to prevent Alice (and his other little girl friends) from growing up and leaving him. He therefore tried to build his own future into *Through the Looking Glass*, to triumph over the destructions of time by becoming the White Knight. Alice's response to the

White Knight is Carroll's paradigm for his own impact upon his child-friends:

> Of all the strange things that Alice saw in her journey Through the Looking-Glass, this was the one that she always remembered most clearly. Years afterwards she could bring the whole scene back again, as if it had been only yesterday—the mild blue eyes and kindly smile of the Knight—the setting sun gleaming through his hair, and shining on his armour in a blaze of light that quite dazzled her—the horse quietly moving about, with the reins hanging loose on his neck, cropping the grass at her feet—and the black shadows of the forest behind—all this she took in like a picture, as, with one hand shading her eyes, she leant against a tree, watching the strange pair, and listening, in a half-dream, to the melancholy music of the song. (307)

Again, Carroll invokes a spatial image ("like a picture," like a photograph) in his desire to arrest time, to arrange the chaotic flux of becoming into a composition of which he is the central figure, a composition much admired and never forgotten by his child-love.

Carroll's personal attempt to control time extends beyond his own future to Alice's life as well. In the opening poem, "Child of the pure unclouded brow," he builds Alice's future into his dream. She will either die a virginal death or live to regret an unhappy marriage:

> Come, hearken then, ere voice of dread,
>   With bitter tidings laden,
> Shall summon to unwelcome bed,
>   A melancholy maiden!
> We are but older children, dear,
> Who fret to find our bedtime near.   (173)

The concluding metaphor (adults are children whose anxiety-provoking death is a "fretful" bedtime) encourages us to read Alice's own "unwelcome bed" on several levels. The "voice of dread" is literally the voice of Alice's nannie, summoning her away from the bedtime storytelling hour to sleep; but it is also the voice of death summoning a still virginal "melancholy maiden," as well as the voice of the dreaded lover / husband summoning his reluctant and still chaste bride.

Lewis Carroll's attempts to stop the flux of time and space by fixing them within a self-serving linguistic system failed on the personal level: his little girls always grew up and left him for fuller lives elsewhere. But his vivid vision of the chaos lying beneath our merely relative social and linguistic axioms—and of the anxiety and terror that such a romantic-ironic vision can invoke in a sexually repressed person and culture—

remains an enduring witness to that point, philosophically and historically, where romantic irony gives way to existentialism.

In the same decade in which Carroll wrote his *Alice* books, the first of
the great existentialist thinkers, Søren Kierkegaard, directly attacked the
affirmation of becoming and an abundant chaos that is inherent in romantic irony. Kierkegaard's influential studies of irony argued that the
romantic-ironic mode of consciousness is a condition of existential despair, from which man must turn with deliberate loathing and fear. As a
young man, in rebellion against his bourgeois father and conventionally
Christian society, Kierkegaard had himself experienced the exhilarating
freedom of romantic irony or what he called the "aesthetical life."[28] But
by the time he published his doctoral dissertation, *The Concept of Irony*,
in 1840, Kierkegaard had concluded that the psychology inherent in romantic irony could only produce an individual filled with anxiety, melancholy, boredom, and despair. In *Either/Or* (1843), Kierkegaard portrays the romantic ironist as A, the aesthete whose life is arbitrary and
thus without purpose or historical actuality. As A himself acknowledges,
he is a member of the Symparanekromenoi, the "fellowship of buried
lives" or the living dead.

Why did Kierkegaard equate romantic irony with anxiety and despair?
In *The Concept of Irony*, Kierkegaard distinguished between a positive
or "Socratic" irony and a negative or "romantic" irony. Socratic irony is,
in a phrase Kierkegaard borrowed from Hegel's *Aesthetics*, "infinite absolute negativity": "It is negativity because it only negates; it is infinite
because it negates not this or that phenomenon [but all phenomena *qua*
phenomena]; and it is absolute because it negates by virtue of a higher
which is not . . . It is a divine madness which rages like Tamerlane and
leaves not one stone standing in its wake."[29] As the historical embodiment of this idea of "infinite absolute negativity," Socrates systematically
denied the absolute truth of every object or concept that his contemporaries believed to exist, including the value of life itself. And he did so
without recourse to a "higher" divine being or absolute law. He spoke
only in the name of a "truth" which knows only that nothing can be
known, that the phenomenon or external is never the essence or internal.
Socrates' ironic questioning functioned positively, Kierkegaard argued,
in freeing the mind from overly limited or false conceptions of the self or
society and thus opening the way for new thought and action. But Socrates himself did not create anything new, unlike Plato whose mytholo-
gizing advanced the human conception of the divine Idea. Hence Kierkegaard concluded that Socrates, as the purely ironic subject, had become

estranged from existence and lacked "historical actuality" (276). From Kierkegaard's religious viewpoint, the self can be realized and enjoy a positive freedom only through a lived commitment to the phenomena of a particular time and place. Irony's pure freedom is therefore finally self-destructive: as Kierkegaard insisted, "Irony is free, to be sure, free from all the cares of actuality, but free from its joys as well, free from its blessings. For if it has nothing higher than itself, it may receive no blessings, for it is ever the lesser that is blessed of a greater" (296). And because the ironic self can never become engaged in a concrete historical context, it can never act morally.

At this point, Kierkegaard shifted his attention to negative or romantic irony. The artistic ironist or aesthete who always lives at a distance from his own feelings and actions is completely destructive, both of his own selfhood and of his society. "Because the ironist poetically produces himself as well as his environment with the greatest possible poetic license, because he lives completely hypothetically and subjunctively, his life finally loses all continuity. With this he wholly lapses under the sway of his moods and feelings. His life is sheer emotion" (301). And because this emotion is the pawn of external events, it is arbitrary and contradictory, wholly without permanence or meaning. Hence, Kierkegaard concluded, feeling itself finally has no "reality" for the aesthete, and "Boredom is the only continuity the ironist has" (302). As opposed to the Christian whose feelings grow out of and support an ongoing sense of identity and purpose, the romantic ironist can only undermine his own and others' possible spiritual development. When Kierkegaard commented on Friedrich Schlegel's *Lucinde*, he virulently denounced it as "a very obscene book" (313), an "irreligious" book (312) in which "the flesh negates the spirit" (315) and the ego that has discovered its own freedom and constitutive authority finally arrives not "at a still higher aspect of mind but instead at sensuality, and consequently at its opposite" (316).

Kierkegaard concluded his attack on romantic irony by insisting that such irony must be mastered. The religious life must include irony, for irony "limits, renders finite, defines, and thereby yields truth, actuality, and content; it chastens and punishes and thereby imparts stability, character and consistency" (339). But irony must not be permitted to negate *all* moments: "on the contrary, the content of life must become a true and meaningful moment in the higher actuality whose fullness the soul desires" (341). Thus becoming must finally yield to being: "true actuality becomes what it is, whereas the actuality of romanticism merely becomes" (332). Similarly, "faith becomes what it is; it is not an eternal struggle but a victory which struggles still. In faith the higher actuality of spirit is not merely becoming [*vordende*], but present while yet becoming [*vorder*]" (332).

Kierkegaard's critical portrait of the romantic ironist as the aesthete A in *Either/Or* became the literary prototype of existentialist man living in an absurd universe. Since A denies all necessary connections among past, present, and future, he lives wholly for the immediate moment. He rejects all commitments, all social engagements such as marriage, friendship, work. He is free to do as he likes, but since he ironically reflects upon his desire even as he experiences it, he can never lose himself in pleasure. His present life is "empty," "*idem per idem*," and only the forever-lost past of his youth seems desirable. Hence he is melancholic and bored. As A asserts in one of his Diapsalmata or Schlegelian fragments, "I do not care for anything. I do not care to ride, for the exercise is too violent. I do not care to walk, walking is too strenuous. I do not care to lie down, for I should either have to remain lying, and I do not care to do that, or I should have to get up again, and I do not care to do that either. *Summa summarum:* I do not care at all."[30] And because all action in a chaotic, arbitrary world is meaningless, one can only "regret" everything that one does. A's "ecstatic lecture" can equate intense passion only with regret: "If you marry, you will regret it; if you do not marry, you will also regret it; if you marry or do not marry, you will regret both; whether you marry or do not marry, you will regret both."[31] Nameless (because he possesses no individuality), his papers discovered and arranged "by chance," the victim of contradictory moods, A is the seducer who can never be satisfied with a merely actual object, who must constantly "change fields" according to his Rotation Method, who in his melancholy defines himself as The Unhappiest Man. From the viewpoints of the ethical man (B or Judge William) or the religious man (the Priest of Jutland whose "Edification" concludes *Either/Or*), A can know only boredom and dread. Kierkegaard, through B and the Priest, here rejects the privileging of freedom over belief that is inherent in romantic irony. Instead these spokesmen argue that in a chaotic world, in order to escape despair, one must *choose*. One must totally commit oneself, without irony, to a man-made structure or system—to lasting relationships (such as marriage), contractual obligations, a stable personal identity. But this sense of self, as we are told by the Priest, who corrects B's overly sentimental conception of marriage as completely fulfilling, must be founded on a conviction of spiritual inadequacy: "as against God we are always in the wrong." For Kierkegaard, the self-restraint of romantic irony must become a specifically religious dread, a deep sense of guilt and personal inadequacy. This is the redemptive fear and trembling before God that Kierkegaard described in his later theological, "upbuilding" treatises.[32] Such a religious experience is the result of an emotional commitment to faith in an arbitrary, absurd universe; and only such a leap of faith can give value to human existence.

While not all existentialist philosophers would endorse Kierkegaard's demand that the self make a "leap of faith" into a Christian being, they do agree that the self must, through the passing of time and the ongoing experience of its own phenomenological existence, move toward an ever fuller realization of its own being (what Heidegger called *Dasein*, what Jaspers called *Existenz*, what Sartre called *l'être pour soi*). Unlike Friedrich Schlegel, who celebrated an always changing, always becoming self, these thinkers argue that an authentic self, an "essence," comes into *being* as a result of willed choices and commitments in a chaotic, absurd world: "Existence precedes essence." The romantic-ironic self that "hovers" midway between self-creation and self-destruction comes to seem to these existentialist thinkers to be a self without reality. Its ontological lack of being, they argue, is psychologically experienced as free-floating anxiety or even, as Sartre and Heidegger suggest, as overwhelming nausea or intense deprivation.[33] Thus the existentialists, like the philosophers who preceded Schlegel, ultimately value being over becoming, even though they place far greater emphasis on the process by which the self gains its being.

By the end of the nineteenth century, then, Schlegel's concept of a self always becoming and always free, hovering exultantly over a chaotically abundant *Fülle*, had given way to a self obsessed with its lack of permanence and continuity, a self that experiences such pure freedom as anxiety, dread, or despair. At the risk of oversimplification, we might say that existentialism is the negative view of romantic irony. Existentialism and romantic irony share an ontological vision of the universe as chaotic and incomprehensible. But whereas the romantic ironist embraces this becoming as a merrily multiplying life-process, the existentialist sees it as absurd or benignly indifferent, without inherent meaning for man. In the face of such chaos, the romantic ironist enthusiastically creates and decreates himself and his myths. But the existentialist engages in this same process with anxiety and even fear. Disturbed by the relativity of his self and his systems, he struggles for some sort of permanence or authentic existence in an arbitrary world, either through an irrational leap of faith or through sustained personal and political commitments. For the existentialists, such heuristic behavior is usually accompanied by *angst* (since man can choose not to complete his projects as easily as he can choose to complete them). Thus romantic irony and existentialism confront the same incomprehensible universe, but with very different emotional responses: the romantic ironist delights in its creative possibilities, while the existentialist anxiously seeks to establish at least one still point in the turning world, namely his own identity or essence.

7

A Conclusion in Which
Nothing Is Concluded

In 1885 Friedrich Nietzsche wrote a fragment that might well serve as epigraph to this study of romantic irony. Later made the conclusion to *The Will to Power* by Nietzsche's editors, this fragment powerfully endorses Schlegel's concept of a dynamic universe and always-becoming self:

> And do you know what "the world" is to me? Shall I show it to you in my mirror? This world: a monster of energy, without beginning, without end; . . . a sea of forces flowing and rushing together, eternally changing, eternally flooding back, with tremendous years of recurrence, with an ebb and a flood of its forms; out of the simplest forms striving toward the most complex, out of the stillest, most rigid, coldest forms toward the hottest, most turbulent, most self-contradictory, and then again returning home to the simple out of this abundance, out of the play of contradictions back to the joy of concord, still affirming itself in this uniformity of its courses and its years, blessing itself as that which must return eternally, as a becoming that knows no satiety, no disgust, no weariness: this, my *Dionysian* world of the eternally self-creating, the eternally self-destroying, this mystery world of the twofold voluptuous delight, my "beyond good and evil," without goal, unless the joy of the circle is itself a goal; without will, unless a ring feels good will toward itself —do you want a *name* for this world? A *solution* for all its riddles? A *light* for you, too, you best-concealed, strongest, most intrepid, most midnightly men?—*This world is the will to power—and nothing besides!* And you yourselves are also this will to power—and nothing besides![1]

A book about romantic irony, about the arbitrariness of the universe and the open-endedness of human experience, should have no ending. And I hope that the paradigm of becoming that I have been tracing as both an ontological principle and a literary structure will illuminate many more works and lives than I have been able to discuss.

As a mode of consciousness that finds a corresponding literary mode, romantic irony may constitute the climax of a writer's career; so it was with Byron. Or romantic irony may be only a moment, a phase, in a given artist's work, as with Carlyle. And indeed, few writers have been able to sustain the incredibly difficult balancing between two opposed and unreconciled ideas for a protracted period of time. Most, like Schlegel himself who converted to Roman Catholicism in his later years, have sought refuge in the calmer certainties of an ordered universe. But their retreat from irony in no way invalidates an ontology of becoming or a figural discourse based on the alternation of symbol and metaphor. Both symbolism and allegory, both the rage for order and the rage for freedom, are equally authentic modes of human experience and expression.

Of course, romantic irony itself has more than one mode. The style of romantic irony varies from writer to writer. Byron's divided self (structurally embodied in *Don Juan* in the separate characters of Juan and the narrator) shifts rapidly back and forth between a romantic fantasy of idyllic love and a skeptical melancholy, in an exuberant *mobilité* that acknowledges all the complexities of a constantly changing world. Keats's empathic Greeting of the Spirit enters more directly into the liminal processualism of life. His odes, his love poems, and *The Fall of Hyperion* embrace and record the rhythms of process, both as mental debates and as psychological shifts. Carlyle's irony is directed not at the transcendental goal of life (a total apprehension of the "Divine Idea of the World") but at the limitations of human language and consciousness. Since Carlyle's conception of process is teleological (his self-consuming artifact, by advocating an increasingly dense symbolic language, at least moves closer to a revelation of the absolute Idea), his romantic irony is stylistically less flexible. He questions less than Byron or Keats, and as a result his style is both more ponderous and more sublime (in the sense of the Wordsworthian egotistical sublime or what Thomas Weiskel has called the "positive sublime").[2] And both Coleridge and Carroll approach the vision of a chaotic universe with fear and trembling; hence their romantic irony is hedged round with theological or rhetorical defenses. But however distinctive the voice, a writer is a romantic ironist if and when his or her work commits itself enthusiastically both in content and form to a hovering or unresolved debate between a world of merely man-made being and a world of ontological becoming.

Historically, however, romantic irony was born from the upheavals of the French and Industrial Revolutions, flourished during the early nineteenth century, and was seriously weakened by the violence of World

War I. By 1918, the fear of sudden change that had overwhelmed the timid Lewis Carroll had become a widely shared cultural paranoia. To many people, change meant only destruction. And the absence of onto-logical order meant that the universe was absurd, a conclusion that led many people to a paralysing *angst*. Virginia Woolf lyrically describes the passing of time in the central section of *To the Lighthouse* as a tragic litany of loss. The Victorian assumptions of progress through economic and cultural imperialism were undermined by the Great War and the havoc it wreaked.[3] After such devastation, the romantic ironist's enthusi-astic celebration of process and change seemed callow or philosophically absurd. Writers began to view constant change either as meaningless chaos or as the cyclical recurrence of the disintegration of civilization: "Many ingenious lovely things are gone," lamented Yeats in "Nineteen Hundred and Nineteen." To a universe conceived as having no absolute order or significance, twentieth-century writers have responded with anxiety, anger, terror, despair, or stoical acceptance. Wallace Stevens urged a "violence from within" to confront such "violence from with-out." But the legacy of the Great War, the inescapable knowledge of "in-nocence savaged and destroyed" by the "lunacy of voluntary torment,"[4] sabotaged the romantic ironist's sense of exuberant freedom in an infi-nitely various and infinitely possible world. Instead, in our modern wasteland, Samuel Beckett's characters wait aimlessly in a world where changes occur but have no meaning; Harold Pinter's role-reversals con-demn their participants to a vicious circle of betrayal and cruelty; and revolution, as portrayed in Peter Weiss's *Marat/Sade*, liberates only lunatic violence. Contemporary writers frequently depict a universe in which every object, every relationship, slowly deteriorates (as in John Barth's *End of the Road* or Margaret Drabble's *The Ice Age*); where every character is paranoid or helplessly trapped in absurd conspiracies (as in Thomas Pynchon's *The Crying of Lot 49* or *Gravity's Rainbow*). The dominant modern attitude to change is tersely embodied in Joan Didion's *Play It As It Lays*, in which the protagonist Maria Wyeth repetitiously, compulsively drives the Los Angeles freeways to nowhere, to "nothing."

In the face of such modern despair, of such conviction that the prison-houses of language, of social roles, or psychological and economic deter-minism cannot be broken down, perhaps it is naive to think that we can still profitably learn something from the romantic ironists. Yet an acknowledgment of human limitations *together with* an affirmation of our creative capacities seems more humanly enriching than the lucid madness of pure irony or the alienation of existential *angst* or a reality-denying leap of faith into a comforting myth. Think of the pleasure we derive from the convoluted fictions and ironic love stories of Nabokov or from the word games of Joyce. Genuinely a romantic ironist, Joyce continued to portray the ongoing creative process both skeptically, in the forgings of Stephen Daedalus and Shem the pen man, and enthusiastically, in the all-accepting "yes" of Molly Bloom and the "riverrun" of Anna Livia Plurabelle. Perhaps what we treasure most in our lives is the very *play* between order and chaos—our ability to move in mind and body between a chosen identity and other possible selves, between an imposed socioeconomic role and other possible behaviors. D. W. Winnicott has recently argued that our psychic health depends upon our capacity both as infants and as adults to engage in such play or "illusory experience." Defining play as a dynamic and flexible interaction between the self's inner reality and external life, Winnicott suggests that such play is first enacted in the baby's use of "transitional objects" (a teddy bear, Linus's blanket) and later broadens to include the adult's entire "creative apperception" or capacity to participate, through art or religion or other forms of fantasy, in what Victor Turner has called liminality.[5]

Romantic irony demands just such exuberant playing with the possibilities of an ever-changing world and life, such expanding participation in a variety of selves and modes of consciousness, such openness to new ideas and experiences. In so doing, it embraces a mental habit of tolerance and a discourse of ambiguity. Romantic irony is thus opposed to the "gross dichotomizing" or rigid thinking in polarities that has become the prevailing imaginative structure of modern times.[6] Romantic irony, therefore, can potentially free individuals and even entire cultures from totalitarian modes of thought and behavior.

A genuine participation in romantic irony, then, could bring us pleasure, psychic health, and intellectual freedom. And perhaps its transcendental buffoonery does mimic a chaotically becoming universe and hence has ontological truth. Or if not, perhaps its reward is simply its own exhilarating experience of mental agility or play. Imagine yourself delicately balancing between the given and the possible, enthusiastically creating while skeptically recognizing the limits of everything you create, profoundly involved in a process of self-creation and self-destruction, always moving, never stagnating, always learning. The experience is disorienting, of course, but as Job discovered in the most ironic book of the Bible,[7] the price of wisdom is all that a man hath. Let us listen to Yeats, who toward the very end of his life sounded this authentic note of romantic irony. Yeats's final volume, *New Poems* (1939), includes these self-delighting, self-denying, self-inspiring lines (the last refrain of "What Then?" is sung by Plato's ghost):

> "The work is done," grown old he thought,
> "According to my boyish plan;
> Let the fools rage, I swerved in naught,
> Something to perfection brought";
> *But louder sang that ghost, "What then?"*

Notes

1. The Paradigm of Romantic Irony

1. For useful studies of the political and social changes in England between 1789 and 1815, see Asa Briggs, *The Age of Improvement* (London: Whitefriars, 1959); J. S. Watson, *The Reign of George III* (Oxford: Clarendon Press, 1960), esp. chap. 20; E. J. Hobsbawm, *The Age of Revolution: Europe, 1789-1848* (New York: Praeger, 1962); E. P. Thompson, *The Making of the English Working Class* (London: Victor Gollancz, 1963); and Howard Mumford Jones, *Revolution and Romanticism* (Cambridge, Mass.: Harvard University Press, 1974).

2. Letters to Anabella Milbanke, 6 and 26 September 1813, *Byron's Letters and Journals*, ed. Leslie A. Marchand, III (Cambridge, Mass.: Harvard University Press, 1974), 109, 119.

3. Paul de Man, "The Rhetoric of Temporality," in *Interpretation: Theory and Practice*, ed. Charles S. Singleton (Baltimore: Johns Hopkins Press, 1969), p. 194.

4. Meyer Abrams, *Natural Supernaturalism: Tradition and Revolution in Romantic Literature* (New York: W. W. Norton, 1971).

5. Arnold Van Gennep's pioneering study, *Les rites de passage* (1908), available in English as *The Rites of Passage*, trans. M. Vizedom and G. Caffee (Chicago: University of Chicago Press, 1960), divided rites of passage into three dynamic stages: rites of separation or preliminal rites, transition rites or liminal (threshold) rites, and rites of incorporation or postliminal rites. Victor Turner, in *The Ritual Process: Structure and Anti-Structure* (Chicago: Aldine, 1969), in *Dramas, Fields and Metaphors: Symbolic Action in Human Society* (Ithaca and London: Cornell University Press, 1974), and again in "Variations on a Theme of Liminality," in *Secular Ritual*, ed. Sally F. Moore and Barbara G. Meyerhof (Amsterdam: Van Gorcum, 1977), pp. 36-52, focuses primarily on the social and personal significance of the liminal process, a time between structures when "all previous standards and models are subjected to criticism, and fresh new ways of describing and interpreting sociocultural experience are formulated" (*Dramas*, p. 15). He goes on to identify the liminal experience with "communitas, a spontaneously generated relationship between levelled and equal total and individuated human beings, stripped of structural attributes . . . Communitas . . . is the *fons et origo* of all structures and, at the same time, their critique. For its very existence puts all social structural rules in question and suggests new possibilities. Communitas strains toward universalism and openness" (*Dramas*, p. 202).

6. Friedrich Schlegel, "On Incomprehensibility," trans. Peter Firchow, in *Friedrich Schlegel's Lucinde and the Fragments* (Minneapolis: University of Minnesota Press, 1971), p. 268. The German texts of all of Friedrich Schlegel's works discussed here can be found in *Kritische-Friedrich-Schlegel-Ausgabe*, 22 vols. (Paderborn and Munich: Ferdinand Schöningh, 1958-   ); cited hereafter as KA. The essay "On Incomprehensibility" is in II, ed. Hans Eichner (1967), 126-146.

7. Friedrich Schlegel, *Dialogue on Poetry and Literary Aphorisms*, trans. Ernst Behler and Roman Struc (University Park: Pennsylvania State University Press, 1968), pp. 53-54; cited hereafter as DP.

8. Friedrich Schlegel, "On the Limits of the Beautiful," trans. E. H. Millington, in *The Aesthetic and Miscellaneous Works of Friedrich von Schlegel* (London, 1849), pp. 413n, 418.

9. Friedrich Schlegel, *Transcendental-philosophie (1800-1801)*, in *Friedrich Schlegel: Neue philosophische Schriften*, ed. Josef Körner (Frankfurt: G. Schulte-Bulmke, 1935), pp. 124, 125.

10. Friedrich Schlegel, *Philosophische Lehrjahre*, in KA, XVIII, 283, #1048. Cf. Leonard P. Wessell, Jr., "The Antinomic Structure of Friedrich Schlegel's 'Romanticism,' " *Studies in Romanticism* 12 (1973): 656-663.

11. Friedrich Schlegel, *Critical Fragments* from *The Athenaeum* (1798-1800), in *Lucinde and the Fragments*, no. 51, p. 167; hereafter cited in the text as A with number of fragment.

12. Friedrich Schlegel, *Critical Fragments* from *The Lycaeum*, in *Lucinde and the Fragments*, no. 34, p. 146; hereafter cited in the text as L with number of fragment.

13. Cf. Walter Jackson Bate, *From Classic to Romantic* (1946) (New York: Harper, 1961), chaps. 1, 2.

14. Samuel Taylor Coleridge, *Biographia Literaria*, ed. J. Shawcross (London: Oxford University Press, 1907), I, 202.

15. Friedrich Schlegel, *Literary Notebooks 1797-1801*, ed. Hans Eichner (London: Athlone Press, 1957), no. 1029; cited hereafter as LN.

16. Translated by Raymond Immerwahr in his *Tieck's Fantastic Comedy* (St. Louis: Washington University Studies, 1953), p. 22.

17. "On Incomprehensibility," p. 268.

18. Thomas Carlyle, *Sartor Resartus* (London: J. M. Dent, 1959), p. 140. Cf. Ingrid Strohschneider-Kohrs, *Die Romantische Ironie in Theorie und Gestaltung* (Tübingen: Max Niemeyer, 1960), p. 65, and Lieselotte Dieckmann, "Friedrich Schlegel and Romantic Concepts of the Symbol," *The Germanic Review* 34 (1959): 76-83.

19. "On Incomprehensibility," p. 266.

20. Schlegel defines urbanity as the "wit of harmonious universality, and that is the beginning and the end of historical philosophy and Plato's most sublime music. The humanities are the gymnastics of this art and science" (A, 438).

21. Schlegel, "Über Goethes Meister" (1798) in KA, II, 128-146; trans. in Wessell, "The Antinomic Structure of Schlegel's 'Romanticism,' " p. 664. Cf. Raymond Immerwahr, "Friedrich Schlegel's Essay *On Goethe's Meister*," *Monatschefte* 49 (1957): 1-22.

22. Friedrich Schlegel, *Ideas* (1799-1800), in *Lucinde and the Fragments*, no. 69, p. 247; cited hereafter as *Ideas*.

23. For a famous denunciation of romantic irony, see Irving Babbitt's *Rousseau and Romanticism* (Boston: Houghton Mifflin, 1919), chap. 7.

24. Allardyce Nicoll points out, in *The World of Harlequin—a Critical Study of the Commedia dell'Arte* (Cambridge: The University Press, 1963), p. 217, that the German Romantics who referred affectionately to the commedia dell'arte (including Tieck, Brentano, Grillparzer, and Schiller, among others) almost certainly had Carlo Gozzi's fantastic comedies in mind. Other well-known buffo figures occur in opera (e.g., Leporello in Mozart's *Don Giovanni*) and in the novel (e.g., Sancho Panza in Cervantes's *Don Quixote* and Tristram Shandy in Sterne's *Tristram Shandy*).

25. Schlegel, *Philosophische Lehrjahre*, in KA, XVIII, 85, #668.

26. Strohschneider-Kohrs, *Die Romantische Ironie*, p. 20; Immerwahr, *Tieck's Fantastic Comedy*, pp. 1-45; D. C. Muecke, *The Compass of Irony* (London: Methuen, 1969), p. 164; Ernst Behler, *Klassiche Ironie—Romantische Ironie —Tragische Ironie* (Darmstadt: Wissenschaftliche Buchgesellschaft, 1972); idem, "Techniques of Irony in Light of the Romantic Tradition," *Rice University Studies* 57 (Fall 1971): 1-17. Thomas Rosenmeyer has illuminatingly applied Schlegel's concept of romantic irony or parabasis to Greek tragedy in "Irony and Tragic Choruses," in *Ancient and Modern: Essays in Honor of Gerald F. Else*, ed. John H. D'Arms and J. W. Eadie (Ann Arbor: University of Michigan Press, 1977), pp. 31-44.

27. See Immerwahr, *Tieck's Fantastic Comedy*, pp. 7-21.

28. "On Incomprehensibility," pp. 260, 268-269.

29. D. C. Muecke first used this analogy, *The Compass of Irony*, p. 198.

30. Johann Wolfgang von Goethe, *Von Arabesken*, in *Goethes Sämtliche Werke*, Jubiläums-Ausgabe (Stuttgart and Berlin: J. G. Cotta, 1902-07), XXX, 49-54.

31. Karl Konrad Polheim, *Die Arabeske: Ansichten und Ideen aus Friedrich Schlegels Poetik* (Munich: Ferdinand Schóningh, 1966), chap. 6.

32. Raphael and his contemporaries were attracted by the similarity of these Roman designs to Islamic art; hence the use of the term "arabesque." Schlegel's contemporaries also included Arabic designs in their concept of the arabesque (cf. Polheim, *Die Arabesque*, pp. 17, 21). It is therefore possible that Schlegel may have been aware of what Oleg Grabar, in *The Formation of Islamic Art* (New Haven: Yale University Press, 1973), chap. 7, has recently called "the idea of the arabesque" in early Islamic art. The characteristics of early Islamic decoration or the arabesque are as follows:

1. A *horror vacui*; every object or wall is totally covered with decoration. More precisely, "the relationship found in classical Roman ornament between a background on or against which ornament stands out has been replaced either by a contrast between light and shade . . . or by an impossibility of distinguishing between the two" (198).

2. The ornament is best defined as a relationship among forms rather than as a sum of forms.

3. The ornament is placed in "a symmetry around a variable number of

axes, which serve as the centers around which a motif develops, often almost mirror-reversed. But most of the axes are not finite, physical entities" but rather a "form of the visual imagination for they do not exist by themselves but because of the rest of the design" (199).

4. Since neither the symmetry nor the overall pattern contains within itself a logical end to the design, this ornament exhibits "the possibility of infinite growth"; only "the will of the decorator defines the limits of the design" (199).

5. "A theme from any origin could be and was incorporated in ornament" (200).

6. "Arbitrariness," which in Muslim art has two aspects. First, it is "carried down to the level of the design's composition," and second, it tends "to separate a monument's or object's surface from its shape," so that its surface ornamentation is like a skin that can be removed and changed at will (201). Since the artist made both the object and the decoration, one therefore has to assume "on the part of the artist a sort of double and partly contradictory vision of the finished monument" (201).

In emphasizing the arbitrary and paradoxical nature of arabesque ornament, as well as its movement toward infinity, Grabar has given us a visual analogue for the romantic work of art as Schlegel conceived it. And the relationship between figure and ground, in which neither takes precedence over the other, is an exact analogue for Schlegel's concept of hovering or artistic self-restraint as a balanced (symmetrical) movement between chaos and order.

33. Goethe, *Von Arabesken*, p. 54.

34. Cf. Hans Eichner, *Friedrich Schlegel* (New York: Twayne, 1970), pp. 44-60.

35. Raymond Immerwahr, "Romantic Irony and Romantic Arabesque Prior to Romanticism," *The German Quarterly* 42 (1969): 666-668.

36. F. R. Leavis, *The Great Tradition* (London: Chatto and Windus, 1948), p. 2n and passim.

37. Northrop Frye, *Anatomy of Criticism* (Princeton: Princeton University Press, 1957), pp. 308-312.

38. Peter Firchow, introduction to *Lucinde and the Fragments*, p. 39.

39. Schlegel, *Lucinde*, trans. Firchow, p. 133.

40. Behler, introduction to Schlegel, *Dialogue on Poetry*, p. 12.

41. Cyrus Hamlin, "The Temporality of Selfhood: Metaphor and Romantic Poetry," *New Literary History* 6 (1974): 181; this essay derives from de Man's "The Rhetoric of Temporality," pp. 173-209.

42. For a critique of de Man's reading of Schlegel's concept of romantic irony, see my "On Romantic Irony, Symbolism and Allegory," *Criticism* 21 (Summer 1979): 217-229.

43. This is Coleridge's definition of the symbol, from *The Complete Works of Samuel Taylor Coleridge*, ed. W. G. T. Shedd (New York: Harper, 1871), I, 437-438.

44. Wayne Booth, *A Rhetoric of Irony* (Chicago and London: University of Chicago Press, 1974), p. 259. Morton Gurewitch dismisses Schlegelian irony as spiritually less relevant than Kierkegaardian irony in *European Romantic Irony* (Ann Arbor: University Microfilms, 1957); and Charles I. Glicksberg, in *The Ironic Vision in Modern Literature* (The Hague: Martinus Nijhoff, 1969), chap. 1,

sees romantic irony, with its emphasis on the conflict between the ego's desire for total freedom and the limitations of human finitude, as leading to a modern nihilistic vision of an absurd world accompanied by either cynical laughter or the courageous defiance of despair.

45. Muecke, *The Compass of Irony*, pp. 211, 214-215.

46. Friedrich Schiller, *On the Aesthetic Education of Man in a Series of Letters*, trans. with commentary by Elizabeth M. Wilkinson and L. A. Willoughby (Oxford: Clarendon Press, 1967), p. 80; cited hereafter as AE.

47. I am here using the term "mode" to suggest the interaction of ethos and literary technique. As Paul Alpers has usefully formulated it, "mode is the literary manifestation of the writer's and the ideal reader's assumptions about the world." "Mode in Narrative Poetry," paper delivered at University College, London, 26 April 1973.

48. Wolfgang Köhler, *Gestalt Psychology* (New York: Liveright, 1947), pp. 60-61, 165.

49. For useful summaries of Kant's thought, see Kant's *Prolegomena to Any Future Metaphysics*, trans. Lewis White Beck (New York: Liberal Arts Press, 1950), and Stephen Körner, *Kant* (Harmondsworth: Penguin, 1955).

50. *Friedrich Schlegels philosophische Vorlesungen aus den Jahren 1804 bis 1806*, ed. C. J. H. Windischmann (Bonn, 1836, 1837), II, 19.

51. See Heinrich Heine, "A Revolution in Germany?" trans. Frederic Ewen, in *The Poetry and Prose of Heinrich Heine* (New York: The Citadel Press, 1948), pp. 754-758.

52. For Schiller's influence on Schlegel, see Leonard P. Wessell, Jr., "Schiller and the Genesis of German Romanticism," *Studies in Romanticism* 10 (1971): 176-198.

53. Friedrich von Schiller, *Naive and Sentimental Poetry*, trans. Julius A. Elias (New York: Frederick Ungar, 1966), p. 106; cited hereafter in the text as NSP.

54. Schiller's conception of play as the realization of the individual's highest potential and the basis of human civilization has been more thoroughly developed by Johan Huizinga in *Homo Ludens* (Haarlem: H. D. Tjeenk Willinck, 1938).

55. Friedrich von Schiller, *On the Sublime*, trans. Julius A. Elias (New York: Frederick Ungar, 1966), p. 194; cited hereafter as OS.

56. For the origins of English romantic irony in eighteenth-century Deist critiques of the Bible, see Elinor Shaffer's *"Kubla Khan" and the Fall of Jerusalem: The Mythological School in Biblical Criticism and Secular Literature, 1770-1880* (Cambridge, England: Cambridge University Press, 1975) and her forthcoming essay on the native sources of English romantic irony, in *Romantic Irony*, ed. Frederick C. Garber, to be published under the auspices of the International Comparative Literature Association.

2. Byron: "Half Dust, Half Deity"

1. Jerome J. McGann shrewdly makes this point in *Fiery Dust: Byron's Poetic Development* (Chicago: University of Chicago Press, 1968), pp. 26-27, 286-289.

2. Letter to Lady Melbourne, 1 July 1813, *Byron's Letters and Journals*, ed.

Leslie A. Marchand (Cambridge, Mass.: Harvard University Press, 1973-   ), III (1974), 70.

3. McGann, *Fiery Dust*, p. 49. I have been influenced throughout my discussion of *Childe Harold's Pilgrimage* by McGann's penetrating and thoughtful study.

4. Victor Turner, *Dramas, Fields, and Metaphors: Symbolic Action in Human Society* (Ithaca and London: Cornell University Press, 1974), chap. 5.

5. Letter to Mrs. Catherine Gordon Byron, 2 November 1808, *Letters and Journals*, I, 173.

6. Letters to Annabella Milbanke, 6 and 26 September 1813, *Letters and Journals*, III, 109, 119.

7. As Carl Woodring points out in "Nature, Art, Reason, and Imagination in *Childe Harold*," in *Romantic and Victorian*, ed. W. Paul Elledge and Richard L. Hoffman (Rutherford, N.J.: Fairleigh Dickinson University Press, 1971), p. 150, Byron celebrates the Venus de Medici because it "shows what mind can do," yet at the same time Byron distrusts any art "that has no anchor in fact."

8. McGann, *Fiery Dust*, pp. 43-45.

9. Byron wrote to Thomas Moore on 2 January 1814, "I must admit Childe Harold to be a very repulsive personage." *Letters and Journals*, IV (1975), 14.

10. Byron described *Manfred* as a "dramatic poem" and later asserted that his object in writing drama was to create not a stageable production but a *"mental* theatre." Letters to John Murray, 28 February 1817, and 23 August 1821, *Letters and Journals*, V (1976), 178; VIII (1978), 185. While Byron did hope that his plays would be successfully performed, he intended their impact to be intellectual or "poetic." He hoped to arouse his audience to a higher state of self-consciousness and a more subtle comprehension of the workings of the universe. Cf. McGann, *Fiery Dust*, p. 227, and David Erdman, "Byron's Stage Fright," *ELH* 6 (1939): 219-243.

11. In the Alpine Journal he kept for Augusta Leigh, Byron described his own "wretched identity" while composing Manfred: "I am a lover of Nature— and an Admirer of Beauty—I can bear fatigue—& welcome privation—and have seen some of the noblest views in the world.—But in all this—the recollection of bitterness—& more especially of recent & more home desolation—which must accompany me through life—have preyed upon me here—and neither the music of the Shepherd—the crashing of the Avalanche—nor the torrent—the mountain —the Glacier—the Forest—nor the Cloud—have for one moment—lightened the weight upon my heart—nor enabled me to lose my own wretched identity in the majesty & the power and the Glory—around—above—& beneath me." 28 September 1816, *Letters and Journals*, V, 104-105.

12. Stuart M. Sperry, "Byron and the Meaning of 'Manfred,' " *Criticism* 16 (1974): 189-202.

13. Letter to John Murray, 15 February 1817, *Letters and Journals*, V, 170.

14. Leslie Marchand, Introduction to *Byron's Letters and Journals*, I, 1. Byron himself told Thomas Moore as much on 5 July 1821: "I can never get people to understand that poetry is the expression of *excited passion*, and that there is no such thing as a life of passion any more than a continuous earthquake, or an eternal fever. Besides, who would ever *shave* themselves in such a state?" (*Letters and Journals*, VIII, 146).

15. Letter to Hobhouse and Kinnaird, 19 January 1819, *Letters and Journals*, VI (1976), 90.

16. Byron himself stressed Cain's "dissatisfaction" with his lot, his "rage and fury against the inadequacy of his state to his Conceptions" in his comments on the poem. See his letters to Moore, 19 September 1821, and to Murray, 3 November 1821, *Letters and Journals*, VIII, 216; IX (1979), 54.

17. In Thomas Medwin's not necessarily reliable account of Byron's projected ending for *Heaven and Earth*, Byron proffers a more pessimistic and ironic vision of the lovers' fate: as the floodwaters rise, the lovers are denied admission to various planets and finally are forced to alight on the only peak of earth uncovered by water. Here the angels are suddenly summoned away to punishment, leaving Anah and Aholibamah alone. As the waters rise, the Ark appears, with Japhet begging his father to save the two women. Noah refuses; Aholibamah defiantly hurls herself into the waters; and Anah is at last swept from the rock and drowned, leaving Japhet in despair. But Byron then continues, swinging back to the romantic enthusiasm that generated the poem, "I once thought of conveying the lovers to the moon, or one of the planets; but it is not easy for the imagination to make any unknown world more beautiful than this . . . There was another objection: all the human interest would have been destroyed, which I have endeavored to give my Angels." *Medwin's Conversations of Lord Byron*, ed. E. J. Lovell (Princeton: Princeton University Press, 1966), pp. 157-158. By leaving the poem "unfinished," if he did, Byron sustained the romantic-ironic possibility of ever-renewing love in an ever-dying world.

18. McGann, *Fiery Dust*, pp. 201-202.

19. Letter to Teresa Guiccioli, 1 October 1820, *Letters and Journals*, VII (1977), 189.

20. Alvin Kernan, in *The Plot of Satire* (New Haven: Yale University Press, 1965), p. 174, calls attention to the plenitude of the places, persons, and events in *Don Juan* as a satiric attack on dullness and concludes, "This crammed, various creation renders the Romantic view of a world too large in all directions and too complex in its workings to be captured and arranged in any neat system of thought or formal pattern." And Jerome McGann emphasizes throughout his fine *Don Juan in Context* (Chicago: University of Chicago Press, 1976) Byron's rejection of systems, plans, or stable designs in favor of an experimental, open-ended testing of possible hypotheses or fictions (see especially his remarks on the form of the poem, pp. 122-131). M. G. Cooke convincingly concludes that the changes, oppositions, and contradictions of the imagery in *Don Juan* effectively create an "oddly prolific world engendering more than it can reconcile or maintain." *The Blind Man Traces the Circle* (Princeton: Princeton University Press, 1969), p. 116; cf. pp. 99-116. W. Paul Elledge also emphasizes the unreconciled antinomies of Byron's characteristic imagery in *Byron and the Dynamics of Metaphor* (Nashville: Vanderbilt University Press, 1968), pp. 7-12.

21. Cf. *Childe Harold's Pilgrimage*, 2.7.1-2:

> Well didst thou speak, Athena's wisest son!
> "All that we know is, nothing can be known."

And in his Diary entry for 25 January 1821, Byron confirms: " 'Which is best, life or death, the gods only know,' as Socrates said to his judges, on the breaking up of the tribunal. Two thousand years since that sage's declaration of ignorance have not enlightened us more upon this important point" (*Letters and Journals*, VIII, 35).

22. Ludwig Wittgenstein, *On Certainty*, ed. G. E. M. Anscombe and G. H. von Wright, trans. Denis Paul and G. E. M. Anscombe (Oxford: Basil Blackwell, 1969), nos. 622, 633, 608-609, and passim. Wittgenstein's debt to Kant in *On Certainty* was pointed out by A. J. Ayer in a paper entitled "Wittgenstein on Certainty," delivered at University College, London, 5 May 1973. In this last book Wittgenstein restricts to the phenomenological realm his earlier, logical positivist claims in the *Tractatus Logico-Philosophicus* (1921) and *Philosophical Investigations* (1945-49) that logic and the total family of language-games constitute all knowable, hence meaningful, reality. (Cf. "Whereof one cannot speak, thereof one must be silent," *Tractatus*, #7).

23. Thomas Moore's annotation to his edition of *The Works of Lord Byron* (London: John Murray, 1833) gives the source of Byron's image: "A short time before his death, [Newton] uttered this memorable sentiment:—"I do not know what I may appear to the world; but to myself I seem to have been only a boy playing on the sea-shore, and diverting myself in now and then finding a smoother pebble or a prettier shell than ordinary, whilst the great ocean of truth lay all undiscovered before me" (later recorded in Sir David Brewster's *Memoirs of Sir Isaac Newton*, Edinburgh: T. Constable, 1860, II, 331).

24. The narrator's contempt for the "moderate bather" was stronger in the original (but unmetrical) version of this final line: "is best for timi [timid] bathers."

25. See my discussion of Schiller's concept of art as play in chapter 1, p. 24.

26. Schiller, NSP, 176-190. Cf. my discussion of Schiller's concept of the naive in chapter 1, pp. 28-30.

27. Byron may have seen performances of Mozart's *dramma giocoso, Don Giovanni,* and of Tirso de Molina's *El Burlador de Sevilla,* according to Willis Pratt, *Byron's Don Juan—A Variorum Edition,* IV (Austin: University of Texas Press, 1957), pp. 15-16; or, more likely, he was thinking of the newspaper accounts of the London harlequin pantomimes featuring Don Juan in 1817—see Fred Beaty, "Harlequin Don Juan," *JEGP* 67 (1968): 395-405.

28. Leo Weinstein's *The Metamorphoses of Don Juan* (Stanford: Stanford University Press, 1959) traces the development of the Don Juan tradition from Tirso de Molina's *El Burlador de Sevilla,* which presents Don Juan Tenorio as a young, carefree madcap whose greatest pleasure is "to deceive a woman and leave her dishonoured," through Molière's *Don Juan, ou le Festin de Pierre,* which depicts the Don as a cynical and witty libertine intent on living according to his pleasure, to E. T. A. Hoffman's romanticized image of Don Juan as the irresistible lover who seeks, but never finds, the ideal woman and is consequently filled with rage at both God and the women who consistently disappoint his transcendental desire (pp. 11-20, 68-77, and passim). Byron, of course, would not have known of Hoffman's reinterpretation of Don Juan. Cf. Oscar Mandel, ed., *The Theatre of Don Juan* (Lincoln: University of Nebraska Press, 1963).

29. Denis de Rougemont, in *Love in the Western World,* rev. ed. (New

York: Pantheon Books, 1956), discusses the association of erotic passion with death in the Tristan and Isolde myth, in the Neoplatonic Manichaean and catharist heresies of the middle ages, in the cult of Courtly Love, in the nineteenth century's glorification of the perfect woman, and even in Freud's linking of the pleasure principle with death. De Rougemont analyses the eighteenth-century Don Juan as an inversion of Tristan but does not comment on the nineteenth-century romanticized version of Don Juan.

30. Byron was well aware of the danger of self-destruction inherent in erotic desire. As he commented to John Cam Hobhouse on his affair with Teresa Guiccioli: "I feel & I feel it bitterly—that a man should not consume his life at the side and on the bosom—of a woman—and a stranger—that even the recompense and it is much—is not enough—and that this Cisisbean existence is to be condemned. —But I have neither the strength of mind to break my chain, nor the insensibility which would deaden it's weight." (Letter of 23 August 1819, *Letters and Journals*, VI, 214.)

31. Cf. M. G. Cooke, *The Blind Man Traces the Circle*, pp. 143-144.

32. Byron swam the Hellespont with Lieutenant Ekenhead of the Salsette on 3 May 1810 (cf. letters to H. Drury, 3 May and 17 June 1810, *Letters and Journals*, I, 237, 246). Several details of the shipwreck in Canto II were taken from "A Narrative of the Honourable John Byron (Commodore in a late expedition round the world), containing an account of the great distresses suffered by himself and his companions on the coast of Patagonia, from the year 1740, till their arrival in England, 1746; written by Himself" (London, 1768; cf. *Variorum Edition of Don Juan*, IV, 75).

33. Byron himself insisted on the distance between his own experiences and those of his fictional characters. Referring to his affair with Teresa Guiccioli, he wrote John Murray: "I cannot tell how our romance will end—but it hath gone on hitherto most *erotically*—such perils—and escapes—Juan's are a child's play in comparison.—The fools think that all my *Poeshie* is always allusive to my *own* adventures—I have had at one time or another better—and more extraordinary—and perilous—and pleasant than those any day of the week,—if I might tell them,—but that must never be." (Letter of 9 August 1819, *Letters and Journals*, VI, 206.) The narrator's claim to have seen a harem (6.51.3-4) clearly goes beyond what the historical Byron could have experienced.

34. Cf. Byron's comments on Mr. Sotheby: "He may be an amiable man—a moral man—a good father—a good husband—a respectable & devout individual —I have nothing to say against all this—but I have something to say of Mr. S's literary foibles—and of the wretched affectation & systematized Sophistry of many men women & Children now extant & absurd in & about London & elsewhere;—which & whom in their false pretensions & nauseous attempts to make Learning a nuisance—& society a Bore—I consider as fair Game—to be brought down on all fair occasions . . ." (Letter to John Murray, 23 April 1818, *Letters and Journals*, VI, 36).

35. Letter to John Murray, 9 May 1817, *Letters and Journals*, V, 221.

36. Byron defined *mobilité*—a quality attributed to Lady Adeline—as "an excessive susceptibility of immediate impressions—at the same time without *losing* the past; and is, though sometimes apparently useful to the possessor, a most

painful and unhappy attribute" (note to *Don Juan*, 16.97.4). Lady Adeline's excessive involvement in *present* events may involve a painful failure of self-coherence, even conscious hypocrisy. Nonetheless, the capacity to live in the present without either forgetting the past or imposing a system derived from the past upon each passing moment is a capacity that the romantic ironist cultivates and that Byron himself possessed to a remarkable degree.

37. Byron was well aware of the necessity for a comic, buffoonish style to convey his ideas. As he wrote to John Murray, "You ask me for the plan of Donny Johnny—I *have* no plan—I *had* no plan—but I had or have materials—though if like Tony Lumpkin—I am "to be snubbed so when I am in spirits" the poem will be naught—and the poet turn serious again.—If it don't take I will leave it off where it is with all due respect to the Public—but if continued it must be in my own way—you might as well make Hamlet (or Diggory) "act mad" in a strait waistcoat—as trammel my buffoonery—if I am to be a buffoon—their gestures and my thoughts would only be pitiably absurd—and ludicrously constrained.—Why Man the Soul of such writing is it's licence?—at least the *liberty* of that *licence* if one likes—*not* that one should abuse it . . . (Letter of 12 August 1819, *Letters and Journals*, VI, 207-208.)

38. I am indebted to Joel Black's doctoral dissertation (Stanford University, 1978), "The Literature of Truancy: Digression, Involution and Duplication in the Biographical Romance," for these remarks on the literary history of the digression.

39. Jerome McGann has described the pornographic and theological implications of this passage (*Fiery Dust*, pp. 294-296).

40. Letter to John Murray, 12 August 1819, *Letters and Journals*, VI, 207. Byron later provided Murray with more of the materials for *Don Juan*, but always refrained from identifying a controlling design or philosophical purpose in the poem. His later remarks do confirm, however, a pattern of growing self-consciousness in Juan, although they tell us nothing of the development of the narrator, an equally (and perhaps more) important character: "The 5th. [Canto] is so far from being the last of D. J. that it is hardly the beginning.—I meant to take him the tour of Europe—with a proper mixture of siege—battle—and adventure —and to make him finish as *Anacharsis Cloots*—in the French revolution.—To how many cantos this may extend.—I know not.—nor whether (even if I live) I shall complete it.—but this was my notion.—I meant to have made him a Cavalier Servente in Italy and a cause for a divorce in England—and a Sentimental "Werther-faced man" in Germany—so as to show the different ridicules of the society in each of those countries—and to have displayed him gradually gâté and blasé as he grew older—as is natural.—But I had not quite fixed whether to make him end in Hell—or in an unhappy marriage,—not knowing which would be the severest.—The Spanish tradition says Hell—but it is probably only an Allegory of the other state.—You are now in possession of my notions on the subject. (Letter to John Murray, 16 February 1821, *Letters and Journals*, VIII, 78.) Rowland E. Prothero, in *The Works of Lord Byron*, V, (London: John Murray, 1901), p. 242, provides the following note on this passage: "Jean Baptiste Clootz . . . was, in March, 1794, condemned to death by Robespierre. On the scaffold, he begged the executioner to decapitate him last, alleging that he wished to make

some observations essential to the establishment of certain principles, while the heads of his companions were falling. The request was complied with."

41. See George M. Ridenour, *The Style of Don Juan* (New Haven: Yale University Press, 1960), chap. 1 and passim.

42. Jerome McGann's superb study of *Don Juan* does full justice to the poem's alternation between the plain and the elevated style (*Don Juan in Context*, pp. 68-99).

43. Robert F. Gleckner reads *Don Juan* (and Byron's poetry as a whole) as "despairing" in *Byron and the Ruins of Paradise* (Baltimore: Johns Hopkins Press, 1967), p. 330 and passim; George Ridenour dismisses the poem as a spiritual dead end in *The Style of Don Juan*, p. xiii. For similar readings of the tone of *Don Juan* as fundamentally pessimistic, see T. G. Steffan, *Byron's Don Juan, I, The Making of a Masterpiece* (Austin: University of Texas Press, 1957), 283; Harold Bloom, *The Visionary Company* (Garden City, N.Y.: Doubleday, 1961), p. 258; E. E. Bostetter, *The Romantic Ventriloquists* (Seattle: University of Washington Press, 1963), pp. 254-268; Brian Wilkie, *The Romantic Poets and Epic Tradition* (Madison: University of Wisconsin Press, 1965), pp. 188-226; and Cooke, *The Blind Man Traces the Circle*, pp. 128-174.

For more positive readings of the tone and imagery of *Don Juan*, which support my interpretation, see Jerome McGann, *Fiery Dust*, pt. 5, p. ix and passim, and *Don Juan in Context*, pp. 138-148; Kernan, *The Plot of Satire*, p. 199; and E. D. Hirsch, "Byron and the Terrestrial Paradise," in F. W. Hilles and H. Bloom, eds., *From Sensibility to Romanticism* (New Haven: Yale University Press, 1965), pp. 467-486.

44. Letter to Thomas Moore, 10 March 1817, *Letters and Journals*, V, 186.

45. *Letters and Journals*, VIII, 20.

46. Alvin Kernan, in *The Plot of Satire*, pp. 197-199, stresses the tonal significance of the encounter with the Black Friar/Lady Fitz-Fulke as a comic affirmation of life over death.

47. I quote the preface from *Byron's Don Juan—A Variorum Edition*, ed. T. G. Steffan and W. W. Pratt (Austin: University of Texas Press, 1957), II, 5-7.

48. McGann, *Don Juan in Context*, pp. 161-165.

3. Keats and the Vale of Soul-Making

1. *The Letters of John Keats, 1814-1821*, ed. Hyder Edward Rollins, 2 vols. (Cambridge, Mass.: Harvard University Press, 1958), I, 281. References by volume and page number to this edition are hereafter included in the text.

2. John Middleton Murry, *Keats and Shakespeare* (London: Oxford University Press, 1925), pp. 72-73.

3. David Perkins, *The Quest for Permanence: The Symbolism of Wordsworth, Shelley, and Keats* (Cambridge, Mass.: Harvard University Press, 1959), pp. 228-257, 299-301. This analysis of the Odes' structure has been accepted by many other critics, including Walter Jackson Bate in *John Keats* (Cambridge, Mass.: Harvard University Press, 1963), p. 500, and Stuart Sperry in *Keats the Poet* (Princeton: Princeton University Press, 1973), pp. 242-291.

4. Stuart Sperry also makes this point in *Keats the Poet*, pp. 244-246.

5. The extent of Keats's empathic response to the urn has been emphasized by James Dickie. In "The Grecian Urn: An Archeological Approach," *Bulletin of the John Rylands Library* 52 (1969): 96-114, Dickie suggests that the primary sources for Keats's descriptions of his Grecian urn were not real marble urns or pottery vases so much as the engravings of Etruscan urns published by Piranesi in *Vasi, candelabri, cippi, sarcofagi, tripodi, lucerne, ed ornamenti antiche disegnati ed incisi dal cav. Gio. Batt. Piranesi* (Rome, 1778) and by Henry Moses in *A Collection of Antique Vases, Altars, Paterae, Tripods, Candelabra, Sarcophagi, etc.* (London, 1814). Keats's imagery is based primarily upon the engravings of the Borghese and Holland House vases, both presented in Piranesi's and Moses's volumes. However, Keats's eclectic imagination also drew on details he had observed in Claude's "Priests sacrificing to Apollo" and "View of Delphi, with a Procession" as well as in the engravings included in *Les Monumen[t]s antiques du Musée Napoléon, dessinés et gravés par Thomas Piroli* (Paris, 1804-06).

6. Lady Emma Hamilton's Attitudes or pantomime performances of classical Greek poses copied from Greek and Roman vases and wall-paintings were legendary in Keats's day. The most famous description of these Attitudes, and of the woman who created them, occurs in Goethe's letters. On 16 March 1787 he reported from Naples: "Sir William Hamilton, who is still living here as English ambassador, has now, after many years of devotion to the arts and the study of nature, found the acme of these delights in the person of an English girl of 20 with a beautiful face and a perfect figure. He has had a Greek costume made for her which becomes her extremely. Dressed in this, she lets down her hair and with a few shawls gives so much variety to her poses, gestures, expressions, etc., that the spectator can hardly believe his eyes. He sees what thousands of artists would have liked to express realised before him in movements and surprising transformations—standing, kneeling, sitting, reclining, serious, sad, playful, ecstatic, contrite, alluring, threatening, anxious, one pose follows another without a break. She knows how to arrange the folds of her veil to match each mood, and has a hundred ways of turning it into a headdress. The old knight idolises her and is enthusiastic about everything she does. In her he has found all the antiquities, all the profiles of Sicilian coins, even the Apollo Belvidere. This much is certain: as a performance it's like nothing you ever saw before in your life. We have already enjoyed it on two evenings." Johann Wolfgang Goethe, *Italian Journey 1786-1788*, trans. W. H. Auden and Elizabeth Mayer (London: Collins, 1962), pp. 199-200.

But Goethe was far less enthusiastic about Emma herself. After a two months' acquaintance, he wrote on 27 May, "I must confess that our fair entertainer seems to me, frankly, a dull creature. Perhaps her figure makes up for it, but her voice is inexpressive and her speech without charm. Even her singing is neither full-throated nor agreeable" (p. 312). And Goethe was not the only one to be appalled by Emma Hart Hamilton's Cheshire accent and lower-class manners. Lady Holland recorded in her journal: "Just as she was lying down, with her head reclining upon an Etruscan vase to represent a water-nymph, she exclaimed in her provincial dialect: 'Doun't be afeared Sir Willum, I'll not crack your *joug*.' I turned away disgusted . . ." *Journal of Elizabeth, Lady Holland*, ed. Earl of Ilchester (London, 1908), I, 243.

For a detailed account of Emma Hamilton's career and Attitudes, see Patricia Jaffe, *Lady Hamilton in Relation to the Art of Her Time*, a catalogue for The Arts Council of Great Britain exhibition at Kenwood, 18 July-16 October 1972.

7. Friedrich Schlegel, *Über Goethes Meister*, trans. Leonard P. Wessell, Jr., "The Antinomic Structure of Friedrich Schlegel's 'Romanticism,' " *Studies in Romanticism* 12(1973): 664.

8. In Greek temples, shrines were usually set up to deities closely associated with, or subservient to, the temple's titular deity.

9. "O thou whose face hath felt the Winter's wind," ll. 9, 14; first included in Keats's 19 February 1818 letter to Reynolds (I, 233).

10. Morris Dickstein, *Keats and His Poetry: A Study in Development* (Chicago and London: University of Chicago Press, 1971), p. 125.

11. Endymion's shift from a Neoplatonic quest to a debate between the ideal and the real, between the moon-goddess and the sorrowing Indian Maiden, was first emphasized by Glen O. Allen in "The Fall of Endymion: A Study in Keats's Intellectual Growth," *Keats-Shelley Journal* 6 (1957): 37-58.

12. This point has been convincingly made by Morris Dickstein in *Keats and His Poetry*, pp. 106-115.

13. Earl R. Wasserman, *The Finer Tone—Keats' Major Poems* (Baltimore: Johns Hopkins Press, 1953), pp. 84-137.

14. Jack Stillinger, *The Hoodwinking of Madeline and Other Essays on Keats's Poems* (Urbana: University of Illinois Press, 1971), pp. 67-93.

15. I am indebted for these observations to Craig Seligman's Honors Essay, "Romantic Irony in the Poetry of Keats," Stanford University, 1975.

16. Keats's deliberate refusal to characterize Porphyro and Madeline in detail makes it possible for them to play many, and contradictory, roles. Jack Stillinger has emphasized the thematic role of the bird imagery in the poem (*The Hoodwinking of Madeline*, p. 76).

Keats's obscure reference to Merlin is probably based on a conflation of the two conflicting versions of Merlin's death popularly known in Keats's day. One derived from the Anglo-Norman romance, *Lestroire de Merlin*—i.e., the Vulgate Merlin published by H. O. Sommer, *The Vulgate Version of the Arthurian Romances* (Washington, 1908), vol. II—depicts Merlin's lover Nimiane as a beautiful, loving girl who uses the magic Merlin agrees to teach her in return for her love and sexual favors to enchant him forever within a paradisiacal tower in the forest of Broceliande. This Nimiane imprisons Merlin out of love, because she cannot bear to be separated from him. The other version of Merlin's death recorded in Thomas Malory's famous *The Tale of King Arthur* (two editions of Malory were published in London in 1816), depicts Merlin as the foolish, "assotted" lover of the indifferent Nyneve, the Lady of the Lake. In order to rid herself of Merlin's persistent and unwelcome attentions, the Lady uses the magical knowledge Merlin has freely and foreknowingly given her to imprison him forever under a rock.

In identifying Merlin and his demon as lovers who meet in enchanted times ("Never on such a night have lovers met") and who have made a contract ("debt"), Keats invokes the Anglo-Norman romance tradition. But in identifying Merlin's lover as a "demon" and his debt to her as "monstrous," Keats has invoked Malory's image of the heartless lady (a belle dame sans merci) who effectively destroys Merlin by imprisoning him forever. Keats's allusion thus serves to remind us that Porphyro, as well as Madeline, is in danger of being enchanted by his love into a kind of living death or "fairyland forlorn" from which he may not be able to return to ordinary human reality.

17. See, for example, Sperry, *Keats the Poet*, pp. 234-240; Dickstein, *Keats and His Poetry*, pp. 108-109; Bate, *John Keats*, pp. 478-481; Charles Patterson, Jr., *The Daemonic in the Poetry of John Keats* (Urbana: University of Illinois Press, 1970), pp. 141-143. These readings do not take into account the published, *Indicator* version of the poem in which the knight is treated more scornfully by the narrator (he is addressed as a "wretched wight") and the lady's responsibility for the outcome is lessened. Rather than having "wept and sighed full sore" (l. 30, a possible sign of her knowledge of an impending cruel separation), she merely "gaz'd and sighed deep," perhaps in passionate love. More significantly, in the *Indicator* version, the dame does not "lull" or entice the "wight" to sleep—rather the lovers together "slumber'd on the moss" (l. 33).

18. In Alain Chartier's lyric, the belle dame justifies at length her refusal to respond to her lover: she does not love him; his love is unsolicited and capricious, based on the eye alone; and his threat of suicide is a form of emotional blackmail. Keats probably read Chartier's poem in the translation by Sir Richard Ros that was originally attributed to Chaucer; for the text of this translation, see *The Works of Chaucer*, ed. W. W. Skeat, VII (Oxford: Clarendon Press, 1897), 299-326.

19. Keats's publisher, John Taylor, rejected the proposed changes in the love scene on moral grounds: "This Folly of Keats is the most stupid piece of Folly I can conceive . . . if he will not so far concede to my Wishes as to leave the passage as it originally stood, I must be content to admire his Poems with some other Imprint" (II, 182-183). Richard Woodhouse talked Keats out of changing the ending, arguing that the original had succeeded in achieving the desired change of sentiment.

20. See, for example, Bate, *John Keats*, p. 556; Sperry, *Keats the Poet*, p. 299; Stillinger, *The Hoodwinking of Madeline*, p. 59; Claude L. Finney, *The Evolution of Keats's Poetry* (Cambridge, Mass.: Harvard University Press, 1936), II, 698.

21. Stuart Sperry has perceptively analyzed Keats's use of chemical and other scientific terminology in his letters and poems. For his discussion of the meaning of "evaporate" in Keats's letter, see *Keats the Poet*, pp. 44-45.

22. For the identification of Moneta with the Athena Parthenos and the goddess of Wisdom, see my "Keats's Face of Moneta: Source and Meaning," *Keats-Shelley Journal* 25 (1976): 65-73.

23. Frank Kermode, *The Romantic Image* (London: Routledge and Paul, 1957), pp. 8-9.

24. Thomas Weiskel has defined this affirmation of the signifying imagination as the positive or egotistical sublime (as opposed to the negative or Kantian/Burkean sublime) in *The Romantic Sublime: Studies in the Structure and Psychology of Transcendence* (Baltimore: Johns Hopkins University Press, 1976), pp. 28-80. Cf. Stuart Ende, *Keats and the Sublime* (New Haven: Yale University Press, 1977).

25. For an illuminating discussion of these processual patterns in the poem, see Virgil Nemoianu's "The Dialectics of Movement in Keats's 'To Autumn,' " *PMLA* 93 (1978): 205-214.

26. "To Autumn," like "The Eve of St. Agnes" and Keats' open-ended Odes, has led critics to radically opposed interpretations. Aileen Ward has seen the poem pessimistically, as an acceptance of death, in *John Keats: The Making of a Poet* (New York: Viking Press, 1973), p. 322, while James Benziger has read it as a portrayal of immortality in *Images of Eternity* (Carbondale: Southern Illinois University Press, 1964), p. 30. See Herbert Lindenberger's "Keats's 'To Autumn' and Our Knowledge of a Poem," *College English* 32 (1970): 123-134, for a perceptive analysis of the full range of responses to this poem.

4. Carlyle's *Sartor Resartus:* A Self-Consuming Artifact

1. Thomas Carlyle, "Signs of the Times," in *The Works of Thomas Carlyle* (New York: Collier, 1897), XIV, 473. Cited hereafter as *Works*.

2. Ibid., pp. 476, 478, 486.

3. "On History," in *Works*, XIV, 551, 552.

4. Thomas Carlyle, "Characteristics," in *Works*, XV, 210.

5. See Geoffrey Hartman, "Romanticism and Anti-Self-Consciousness," in *Beyond Formalism—Literary Essays 1958-1970* (New Haven: Yale University Press, 1970), pp. 298-310.

6. Carlyle, "Characteristics," pp. 209, 210, 215, 243, 209. Carlyle's familiarity with Schlegel's writings extended well beyond the *Philosophische Vorlesungen* or *Philosophical Lectures* (1830), which he hailed in the *Edinburgh Review* of December 1830 as "the apotheosis of Spiritualism," as an exactly and dexterously written work, "full of deep meditation, wherein the infinite mystery of Life, if not represented, is decisively recognized," despite what he saw as Schlegel's desperate and futile conversion to Catholicism (pp. 239-240). As early as January 1826 Carlyle had confided to Jane Welsh his aspiration to follow in the footsteps of "the great Schlegel" and publish a literary newspaper like the *Athenaeum*; and in June 1830 he asked Henry Inglis to send him Schlegel's *Lessings Geist.* See *Collected Letters of Thomas and Jane Welsh Carlyle,* ed. C. R. Sanders (Durham, N.C.: Duke University Press), IV (1970), 22; V (1976), 114. Carlyle repeatedly urged his brother, Dr. John Carlyle, to visit Friedrich Schlegel during his sojourn in Germany, but Schlegel died before the visit could take place (*Letters,* IV, 424; V, 7n13). John Carlyle did visit A. W. Schlegel and conveyed to Carlyle their conversation concerning Friedrich Schlegel's review of Goethe's *Wilhelm Meister;* see John Clubbe's "John Carlyle in Germany and the Genesis of *Sartor Resartus,*" in *Romantic and Victorian,* ed. W. Paul Elledge and Richard L. Hoffman (Rutherford, N.J.: Fairleigh Dickinson University Press, 1971), p. 268. The influence of Schlegel's aphoristic style, as well as of Jean Paul Richter's Schlegelian "transcendental buffoonery," is apparent both in Carlyle's essays and in *Sartor Resartus*.

7. Philip Rosenberg, *The Seventh Hero: Thomas Carlyle and the Theory of Radical Activism* (Cambridge, Mass.: Harvard University Press, 1974) p. 10.

8. Thomas Carlyle, *The French Revolution,* in *The Centenary Edition of Works by Thomas Carlyle,* ed. H. D. Traill (New York: C. Scribner's Sons, 1896-

99), IV, 26.

9. Rosenberg, *The Seventh Hero*, p. 101.

10. Carlyle, *The French Revolution*, IV, 114; II, 251. As John Holloway emphasizes, in *The Victorian Sage* (London: Macmillan, 1953), pp. 61-75, for Carlyle the French Revolution was an inevitable phase in the historical process.

11. Carlyle, "The Diamond Necklace," in *Works*, XV, 561-562, 563.

12. [William Maginn], "A Literary Portrait of Thomas Carlyle," *Fraser's Magazine* 7 (June 1833): 706.

13. Thomas Carlyle, "Jean Paul Friedrich Richter" (1827), in *Works*, XIV, 20, 13, 14, 15; and Thomas Carlyle, "Jean Paul Friedrich Richter" (1830), in *Works*, XIV, 623.

14. Thomas Carlyle, Letter to Mr. Fraser, 27 May 1833, in *Letters of Thomas Carlyle, 1826-1836*, ed. Charles Eliot Norton (London: Macmillan, 1889), pp. 365-366. Carlyle had earlier written to Goethe, on the eve of beginning *Sartor*, that the doctrine of "natural Supernaturalism" was his own belief, born of his own internal chaos: "When I look at the wonderful Chaos within me, full of natural Supernaturalism, and all manner of Antediluvian fragments; and how the Universe is daily growing more mysterious as well as more august, and the influences from without more heterogeneous and perplexing; I see not well what is to come of it all, and only conjecture from the violence of the fermentation that something Strange may come." *Goethes Briefwechsel mit Thomas Carlyle* (Dachau: Einhorn-Verlag, 1913), p. 44; dated 31 August 1830.

15. Carlyle, Letter to Mr. Fraser, p. 365.

16. It is ironic that Meyer Abrams chose Teufelsdröckh's phrase as the title of his study of Romantic myths of progress and human perfectibility, since Carlyle himself was deeply skeptical of the adequacy of any poetic, let alone discursive, formulation of this vision.

17. For the influence upon Carlyle of the German Idealist tradition and his native Puritan tradition, see Charles Frederick Harrold, *Carlyle and German Thought: 1819-1834* (New Haven: Yale University Press, 1934), and A. Abbott Ikeler, *Puritan Temper and Transcendental Faith—Carlyle's Literary Vision* (Columbus: Ohio State University Press, 1972).

18. Thomas Carlyle, *Sartor Resartus*, introd. by W. H. Hudson (London: J. M. Dent, Everyman's Library, 1959 ed.), p. 33. Hereafter, all page references to *Sartor Resartus* will be given in parentheses in the text and will refer to this edition.

19. Shelley invokes Prometheus as man's savior in *Prometheus Unbound*, where he also celebrates the poet's creative use of language as a "perpetual Orphic song, / Which rules with Daedal harmony a throng / Of thoughts and forms, which else senseless and shapeless were" (*PU*, 4.415-417). And Byron hailed Prometheus as "a symbol and a sign / To Mortals of their fate and force; / Like thee, Man is in part divine" ("Prometheus," ll. 45-47).

20. G. B. Tennyson makes this point in *Sartor Called Resartus: The Genesis, Structure, and Style of Thomas Carlyle's First Major Work* (Princeton, N.J.: Princeton University Press, 1965), p. 187.

21. John Holloway, *The Victorian Sage*, pp. 23-30.

22. When John Sterling criticized the style of *Sartor Resartus* as capricious,

lawless, too emphatic, even "barbarous," Carlyle replied: "But finally, do you reckon this really a time for Purism of Style; or that Style (mere dictionary Style) has much to do with the worth or unworth of a Book? I do not: with whole ragged battalions of Scott's-Novel Scotch, with Irish, German, French, and even Newspaper Cockney (when 'Literature' is little other than a Newspaper) storming in on us, and the whole structure of our Johnsonian English breaking up from its foundations, —revolution *there* as visible as anywhere else!" Sterling's letter and Carlyle's response are both included in C. F. Harrold's edition of *Sartor Resartus* (New York: Odyssey Press, 1937); the passage quoted here appears on p. 317.

23. For example, Teufelsdröckh says, "Philosophy complains that Custom has hood-winked us, from the first; that we do everything by Custom, even believe by it; that our very Axioms, let us boast of Free-thinking as we may, are oftenest simply such Beliefs as we have never heard questioned. *Nay*, what is Philosophy throughout but a continual battle against Custom; an ever-renewed effort to *transcend* the sphere of blind Custom, and so become Transcendental?" (194).

24. Leonard Deen, "Irrational Form in *Sartor Resartus*," *Texas Studies in Literature and Language* 5 (Autumn 1963): 439-440.

25. This point has been argued by both George Levine, in *The Boundaries of Fiction: Carlyle, Macauley, Newman* (Princeton: Princeton University Press, 1968), p. 55, and Jerry Allen Dibble, in "Carlyle's 'British Reader' and the Structure of *Sartor Resartus*," *Texas Studies in Literature and Language* 16 (1974): 300.

26. *Carlyle's Letters to Mill, Sterling, and Browning*, ed. Alexander Carlyle (London: Frederick A. Stokes, 1923), p. 74; cf. George Levine, *The Boundaries of Fiction*, pp. 43-45.

27. That Carlyle is here describing his personal sense of authorial inadequacy becomes clear when we compare this passage to his description of *Sartor* in his letter to Goethe on 10 June 1831: "But for these last months I have been busy with a Piece more immediately my own: of this, should it ever become a printed volume, and seem in the smallest worthy of such honour, a copy for Weimar will not be wanting. Alas! It is, after all, not a Picture that I am painting; it is but a half-reckless casting of the brush, with its many frustrated colours, against the canvas: whether it will make good Foam is still a venture" (*Goethes Briefwechsel mit Thomas Carlyle*, p. 62).

28. Interestingly, Roland Barthes has also chosen to analyze clothing fashions as a paradigmatic semiotic system, in *Système de la mode* (Paris: Seuil, 1967).

29. Ferdinand de Saussure, *Course in General Linguistics*, ed. Charles Bally and Albert Sechehave, trans. Wade Baskin (New York: McGraw-Hill, paper, 1966), pp. 67-70.

30. Carlyle, "On History," p. 551.

31. Meyer Abrams has discussed Teufelsdröckh's crisis autobiography in *Natural Supernaturalism* without acknowledging the ironic treatment it here receives from Carlyle (pp. 308-311).

32. Carlyle associated the East with the glorious innocence of youth and the beauty of Aurora in an earlier letter to Jane Welsh (2 September 1824), in *The Collected Letters of Thomas and Jane Welsh Carlyle*, III, 145.

33. G. B. Tennyson has drawn attention to the significance of the frequent allusions to the Wandering Jew (*Sartor Called Resartus*, pp. 201-207). Teufelsdröckh is not only an angst-ridden wanderer (57, 117); he is also associated with the Jewish old-clothes peddlers on Monmouth Street, the "High Priests" who summon the past to judgment and prophesy the messiah to come (181).

34. Philip Rosenberg, *The Seventh Hero*, pp. 3, 52.

35. This conception of the structure of *Sartor Resartus* has been put forth in Janice L. Haney's " 'Shadow-Hunting': Romantic Irony, *Sartor Resartus*, and Victorian Romanticism," *Studies in Romanticism* 17 (Summer 1978): 319-320.

36. G. B. Tennyson has perceptively analyzed this tripartite structure in *Sartor Called Resartus*, pp. 167-171.

37. Jerry Dibble points out this "metamorphosis in character" between Teufelsdröckh and the Editor in "Carlyle's 'British Reader,' " p. 303.

38. G. B. Tennyson has most fully explicated the significance of Teufelsdröckh's name, in *Sartor Called Resartus*, pp. 220-222.

39. Rosenberg, *The Seventh Hero*, pp. 51-62.

40. A. Abbott Ikeler errs, I believe, in *Puritan Temper and Transcendental Faith*, pp. 20, 24, and passim, in attributing Carlyle's discomfort with literature and language to a Puritan hostility to the sensuous pleasures provided by literature rather than to his profound awareness of the limits of linguistic expression.

41. Stanley E. Fish, *Self-Consuming Artifacts—The Experience of Seventeenth Century Literature* (Berkeley: University of California Press, 1972), pp. 1-4.

42. "Wovon man nicht sprechen kann, darüber muss man schweigen." Ludwig Wittgenstein, *Tractatus Logico-Philosophicus*, trans. C. K. Ogden (London: Routledge and Kegan Paul, 1922), pp. 188-189, #7.

43. This has led at least one critic to overlook all the irony in *Sartor Resartus* and to describe the book as a purely "persuasive essay" designed to convert the reader to Carlyle's view of the universe. See Gerry H. Brookes, *The Rhetorical Form of Carlyle's 'Sartor Resartus'* (Berkeley: University of California Press, 1972), p. 8 and passim.

5. Guilt and Samuel Taylor Coleridge

1. S. T. Coleridge, *Biographia Literaria*, ed. J. Shawcross (Oxford: Oxford University Press, corrected ed., 1962; 1st ed., 1907), II, 235; Owen Barfield has drawn attention to the significance of this passage in *What Coleridge Thought* (London: Oxford University Press, 1972), p. 27. It is a mistake, I think, to read Coleridge's later ideas back into his early poems, and I have tried to restrict my use of terminology gleaned from his later philosophical writings to instances where the concepts are already present in the poetry.

2. It is possible that Coleridge read Schlegel's *Athenaeum* and *Lyceum* fragments when he was in Germany in 1798-99, although he did not annotate Joseph Henry Green's copy of the *Athenaeum* before the summer of 1817 and even then did not comment upon Schlegel's most famous aphorisms on romanticism and irony. Coleridge's annotated copy of the *Athenaeum* is in the British Museum (no. C 132 c 2). Professor George Whalley, who is editing Coleridge's

marginalia for the Bollingen *Collected Coleridge*, has most graciously permitted me to see a typescript of his notes on this volume, which is being subedited by Hans Eichner. Coleridge did mark the following passage by Schelling with an *N* (*Nota Bene*): "Humour is the result of a free mingling of the conditioned and the unconditioned . . . Where imagination and judgement come into touch, wit arises; where reason and caprice come together, there arises humour . . . What Friedrich Schlegel characterises as irony is to my mind nothing but the consequence, the character of circumspection, of true presence of mind. Schlegel's irony seems to me to be genuine humour. More than one name is of advantage to an idea" (trans. Hans Eichner). But in the summer-autumn of 1817, the date Whalley conjectures for these annotations, Coleridge seems to have been more interested in distinguishing genius from talent than in analyzing Schlegel's concept of irony.

Laurence S. Lockridge, in *Coleridge the Moralist* (Ithaca: Cornell University Press, 1977), p. 55 and passim, has emphasized Coleridge's belief that the unconscious human will is a "primordial energic principle" or libidinal power that is both "the ground of selfhood and freedom" and "the source of evil."

3. *Biographia Literaria*, II, 5.

4. Coleridge's poems and notebooks record both the anxieties aroused in him by solitude ("Fears in Solitude") and his recurrent feelings of loneliness and alienation from loved ones: "Yet at times / My soul is sad, that I have roamed through life / Still most a stranger, most with naked heart / At mine own home and birthplace" ("To the Rev. George Coleridge"). Cf. "Lines, written at the King's Arms, Ross," "The Blossoming of the Solitary Date-tree," and *Notebooks*, I, #1082(6) and #1463.

5. Richard Haven, in *Patterns of Consciousness* (Amherst: University of Massachusetts Press, 1969), pp. 23-29, has perceptively compared the Mariner's experience of isolation and communion to John Custance's description in *Wisdom, Madness and Folly* of the depression and mania undergone during psychosis.

6. The Mariner's limited perspective on his own experience has been reemphasized by Sara Dyck in "Perspective in 'The Rime of the Ancient Mariner,' " *Studies in English Literature* 13 (Autumn 1973): 591-604. This essay develops the earlier comments on this point made by William H. Marshall in "Coleridge, The Mariner and Dramatic Irony," *The Personalist* 42 (1961): 524-532 and by Lionel Stevenson in " 'The Ancient Mariner' as a Dramatic Monologue," *The Personalist* 30 (1949): 34-44.

7. *The Notebooks of Samuel Taylor Coleridge*, ed. K. Coburn (New York: Bollingen, 1957), I, #45n.

8. *Biographia Literaria*, I, 132-134.

9. Kathleen Coburn has found manuscript evidence to support John Livingston Lowes's suggestion that the Ancient Mariner is derived in part from the romance of the Wandering Jew. The Ancient Mariner "was in my mind the everlasting wandering Jew—had told this story ten thousand times since the voyage, which was in his early youth and 50 years before," wrote Coleridge (*Notebooks*, I, #45n).

10. Although they do not distinguish between the 1798 and later editions of

"The Rime of the Ancient Mariner," both Edward Bostetter and James Boulger have read the poem as a denial or questioning of orthodox Christianity. Bostetter, in *The Romantic Ventriloquists* (Seattle: University of Washington Press, 1963), p. 115, concludes that "the total impression . . . we get of the universe in "The Rime" is of unpredictable despotic forces." And James Boulger, in the Introduction to *Twentieth Century Interpretations of The Rime of the Ancient Mariner* (Englewood Cliffs, N.J.: Prentice-Hall, 1969), p. 20, describes "The Rime" as "an original parable in epic structure of the uneasy religious scepticism and faith that has been with us since Newton and Kant." William Empson, who does comment on the changes in later editions of the poem, also insists on the inadequacy of a Christian interpretation in his Introduction to *Coleridge's Verse: A Selection*, ed. W. Empson and D. Pirie (London: Faber, 1972), pp. 27-81.

11. William Wordsworth, Notes to "The Ancient Mariner," *Lyrical Ballads* (London, 1800), I, 214-215.

12. *The Early Letters of William and Dorothy Wordsworth (1787-1805)*, ed. Ernest de Selincourt (Oxford: Clarendon Press, 1935), pp. 226-227.

13. Robert Southey, review of *Lyrical Ballads* (1798) in *The Critical Review* 24 (October 1798): 201. Southey's attack, together with the negative reviews of *Lyrical Ballads* in the December 1798 issues of *Monthly Magazine* and *The Analytical Review*, both of which singled out "The Rime of the Ancyent Mariner" for condemnation, led Sara Fricker Coleridge to write harshly but accurately to Thomas Poole: "The Lyrical Ballads are laughed at and disliked by all with very few excepted." *Minnow among Tritons: Mrs. S. T. Coleridge's Letters to Thomas Poole, 1799-1834*, ed. Stephen Potter (London: Nonesuch, 1934), p. 4; dated March 1799. Further hostile reviews of "The Ancient Mariner" occurred in *The Monthly Review* (May 1799), which described the poem as "the strangest story of a cock and bull that we ever saw on paper," and in *The British Critic* (October 1799). Cf. J. R. de J. Jackson, ed., *Coleridge—The Critical Heritage* (New York: Barnes and Noble, 1970), pp. 51-61.

14. Walter Jackson Bate, *Coleridge* (New York: Macmillan, 1968), pp. 1-2. For Coleridge's recurring concern with the hostile reviews of "The Ancient Mariner," see the *Collected Letters of Samuel Taylor Coleridge*, II, ed. E. L. Griggs (Oxford: Clarendon Press, 1959), 203, 316.

15. Charles Lamb felt this keenly. "I am sorry that Coleridge has christened his *Ancient Marinere*, a Poet's Reverie; it is as bad as Bottom the Weaver's declaration that he is not a Lion but only the scenical representation of a Lion. What new idea is gained by this title but one subversive of all credit—which the tale should force upon us—of its truth," wrote Lamb to Wordsworth soon after receiving his copy of the 1800 *Lyrical Ballads*. *Letters of Charles Lamb*, ed. E. V. Lucas (London: Methuen, 1935), I, 240; dated January 1801.

16. The entire Latin text is in Thomas Burnet's *Archeologiae Philosophicae: Sive Doctrina Antiqua de Rerum Originibus*, II, London, 1692, book I, pp. 68-69. Cf. *Notebooks*, I, #1000H, 1000H n.

17. George Watson, *Coleridge the Poet* (London: Routledge and Kegan Paul, 1966), p. 91. Huntington Brown first described the gloss as the work of an imaginary editor and "bookish antiquarian" living around 1650 in "The Gloss to *The Rime of the Ancient Mariner*," *Modern Language Quarterly* 6 (1945): 320.

18. John Livingston Lowes, in *The Road to Xanadu* (Boston: Houghton Mifflin, 1927), pp. 324-325, 575, has noted Coleridge's borrowings in the gloss from the travel books of Gerrit de Veer, Captain Luke Fox, Samuel Purchas, and William Barents.

19. Burnet, *Archeologiae Philosophicae*, p. 68. Stewart Wilcox has translated these lines: "The heathen theologians philosophize much about the invisible world, of Spirits, Genii, Manes, Daemons, Heros, Minds, Noumena, and Gods. For evidence, see the work of Iamblichus on the Egyptian mysteries, of Psellus and Pletho on the Chaldean oracles, and everywhere in Platonic authors." "The Arguments and Motto of *The Ancient Mariner*," *Modern Language Quarterly* 22 (1961): 226.

20. Burnet cites Josephus in the paragraph following Coleridge's epigraph, *Archeologiae Philosophicae*, p. 70.

21. James Boulger has forthrightly dismissed the gloss as "archly pious and disingenuous" in "Christian Scepticism in *The Rime of the Ancient Mariner*," in *From Sensibility to Romanticism*, ed. F. Hilles and H. Bloom (New York: Oxford University Press, 1965), p. 451. But other readers have been persuaded either by the gloss or by the Mariner's own pious credo that the poem is a Christian parable of sin, repentance, penance, and redemption. See, for instance, Robert Penn Warren's influential introduction to *The Rime of the Ancient Mariner*, "A Poem of Pure Imagination: An Experiment in Reading" (New York: Reynal and Hitchcock, 1946), pp. 71-75 and passim. Such diametrically opposed interpretations of the same poem are characteristic responses, as I have suggested earlier, to the open-endedness of romantic-ironic works. Warren does not allow for the amorality of the Mariner's experiences, while Boulger does not acknowledge the extent to which Coleridge was sympathetic to the confident Christianity of the gloss.

22. S. T. Coleridge, *Specimens of the Table Talk*, ed. H. N. Coleridge (London, 1835), I, 154-156; dated 31 May 1830.

23. Laurence S. Lockridge, *Coleridge the Moralist*, pp. 168-170.

24. *Biographia Literaria*, I, 202.

25. Owen Barfield, *What Coleridge Thought*, pp. 76-90 and passim; J. R. de J. Jackson, *Method and Imagination in Coleridge's Criticism* (London: Routledge and Kegan Paul, 1969), pp. 113-125.

26. Barfield, pp. 51-55, 145, and passim.

27. In his discussion of the secondary imagination as evil, Laurence Lockridge fails to acknowledge the extent to which Coleridge is here identifying the artistic with the divine will (*Coleridge the Moralist*, p. 69).

28. Barfield, chap. 8.

29. *Biographia Literaria*, I, 198-201; for Coleridge's authorship of this letter, see Shawcross's note, p. 271.

30. In his *Notebooks*, Coleridge identifies Kublai Khan as "the greatest Prince in Peoples, Cities, & Kingdoms that ever was in the world" (I, #1840) who "ordered letters to be invented for his people" (I, #1281).

31. *Biographia Literaria*, I, 20-21. Reeve Parker, in *Coleridge's Meditative Art* (Ithaca: Cornell University Press, 1975), pp. 68-70, has argued that Coleridge is making a distinction between literary and political activity in this passage, as well as in his much earlier, 1795 poems.

32. Bate, *Coleridge*, p. 78. For other examples of Romantic odal hymns, see Shelley's "Ode to the West Wind" and Keats's "Ode to Psyche."

33. E. H. Coleridge cites a manuscript note (admittedly written over a decade later) that associates the retirement to "Linton and Porlock" with the events of the summer of 1798, rather than 1797. *The Poems of Samuel Taylor Coleridge*, ed. E. H. Coleridge (London: Oxford University Press, 1912), p. 295n2. Even if Coleridge did retire to Ash Farm in November 1797 while on a walking tour with the Wordsworths, as J. B. Beer argues in "Coleridge and Poetry: I. Poems of the Supernatural," in *S. T. Coleridge—Writers and Their Background*, ed. R. L. Brett (London: G. Bell, 1971), pp. 58ff, it is unlikely that he would have carried with him or found there the extremely heavy and rather expensive two-volume edition of Purchas. Beer's dating is supported by the explanatory note on the Crewes holograph manuscript of "Kubla Khan": "This fragment . . . composed . . . at a Farm House between Porlock & Linton, a quarter of a mile from Culbone Church, in the fall of the year, 1797" (published by Alice Snyder, *Times Literary Supplement*, 2 August 1934, p. 541). And Elizabeth Schneider, in *Coleridge, Opium and Kubla Khan* (Chicago: University of Chicago Press, 1953), pp. 28-44, has examined medical evidence that suggests that opium usage is unlikely to activate the creative process.

34. This line appears between l. 252 and l. 253 in MS. W.; see E. H. Coleridge, ed., *The Poems of Samuel Taylor Coleridge*, p. 224.

35. Cf. the excellent discussion of the nature of evil in "Christabel" in Lockridge, *Coleridge the Moralist*, pp. 74-76.

36. James Gillman, *The Life of Samuel Taylor Coleridge* (London, 1838), pp. 301-302. Gillman's version of Coleridge's projected ending, like the gloss for "The Ancient Mariner," imposes a very moral form upon an inherently amoral poem—and thus suggests the guilt Coleridge felt toward his never finished and "obscene" "Christabel" (cf. letter to Southey, 31 January 1819, *Collected Letters*, IV, 918).

37. Norman Fruman, *Coleridge: The Damaged Archangel* (London: George Allen, 1972), pp. 142-143, 355-356, and passim.

38. Bate, *Coleridge*, pp. 68-74.

39. For Newtonian influences on the poem and a fine discussion of "Dejection: An Ode" generally, see George Dekker, *Coleridge and the Literature of Sensibility* (London: Vision Press, 1978), p. 234 and passim.

6. Fear and Trembling: From Lewis Carroll to Existentialism

1. Several Freudian critics have emphasized the extent to which Charles Dodgson created elaborate psychological and verbal defenses to protect himself from the anxiety caused by his repressed and unsatisfied sexual and emotional desires. For the best of these readings, by Paul Schilder, John Skinner, Martin Grotjahn, Phyllis Greenacre, Géza Róheim, Kenneth Burke, and William Empson, see *Aspects of Alice*, ed. R. Phillips (London: Victor Gollancz, 1972), section 7.

2. Kathleen Blake's *Play, Games, and Sport: The Literary Works of Lewis Carroll* (Ithaca: Cornell University Press, 1974) emphasizes Carroll's awareness

that all human endeavors can be regarded as play or games: "His books of geometry and logic show that he has no first principle of reality to assert, because of what he calls the relativity of "axiomaticity." By the same token, he presents logic not as a series of facts but as a series of agreements for the reader to enter into. Once agreed on terms and rules and limits, we have a sort of self-standing system which exists by fiat and can co-exist with any number of possible other and even contradictory systems" (p. 14). Blake goes on to point out that for Carroll play and games are "characterized by a fundamental urge to mastery through incorporation of experience to the ego rather than by adjustment or accommodation of the ego to experience" (p. 18) and that they involve a high degree of aggression or antagonism (p. 64).

3. Derek Hudson, *Lewis Carroll* (London: Constable, 1954), p. 35.

4. For useful accounts of Carroll's mathematical puzzles and logic systems, see Warren Weaver, "The Mathematical Manuscripts of Lewis Carroll," *The Princeton University Library Chronicle* 16 (1954-55): 4-9; and R. P. Braithwaite, "Lewis Carroll as Logician," *Mathematical Gazette* 16 (1932): 174-178.

5. Charles Dodgson, *Symbolic Logic, Part I: Elementary* (1897), 4th ed. (New York: Berkeley Enterprises, 1955), p. 34.

6. All references to *Alice in Wonderland* and *Through the Looking-Glass* (cited hereafter in the text) are to *The Annotated Alice* by Lewis Carroll, illustrated by John Tenniel, with introduction and notes by Martin Gardner (New York: Clarkson N. Potter, 1960), p. 85.

7. Helmut Gernsheim, *Lewis Carroll, Photographer*, rev. ed. (New York: Dover, 1969), p. 29.

8. *The Letters of Lewis Carroll*, ed. Morton N. Cohen (New York: Oxford University Press, 1979), I, 64; cf. Gernsheim, pp. 20, 54. For Carroll's only surviving nude photographs of young girls, see Morton N. Cohen's *Lewis Carroll, Photographer of Children: Four Nude Studies* (New York: Clarkson Potter, 1979).

9. Facsimile reprinted in *Letters of Lewis Carroll*, I, 33.

10. Michael Holquist, "What is a Boojum? Nonsense and Modernism," *Yale French Studies* 43 (1969): 147-148.

11. Elizabeth Sewell, *The Field of Nonsense* (London: Chatto and Windus, 1952), p. 181.

12. *Letters of Lewis Carroll*, I, 4; cf. Derek Hudson, *Lewis Carroll* (London: Longmans, 1958), pp. 6-7.

13. Sewell, *The Field of Nonsense*, p. 5.

14. Peter Alexander, in "Logic and the Humour of Lewis Carroll," *Proceedings of the Leeds Philosophical and Literary Society* 6 (May 1961): 551, has noted that Carroll has constructed in *Alice in Wonderland* "a setting within which inconsistency would appear inevitable."

15. Donald Rackin, "Alice's Journey to the End of Night," *PMLA* 81 (October 1966): 313-326.

16. Alexander L. Taylor, *The White Knight—A Study of C. L. Dodgson (Lewis Carroll)* (Edinburgh and London: Oliver and Boyd, 1952), pp. 46-47.

17. As Kathleen Blake points out, since the caucus-race is both egotistical (everyone does as he likes) and social (it includes a concept of competition and

winning), "its two aspects—of chaotic freedom and of ordered ranking of outcomes—are incompatible" (*Play, Games, and Sport*, p. 114).

18. Quoted by Robert D. Sutherland in *Language and Lewis Carroll*, vol. 26 of *Janua Linguarum*, ed. C. H. Van Schooneveld (The Hague and Paris: Mouton, 1970), p. 97.

19. Dodgson, *Symbolic Logic*, p. 166.

20. Carl Hempel, in "Problems and Changes in the Empiricist Criterion of Meaning," *Revue Internationale de Philosophie* 2 (1950): 41, defined the fundamental principle of logical positivism thus: "a sentence fails to make a cognitively meaningful assertion unless it is 'capable, at least in principle, of experimental test.' "

21. Daniel F. Kirk, *Charles Dodgson, Semeiotician* (Gainesville: University of Florida Press, 1962), p. 53.

22. Robert Sutherland discusses this error in *Language and Lewis Carroll*, pp. 102-110.

23. Cf. Blake, *Play, Games, and Sport*, p. 130.

24. Gernsheim, *Lewis Carroll, Photographer*, p. 49.

25. Cf. Kirk, *Charles Dodgson, Semeiotician*, p. 64 and Sutherland, *Language and Lewis Carroll*, p. 198.

26. Cf. Helene Cixous, "Au sujet de Humpty Dumpty toujours déjà tombé," in *Lewis Carroll*, ed. Henri Parisot (Paris: Editions de l'Herne, 1971), pp. 14-16.

27. The phrase is Meyer Abrams's, *Natural Supernaturalism* (New York: W. W. Norton, 1971), p. 335.

28. See Gregor Malantschuk, *Kierkegaard's Thought*, ed. and trans. Howard V. Hong and Edna H. Hong (Princeton: Princeton University Press, 1971), p. 202; cf. Walter Lowrie, *A Short Life of Kierkegaard* (Princeton: Princeton University Press, 1942).

29. Søren Kierkegaard, *The Concept of Irony, with Constant Reference to Socrates*, trans. Lee M. Capel (Bloomington: Indiana University Press, 1965), p. 278. References to this work by page number hereafter appear in the text.

30. Søren Kierkegaard, *Either/Or*, trans. David F. Swenson and Lillian Marvin Swenson (Garden City, N.Y.: Doubleday Anchor, 1959), I, 20.

31. I, 37. Louis Mackey has ably described A's despair in "Søren Kierkegaard: The Poetry of Inwardness," in *Existential Philosophers: Kierkegaard to Merleau-Ponty*, ed. G. A. Schrader, Jr. (New York: McGraw-Hill, 1967), pp. 46-77.

32. See Malantschuk, pp. 307-362, for a penetrating study of Kierkegaard's theological, "upbuilding" (*opbyggende*) or edifying authorship.

33. See, e.g., Jean-Paul Sartre's *L'Être et le Neant* (Paris: Gallimard, 1943) and *La Nausée* (Paris: Gallimard, 1938); Martin Heidegger's *Sein und Zeit* (Tübingen: M. Niemeyer, 1927); and Karl Jasper's *Philosophie* (Berlin: J. Springer, 1932) and *Existenzphilosophie* (Berlin and Leipzig: W. de Gruyter, 1938).

7. A Conclusion in Which Nothing Is Concluded

1. Friedrich Nietzsche, *The Will to Power*, trans. Walter Kaufmann and R. J. Hollingdale (New York: Vintage, 1967), #1067. This passage is discussed by

John Foster in his forthcoming *Heirs to Dionysus: A Nietzschean Tradition in Literary Modernism* (Princeton: Princeton University Press, 1981), chap. 2.

2. Thomas Weiskel, *The Romantic Sublime* (Baltimore: Johns Hopkins University Press, 1976), pp. 54-62.

3. Cf. Paul Fussell's study of the way that World War I propagated a purely ironic (or skeptical) consciousness, *The Great War and Modern Memory* (New York and London: Oxford University Press, 1975), p. 8 and passim.

4. The phrases are Fussell's, *The Great War*, pp. 335, 328.

5. Donald W. Winnicott, *Playing and Reality* (New York: Basic Books, 1971), pp. 1-9, 89-103. Winnicott contrasts such healthy playing to a self-destructive submission to an external reality principle or super-ego: "It is creative apperception more than anything else that makes the individual feel life is worth living. Contrasted with this is a relationship to external reality which is one of compliance, the world and its details being recognized but only as something to be fitted in with or demanding adaptation. Compliance carries with it a sense of futility for the individual and is associated with the idea that nothing matters and that life is not worth living. In a tantalizing way many individuals have experienced just enough of creative living to recognize that for most of their time they are living uncreatively, as if caught up in the creativity of someone else, or of a machine" (p. 65).

6. Fussell, *The Great War*, p. 75. He continues, "the mode of gross dichotomy came to dominate perception and expression elsewhere, encouraging finally what we can call the modern *versus* habit: one thing opposed to another, not with some Hegelian hope of synthesis involving a dissolution of both extremes (that would suggest "a negotiated peace," which is anathema), but with a sense that one of the poles so embodies so wicked a deficiency or flaw or perversion that its total submission is called for" (p. 79). Such binary thinking traces its ancestry back to antiquity, of course (cf. Plato, Aristotle, the Sophists, Galen, among others).

7. Cf. Edwin M. Good, *Irony in the Old Testament* (Philadelphia: Westminster Press, 1965), chap. 7.

Index